Translation and Identity

Identity is one of the most important political and cultural issues of our time. *Translation and Identity* looks at how translation has played a crucial role in shaping debates around identity, language and cultural survival in the past and in the present.

The volume explores how everything, from the impact of migration to the curricula for national literature courses to the way in which nations wage war in the modern era, is bound up with urgent questions of translation and identity. The book examines translation practices and experiences across continents to show how translation is an integral part of how cultures are evolving, offering new perspectives on how translation can be a powerful tool both to enhance difference and to promote intercultural dialogue.

Drawing on a wide range of materials from official government reports to Shakespearean drama to Hollywood films, *Translation and Identity* demonstrates that translation is central to any proper understanding of the emergence of cultural identity in human history, and offers an innovative and positive vision of the way in which translation can be used to deal with one of the most salient issues in an increasingly borderless world.

Michael Cronin is Director of the Centre for Translation and Textual Studies, Dublin City University. He is the author of *Translating Ireland* (1996), *Across the Lines: Travel, Language and Translation* (2000) for which he was awarded the CATS Vinay Darbelnet Prize, and *Translation and Globalization* (2003).

Translation and Identity

Michael Cronin

Routledge
Taylor & Francis Group

LONDON AND NEW YORK

First published 2006
by Routledge
2 Park Square, Milton Park, Abingdon, Oxon OX14 4RN

Simultaneously published in the USA and Canada
by Routledge
270 Madison Ave, New York, NY 10016

Routledge is an imprint of the Taylor & Francis Group, an informa business

Typeset in Times New Roman by
Keystroke, Jacaranda Lodge, Wolverhampton
Printed and bound in Great Britain by
The Cromwell Press, Trowbridge, Wiltshire

British Library Cataloguing in Publication Data
A catalogue record for this book is available from the British Library

Library of Congress Cataloging in Publication Data
Cronin, Michael, 1960–
    Translation and identity / Michael Cronin.
        p. cm.
    Includes bibliographical references.
    ISBN 0–415–36465–5 (pb) — ISBN 0–415–36464–7 (hb)
1. Translating and interpreting—Social aspects. 2. Pluralism (Social sciences)
3. Identity (Psychology) I. Title.
    P306.97.S63C76 2006
    418′.02—dc22   2005030926

ISBN10: 0–415–36464–7 (hbk)
ISBN10: 0–415–36465–5 (pbk)
ISBN10: 0–203–01569–X (ebk)

ISBN13: 978–0–415–36464–5 (hbk)
ISBN13: 978–0–415–36465–2 (pbk)
ISBN13: 978–0–203–01569–8 (ebk)

For Evelyn, Barra and Peter, *dlúthchairde*

Contents

viii *Contents*

Acknowledgements

A recurrent theme of *Translation and Identity* is the constant interaction between the local and the global. In writing the work it has been my own good fortune to benefit from local friendships and global supports. I would first like to record my gratitude to the Governing Authority of Dublin City University which granted me sabbatical leave for the academic year 2004–5, thus allowing me to finish work on the book. I would also like to acknowledge the encouragement and inspiration offered by my colleagues in the Centre for Translation and Textual Studies and in the School for Applied Language and Intercultural Studies, Dublin City University. Special mention must also be made of the DCU/St Patrick's College Philosophy Reading Group which has been a recurrent source of fresh and innovative thinking.

In working through the issues that inform the present volume I am particularly grateful to colleagues and institutions around the world that have helped me arrive at a clearer understanding of the global dimension to the questions addressed. Among the institutions and bodies I would like to thank are: University of Wolverhampton; Sheffield Hallam University; Università degli Studi Roma Tre; Queen's University, Belfast; Concordia University; Université de Moncton; University of Toronto; Heriot-Watt University; University of Edinburgh; Universitat Rovira i Virigili; National University of Ireland, Galway; University of Salford; University of Lisbon; University of Oporto; Princess Grace Irish Library, Monaco; St Mary's University, Halifax; University of Warwick; Academy of Irish Heritages, University of Ulster; University of Utrecht; Royal Irish Academy; Université de Paris III-Sorbonne Nouvelle; Centre for Asian and African Literatures, SOAS, and University College London. I would particularly like to thank Gavan Titley, Michelle Woods, Rita McCann, Sylvie Kleinman and Caoimhghín Ó Croidheáin for the privilege of their company and their conversation as we explored the territory of our common research interests. A special word of thanks also to the editorial staff at Routledge for their kindness and patience in bringing the book to publication.

The book is dedicated to Evelyn Conlon, Barra Ó Séaghdha and Peter Sirr who have been unstinting in their friendship and support through the years.

Sections of chapters 1 and 3 have appeared in earlier versions in *Languages and Intercultural Communication*, vol. 5, no. 2; *Translation Ireland Yearbook 2004*,

Dublin: Irish Translators Association, 2004; Niall Ó Ciosáin (ed.) *Explaining Change in Cultural History*, Dublin: University College Dublin Press, 2005; Jean Morencey, Hélène Destrempes, Denise Merkle and Martin Pâquet (eds) *Des cultures en contact: Visions de l'Amérique du Nord francophone*, Québec: Nota bene, 2005; Paul St-Pierre and Prafulla C. Kar (eds) *In Translation: Reflections, Refractions, Transformations*, Delhi: Pencraft International, 2005; *New Hibernia Review*, vol. 8, no. 4; Alyce von Rothkirch and Daniel Williams (eds) *Beyond the Difference: Welsh Literature in Comparative Contexts Essays for M. Wynn Thomas at Sixty*, Cardiff: University of Wales Press, 2004; Maria Tymoczko and Colin Ireland (eds) *Language and Tradition in Ireland*, Amherst and Boston: University of Massachusetts Press, 2003.

All translations, unless otherwise stated, are my own.

Introduction
Identity papers

Augustine of Hippo did not believe in language miracles. In sketching a map of human community from the household to the world, he saw diversity of languages as what most obviously set humans apart from each other:

> For if two men meet, and are forced by some compelling reason not to pass on but to stay in company, then if neither knows the other's language, it is easier for dumb animals, even of different kinds, to associate together than these men, although both are human beings. For when men cannot communicate their thoughts to each other, simply because of difference of language, all of the similarity of their common human nature is of no avail to unite them in fellowship. So true is this that a man would be more cheerful with his dog for company than with a foreigner.
>
> (Augustine 1984: 861)

Augustine is attentive, however, to what the 'Imperial City' has done to solve this problem, namely impose a common language. For the North African Doctor of the Latin Church, coercion in matters of language is rarely a happy affair and he remarks, 'think of the cost of this achievement! Consider the scale of these wars, with all that slaughter of human beings, all the human blood that was shed' (ibid., 861). So language contact and language change are not innocent transactions as language itself is intimately bound up with what makes humans different from each other. Missing from the account above is, of course, the translator. *Translation and Identity* is about the role of Augustine's missing link and how, from the household to the city to the world, translation must be at the centre of any attempt to think about questions of identity in human society.

In order to do this, it is worth considering why identity has emerged as such an important issue in contemporary debate both inside and outside the academy. The end of what the political scientist Philip Bobbitt has called the Long War, with the signing of the Charter of Paris allowing for parliamentary institutions in all the participating member states of the Conference on Security and Cooperation in Europe, also signalled a decisive shift in the categories that would now be used to interpret the world (Bobbitt 2002: 61). If previously ideology had been the principal way of structuring political communication, identity has now taken over. This is not to say, of course, that the issues raised by ideological critiques somehow disappeared or were no longer important but issues such as marginalization, dispossession, powerlessness were increasingly mediated through discourses of identity.

In the words of Gerard Delanty, '[t]he older ideologies of modernity – capitalist liberal democracy and state socialism – and their geopolitical foundations in east versus west appear to have dissolved into new kinds of binary opposites, such as those of *self* and *other*' (Delanty 2000: 130). The attempts to think through the theoretical and practical implications of notions of citizenship that acknowledge both individual and collective rights and that conceive politics to be as much a striving after equality as a safeguarding of difference have become increasingly common in a post-Cold War world. Views of identity are, of course, in part determined by local place and local histories, but one of the central insights of Renaissance humanism and by extension translation practice is that we need not always be bound by the circumstances of our origin. The ways in which people represent themselves to each other and themselves is not just a function of different histories; it is also bound up with the way in which in the contemporary world they are invited, encouraged or obliged to participate in the economy and society. One of the questions this book asks is what kinds of identity emerge in industrial and post-industrial economies and societies and where does translation feature in their formation.

Richard Sennett has argued, for example, that one of the features of society and the economy in the era of globalization is that there is no longer such a thing as the long term: '[i]n work, the traditional career progressing step by step through the institutions is withering; so is the deployment of a single set of skills throughout the course of a working life' (Sennett 1998: 22). Nowadays, young Americans with at least two years of university education can expect to change jobs at least eleven times in the course of their working life and radically change their skill base at least three times during forty years of labour. Subcontracting is the order of the day, temping agencies are everywhere and what governs managerial policy is less the long-term interests of its workforce than the short-term interests of its shareholders.

For proponents of the new economy the watchwords are flexibility, opportunity, lifelong learning and mobility. These are indeed attractive concepts, particularly when contrasted with what is presented as the disabling fatalism of the grey years of rigid, hierarchical, Fordist working practices. However, there are real consequences for people's lives in these new economic arrangements and these include vastly increased uncertainty over long-term employment futures, harmful relational and familial consequences of 7/24 working practices and changing attitudes to trust and commitment due to the fickleness of equity-driven corporate policies (making a profit is no guarantee of keeping your job if even more profit can be made out of the same job being done elsewhere). In short, as Sennett asks:

> How do we decide what is of lasting value in ourselves in a society which is impatient, which focuses on the immediate moment? How can long-term goals

be pursued in an economy devoted to the short term? How can mutual loyalties and commitments be sustained in institutions which are constantly breaking apart or continually being redesigned?

(ibid., 10)

These developments in business, the economy and society obviously make the working out of any kind of identity – which implies a sense of continuity over time – problematic. In a sense, the difficulty may be not so much in deciding whether you are Irish or Chinese or European or Australian but in retaining the possibility of working out any kind of identity at all. The danger is that as a sense of uncertainty or risk becomes more and more prevalent, the temptation is to reach for a notion of identity which is wholly concerned with economic entitlement and detaches identity from any idea of collective, social transformation which goes beyond the needs of the market. Once we have individuals as consumers rather than as citizens, who are defined by what they have and will have rather than by what they are and, more importantly, might be, then we run the paradoxical risk of increasingly virulent forms of nationalism in a globalized world with its much vaunted decline of the nation-state. Identity in this scenario is the bleak, defensive interface between a global economy and infinitely malleable human material. It is in this context that the contribution of translation is paramount in describing both how certain forms of identity have come into being and how they are being shaped. Equally important is the manner in which translation theory and practice can point the way to forms of coexistence that are progressive and enabling rather than disabling and destructive.

Chapter 1 begins by situating translation in the context of debates on identity in the modern world. The chapter examines in particular the renewed contemporary interest in the notion of cosmopolitanism in cultural studies and in political science. The chapter considers some of the more negative connotations of the notion of the cosmopolitan, particularly its association with privilege, before reworking the concept to make it more relevant to the contemporary world and the concerns of translators and students of translation. A core concern in this chapter is how best to think about the relationship between the local and the global and, in this context, we will be advancing an argument for a new form of micro-cosmopolitanism based on the dual nature of cultural experience, both specific and connected. To demonstrate how cosmopolitan thinking on translation can illuminate particular (trans)national histories of translation, episodes from the translation history of Ireland and China are highlighted. The chapter proceeds from the argument for the historical duality of translation practice to how we might best conceptualize translation in a contemporary world of ceaseless change. It is argued that the alleged inadequacy or shortcoming of translation belies the fact that it is a practice not only eminently suited to contemporary conditions but capable too of explaining a number of the particularities of the present situation. The chapter then examines three specific areas where a reworked cosmopolitan version of translation theory can contribute to debate, namely, localization practice, curricular reform of national literature courses and the formulation of translation policy for supra-national institutions. The primary concern of the chapter is to develop a number of conceptual tools that will allow translation to contribute to and inflect mainstream political debates on the role of cultural and linguistic diversity in the societies of the present and the future.

Chapter 2 moves to consider the implications of the phenomenon of migration for debates around identity, translation and language. The chapter begins by showing the centrality of migration to the myth of Babel itself before assessing the extent of migration in the contemporary world. It then explores how migration brings to the fore issues around language, identity, multiculturalism and interculturalism and how a crucial dimension to these questions is the relationship between the local and the global. One specific instance of the local engagement with this global phenomenon is the change in certain countries such as Ireland from being countries of emigrants to being countries of immigrants; the consequences of this are explored in detail. The chapter looks at the variety of translation strategies employed by immigrants as they settle down in new societies. The manner in which a migratory present can influence the perception of a national past, the influence of transculturalism and the shift from translation within countries to translation between countries are explored in this context. The consequences of migration for identity and translation in the specific arenas of urban spaces and educational curricula are then examined to see how translation can contribute to inclusive forms of citizenship. It is argued, in the chapter, that there can be no proper theory of political justice in migratory settings if there are not effective and enabling theories and practices of translation. To this end, translators must not only be seen but be heard and the audibility of the translator is a key element in politically situating the translator in the modern world.

Chapter 3 examines the position of those translators who are both seen and heard in the contemporary world, namely interpreters. In a world where orality in its various forms is still hugely important, the chapter argues for the necessity of properly understanding the role of interpreters through history as they negotiate the conflicting pressures of identity, allegiance and power. The chapter begins by exploring the conflicting interests of interpreters and argues for the necessity of seeing interpreters as embodied agents. The chapter then traces the consequences of this embodiment in a number of situations of conflict so that we emerge with a more complex and nuanced conception of the interpreter's identity. Central to the examination of the role of the interpreter is the relationship between language and power in periods of tension and struggle. The chapter analyses a number of Shakespearean plays with a view to arriving at a more detailed understanding of the impact of translation and interpreting on questions of identity in periods of violent conflict. Part of the argument of the chapter is that translation theory needs not simply to discuss the translation of literary texts but to look at what these texts have to say about translation practices. The chapter then moves from the world of Shakespeare to another theatre of war, Iraq. In this section, the focus is on the changing nature of conflict and the implications this has for the future identity and position of translators and interpreters in war zones. In situations where interpreters pay with their lives for issues of identity and allegiance, discussions around the role and position of translation take on an urgent and pressing meaning. Since one of the dangers of interpreting in times of conflict is the relative visibility of the interpreter the chapter concludes with the ultimately visible interpreter, Nicole Kidman, in Sydney Pollack's film, *The Interpreter* (2004). Analysis of the film shows that the question of the identity of the interpreter is inseparable from the practice of interpreting as interpreted by the other protagonists in the film. Indeed, the chapter shows that from Shakespeare's dramas to the death camps of Auschwitz to the killing fields of Iraq and Nicole Kidman's United Nations, the question of translation is central to the negotiation of identity and power in a fractured world.

Chapter 4 then asks how we can think about translation in a way that will help us to deal with the fraught issues of identity and representation which can lead to dissension and violence. The chapter begins by examining the key notions of 'bridge' and 'door' as presented by the German sociologist Georg Simmel and considers ways in which they can enable us to think more fruitfully about translation and identity. In particular, the chapter focuses on the contemporary debates around 'world literature' and on the putative bridge-building or door-opening role of translation. It is argued in this chapter that one of the functions of translation is to challenge entropic views of cultural mediation and exchange which present diversity as always already and everywhere under threat and which see translation as at best a poor imitation and at worst a dangerous sop. Central to the presentation of an anti-entropic or negentropic and holistic version of translation practice in this chapter are, again, local and global linkages. This relationship which is discussed in Chapter 1 in the context of cosmopolitanism is revisited in Chapter 4 in the light of work in network theory on small worlds and weak ties. The chapter argues that in a world and in a century where identity has become one of the key sites of struggle translation is particularly well situated to make a positive and enabling contribution to debates around the issue, a contribution which respects complexities of allegiance while demonstrating the need for reciprocity and dialogue.

In Chapter 7, Book XIX of the *City of God*, where Augustine describes the hapless strangers divided by language, he moves from a consideration of language differences to consider the 'grievous evils' of wars. If identity has become a subject of much debate in our time, it is because violent conflicts are still with us and people die and are prepared to die as a result of identity-related issues. Translators and thinkers about translation cannot afford to ignore the obligation to engage with debates about how in our century we are to find ways to live together in our households and in our cities and in our world. If we fail to engage, then there will be no end to the grievous evils that lie ahead.

1 Translation and the new cosmopolitanism

> Herodotus of Halicarnassus here displays his inquiry, so that human achievements may not become forgotten in time, and great and marvellous deeds – some displayed by Greeks, some by barbarians – may not be without their glory; and especially to show why the two peoples fought with each other.
>
> (Herodotus 1996: 3)

The achievements and deeds to be praised in the *Histories* are not only those of the Greeks. Other peoples, other places, will feature in the pantheon of recognition. Herodotus' declaration of faith is partly a result of circumstance, partly an expression of method: a result of circumstance because Halicarnassus was a Dorian town on the western coast of what is now Turkey and in the vicinity were non-Greek Carians (subject to Persian rule) with whom the inhabitants of Halicarnassus had close contact. Herodotus then by virtue of birth finds himself in an intercultural contact zone which will make a life of travel and inquiry into the customs, beliefs and habits of others less a break with a unified past than a continuation of the cultural engagement that was his lot from the beginning. The expression of method is articulated in the word *historia* itself which in its original sense meant 'inquiry' or 'investigation' and was not confined to the later sense of the strict exploration of the past. Herodotus, who appears to have travelled widely throughout the Mediterranean world and beyond, was a disciplinary nomad, an early exponent of what we now call travelling theory, who in his desire to situate the Greeks in the world had to find out for himself what the rest of the known world was like (Lacarrière 1981). To this end, 'his work ranges over many fields and includes geography, anthropology, ethnology, zoology, even fable and folklore' (Marincola 1996: xiii).

What is crucial for the Greek writer is to seek out connections between widely disparate events. Why the dreams and the oracles come to play their role alongside the detailed description of buildings and natural phenomena is because they are all ways of uncovering links and establishing relationships. But even the divine oracles are not immune from the dealings of human language. When Herodotus recounts the story of the oracle at Dodona, he tells of the legend of the black dove 'who perched on an oak, and speaking with a human voice', told the people of

Dodona that on that spot there should be an oracle of Zeus. Herodotus is not convinced and sees the bird as a figurative representation of the female servant of the temple of the Theban Zeus who was carried off by the Phoenicians and sold into slavery. To her new masters, her voice would sound like the twittering of birds, but as she acquired Greek, her language would no longer be heard as 'twittering' but as intelligible human speech. Herodotus adds, 'As to the bird being black, they merely signify by this that the woman was an Egyptian' (Herodotus 1996: 107).

The Greek author is sensitive in this instance not only to the association of language 'lack' with the non-human but to the role of language transfer, translation and cross-cultural communication in the emergence of another contact zone, the oracular, that shifting frontier between human and divine knowledge. Herodotus himself as the bringer of information from elsewhere is close in function to the oracles he describes and like the good people of Dodona must depend for much of his information on what intermediaries can tell him through and in translation (Marincola 1996: xviii).

Herodotus' inquiry entertains few illusions. Not long into his opening remarks we learn that his story has a bad ending and that the Greeks and Persians will go to war. However, he does not allow his Greek sympathies to restrict his human inquisitiveness. If Herodotus inaugurates Douglas Robinson's conspectus of Western translation theory, it is because 'one of Herodotus's central concerns is with cross-cultural communication – how people speaking different languages manage to pass ideas on to each other – and he places that process in an insistently geopolitical context' (Robinson 1997: 1). Herodotus in his seeking after connectedness and in his relentless, cross-disciplinary curiosity is indeed a tutelary figure for thinking about translation. In what follows, however, we want to suggest that it was the intuitions of more marginal members of Greek society that lead us to a more exactly contemporary understanding of the relationship between translation, society and culture.

Cosmopolitanism

It is commonly believed that the notion of cosmopolitanism had its origins in the writings and beliefs of the Cynic philosophers, Antisthenes and Diogenes. For Diogenes, 'all wise men' made up a single, moral community, a city of the world, a city defined by mental compatibility rather than by physical geography. It was he who first explicitly used the idea of the cosmopolitan to describe someone who was not rooted in any contemporary city-state but was 'a citizen of the world' (Sabine 1961: 136–7). Aristippus, the founder of the Cyreniac school, in a more evocative image expressed a similar idea by claiming that the road to Hades was the same distance from any point in the world. The Stoic philosopher Zeno would further develop the idea, claiming that all peoples carried within them the divine spark and all were capable of using *logos* or divine reason (Mason 1999). As Robert Fine and Robin Cohen point out, 'Zeno imagined an expanding circle of inclusion – from self, to family, to friends, to city, to humanity. In this process of enlargement the state itself would disappear, to be replaced by pure reason' (Fine and Cohen 2002: 138).

For the inhabitants of the Athenian city-state, these ideas, though startling, came from social outsiders and were largely ignored. Diogenes was in exile from Sinope in Pontus, Antisthenes was a Thracian and Zeno was a *metic* (resident foreigner) from Citium in Cyprus. These thinkers on the margins of Athenian society were temporarily silenced by their own powerlessness. However, it is Zeno's principles that Cicero would later invoke to argue for the equality of all before the law and Diogenes' declaration would have a long and resonant posterity (Sabine 1961: 164). In 1552, for example, Erasmus refuses the citizenship of the city of Zurich offered by Zwingli, declaring, 'I want to be a citizen not of one single city but of the whole world' (Huizinga 1936: 34). The ideal of humanity as a collection of free and equal beings, possessing the same basic rights and to whom notions of hospitality, openness to others and freedom of movement are primordial, underlies much thinking about translation, cultural contact and the intercultural from antiquity to our own times. Peter Coulmas, in his *Weltbürger: Geschichte einer Menscheitssehnsucht* (1990), offers the reader a historical overview of cosmopolitanism originating in what Fine and Cohen call 'Zeno's moment' (Fine and Cohen 2002: 137) and charting the vicissitudes of cosmopolitan thinking down the centuries. However, rather than replay here the history of cosmopolitan thought we would like to focus on current understandings of what constitutes the cosmopolitan in order to see how differentiated notions of the phenomenon can be used to illuminate debates about translation theory and practice in the contemporary world. To claim that one is a citizen of the world might appear to be a generous and selfless ideal but what does it mean to the state we are in, to the kind of world in which we find ourselves? If the notion of the cosmopolitan is to be of any service then we must have a more fine-grained understanding of what cosmopolitan thinking entails and why the beliefs of Antisthenes, Diogenes and Zeno are still of relevance to contemporary translators and cultural brokers.

The turn of the century has seen a marked renewal of interest in the theory and practice of cosmopolitanism among political scientists, sociologists, philosophers and cultural theorists (Cohen 1996; Brennan 1997; Cheah and Robbins 1998; Zachary 2000; Breckenridge *et al.* 2002). The interest has been prompted by a series of factors that have drawn attention to the necessity for new ways of thinking about the changing circumstances of cultures and societies. First, as early as 1990 Anthony Giddens defined globalization as 'the intensification of worldwide social relations which link distant localities in such a way that local happenings are shaped by events occurring many miles away and vice versa' (1990: 64). Thus, the nation-state system and the sacrosanct principle of national sovereignty which had been elaborated from the Treaty of Westphalia in 1648 onwards came under increasing pressure. The global economy under the regime of what Manuel Castells has called 'informationalism' became a vast, interconnected system operating in real time through the agency of information technology and telecommunications networks (Castells 1996). As evidence of this, if there were approximately 7,000 trans-border corporations in the 1960s, there were 44,000 such corporations by the end of the century (Scholte 2000: 86). Thus, economies or polities could no longer be seen as bounded entities to be described and managed within the framework of the post-Westphalian nation-state.

Second, the end of the Cold War did not result everywhere in an effortless passage to a universal reign of peace and harmony but was characterized, for example in the former Yugoslavia, by the exacerbation of ethnic tensions and the outbreak of extreme interethnic violence. The conflict raised issues about ethnocentric definitions of identity and the consequences of such definitions, and prompted debates about the human rights of individuals versus the sovereign rights of nation-states (Beck 2002: 64–8). Third, the relative hegemony of identity politics, particularly but not only in North America, in the last decade of the twentieth century, led to increasing impatience with static or essentialist notions of identity and a desire to conceive of identity in a more flexible and open fashion (Hollinger 1995). In response to these different phenomena, thinking about the cosmopolitan has taken different forms and we will briefly list these, using a modified form of the classification proposed by Steven Vertovec and Robin Cohen (2002: 8–14).

Cosmopolitanism may be thought of as primarily a *socio-cultural condition*. That is to say, in an era of mass transportation, global tourism, significant migration and the relentless time–space compression of economies driven by information technology, cosmopolitanism is the body of thought most apt to describe our essential connectedness as global producers and consumers. Alternatively, cosmopolitanism may be seen as primarily a *philosophy* or *world-view* which, taking its lead mainly from the writings of Immanuel Kant, sees all of humanity as citizens of the world united by a set of common values, a particular philosophical stance towards others (Reiss 1970). This view can take the form of 'moral cosmopolitanism' which basically urges all humans to respect each other or it can be cast as a type of 'legal cosmopolitanism' which seeks to give expression to shared values in the guise of universal legal rights and duties. A variant on this stance is the idea of a cosmopolitan *attitude* or *disposition* which is not so much the obeying of a moral imperative as the expression of a desire or a willingness to engage with others (Hannerz 1990: 237–51).

Another way in which to present the cosmopolitan is to consider the emergence of *transnational institutions* and the beliefs and practices that these institutions entail. Such institutions include the European Union, the United Nations Organization, the World Bank and the International Monetary Fund but also the different organizations representing global civil society such as Greenpeace, Amnesty International or the Global Social Forum (Delanty 2001). The cosmopolitan political project can equally be envisaged at the level of the subject with the notion of *multiple subjects*. In other words, human subjects have a plurality of different loyalties, a multiplicity of different ways in which they can be described or defined. So, depending on the situation, people might find themselves primarily defined, for example, by their age or their gender or their social class or their ethnicity, or by the neighbourhood in which they live, or by a combination of these different forms of belonging. In this view, cosmopolitanism is a way of thinking through the complexity of a polyidentity rather than accepting single, all-encompassing identities for human subjects based on one variable alone (Cohen 1992: 478–83). Lastly, there is a conception of the cosmopolitan that presents it primarily as a *practice* or a *competence*. That is, it relates to the ability to make one's way into other cultures and to actively engage with those living in or through different cultures, languages or milieux. It is this particular notion of the cosmopolitan that underlies much of the work that goes on in the area of intercultural training. What these contemporary understandings of the cosmopolitan offer is the possibility of thinking about translation as a way not only of thinking but of being and acting in the world. In other words, more complex and differentiated understandings of the concept allow us to escape the idle and dispiriting debates about theory versus practice that have blighted certain kinds of writing over the years.

New cosmopolitan thinking, as we can observe from the classification above, is as concerned with how altered circumstances produce a new kind of world to live and work in as it is with trying to understand what kind of world that might be. It is important at this point to distinguish contemporary cosmopolitan theory from other bodies of thought which seek to describe or account for contemporary multi-ethnic, multicultural and/or multilingual societies. What communitarianism, multiculturalism and pluralism, for example, tend to have in common is the ascription of primary identity to the community of belonging so that an individual's entitlement to certain rights or services (such as 'community' interpreting, for example) is based on the individual's membership of a particular community. The community constitutes both the grounds for access to entitlements and the primary framework for self-definition. In this context, David Hollinger contrasts pluralism or mosaic multiculturalism and cosmopolitan thinking: 'Pluralism respects inherited boundaries and locates individuals within one or another of a series of ethno-racial groups to be protected and preserved. Cosmopolitanism is more wary of traditional enclosures and favours voluntary affiliations' (1995: 3). So the stress in cosmopolitanism is on multiple affiliations and the possibility of individual choice rather than the unwavering cultural determinism of communities of descent.

Another school of thought that cosmopolitanism tends to be associated with is that of universalism. The darker version of universalism is that of an overween-ing humanist enlightenment with a set of prescriptive, 'universal' ideals that provide the alibi for the 'civilizing mission' of imperial and neo-imperial elites. The 'cosmopolitan' in this view is rootless and ruthless, disengaged and disembodied, (falsely) disinterested and (genuinely) disenchanted. A variation on this theme is the ready assimilation of cosmopolitanism to economic and social privilege which is apparent not only in the tirades of the European Far Right but is present also in the analyses of progressive thinkers who are sceptical about the uses to which cosmopolitanism is put by transnational capital. Timothy Brennan, for example, launches a trenchant attack against cosmopolitan thinking in *At Home in the World: Cosmopolitanism Now* (1997) where he denounces the current vogue for cosmo-politanism as simply the well-meaning version of American imperialism which under cover of cultural pluralism wishes to ensure the continued dominance of its political, economic, military and cultural interests. Danilo Zolo in *Cosmopolis:*

Prospects for World Government is similarly hostile to what he sees as Western cosmopolitan visions of a global future which:

> in fact goes no further than a network of connections and functional inter-dependencies which have developed within certain important sectors of the 'global market', above all finance, technology, automation, manufacturing industry and the service sector. Nor, moreover, does it go much beyond the optimistic expectation of affluent westerners to be able to feel universally recognised as citizens of the world – citizens of a welcoming, peaceful, ordered and democratic 'global village' – without for a moment or in any way ceasing to be 'themselves', i.e. western citizens.
>
> (1997: 137)

Craig Calhoun observes that cosmopolitanism is often seen as the 'class consciousness of frequent travellers' (2002: 86–109) and John Micklethwait and Adrian Wooldridge speak of the 'cosmocrats', a highly mobile, meritocratic elite. They are the 'people who attend business-school weddings around the world, fill up the business-class lounges at international airports, provide the officer ranks of most of the world's companies and international institutions' (Micklethwait and Wooldridge 2000: 229).

What the cosmocrats or the new 'hyperbourgeoisie' share is the universalism of social and material self-interest that allows for the easy embrace of a consumer-ist cosmopolitanism where everything from international eateries to the mix 'n' match of world music seems eloquent confirmation of a post-nationalist utopia. However, though the existence of such a class is a recognizable reality and the suspicions of a Brennan or a Zolo are readily understandable, it is important that cosmopolitan thinking be understood on its own terms. Indeed, the history of cosmopolitan critique from the vituperations of the Nazis against the perils of 'cosmopolitan Jewry' to Soviet diatribes from 1949 onwards against the evils of cosmopolitanism associated with Zionism, Pan-Americanism and Catholicism (Carew Hunt 1957: 38) should invite caution in the substitution of caricature for analysis of the cosmopolitan phenomenon. More specifically, it is important to understand the exact nature of the relationship between the local and the global, the particular and the general, the universal and the specific, as it is this relationship which must inevitably be at the heart of how we might conceptualize translation and translation practice in the contemporary period.

David Held in his definition of 'cultural cosmopolitanism' claims that it is *'the ability to stand outside a singular location (the location of one's birth, land, upbringing, conversion) and to mediate traditions'* that lies at its core (2002: 58; his emphasis). In this sense, of course, all translators are cultural cosmopolitans, in that going to the other text, the other language, the other culture, involves that initial journey away from the location of one's birth, language, upbringing. Even if one is translating into the foreign language as a target language, there is still the element of displacement, as the translator moves from the native language to the other language. So standing outside a singular location is an intrinsic part of the translation process, repeated millions of times every day across the planet. But there is of course another dimension which is that translators are expected to be fully in possession of the language and culture of the location of their birth and/or upbringing if they are to function effectively as translators, whether into or out of the native tongue. Indeed, one of the most oft repeated critiques in translation pedagogy is that students of translation fail to recognize the importance of the idiom of the 'singular location' (Seleskovitch 1998: 288).

Held's notion of mediating traditions begins to capture this necessary duality of the translation task but his claim is made more explicit by Stuart Hall in his advocacy of what he terms 'vernacular cosmopolitanism':

> a cosmopolitanism that is aware of the limitations of any one culture or any one identity and that is radically aware of its insufficiency in governing a wider society, but which is nevertheless not prepared to rescind its claim to the traces of difference, which makes its life important.
>
> (Hall 2002: 30)

The 'traces of difference' cannot be ignored, then, in a desire to float free of attachment or through some residual guilt about the pull of a culture or an identity (or a plurality of these) in a world where the fluid and the borderless and the emancipated are held up as virtual synonyms. The difficulty, however, has been to make cosmopolitanism attentive to those differences, to the particular claims of singular locations, without which translation as a meaningful activity would cease to exist. If there are no singular locations, then there is nothing left to mediate and by extension nothing to translate.

If we return to Peter Coulmas, the thinker and historian we mentioned earlier (p. 8), he openly states his preference for a world-view, namely cosmopolitanism, which he believes to be the only one capable of ensuring lasting peace and friendship between the different peoples on the planet. For Coulmas, a decline in cosmo-politanism is always synonymous with the rise of particularism and the birth of nationalism. When he goes on to describe important moments in the history of cosmopolitanism, it is almost invariably in the context of great empires of yester-year, the Greek, the Roman, the Byzantine, the Carolingian, the French, the Spanish, the Austro-Hungarian and the British (Coulmas 1990: 9–13). This approach is not particularly quixotic and it has become a historical commonplace to underline the multi-ethnic and multilingual character of empires, even if the focus is not as resolutely centred on the West as is the case with Coulmas (Fernández Armesto 1996). The version of cosmopolitanism made explicit by Coulmas is what we might term *macro-cosmopolitanism*, namely a tendency to locate the cosmopolitan moment in the construction of empires, in the development of large nation-states (France, Great Britain, Germany) or more recently in the creation of supra-national organizations (European Union/United Nations/World Health Organization).

For the macro-cosmopolitan, it is only large political units which are capable of allowing the development of a progressive and inclusive vision of humanity, even if occasional hegemonic overreaching cannot be ruled out. Small nations, ethnic groups concerned with the protection or preservation of cultural identity, former colonies which still subscribe to an ideology of national liberation are dangerously suspect in this macroscopic conception of cosmopolitanism. Bloody conflicts in the Balkans and in Northern Ireland seem to provide more recent justification for the distrust, in Pascalian terms, of the infinitely great for the infinitely small.

Coulmas evokes the popularity of the motto 'Small is beautiful', associating it with a fashionable interest in local costumes, dances and languages. His verdict is clear: 'this nostalgic looking back is clearly opposed to the onward march of history towards larger political entities'. Worse still, he declares, 'The small state is praised' (Coulmas 1990: 303). These small states have indeed a function which is clearly described in a chapter on the great metropolises of history. The latter benefit from the arrival of immigrants from less important states: 'by means of this brain-drain, many brilliant minds escape their country of origin, particularly, small countries offering few possibilities' (ibid., 272). In *Culture* Raymond Williams offers a similar description of the role of the metropolis, with his notion that those who participated in many avant-garde artistic groups were frequently 'immigrants to such a metropolis, not only from outlying regions but from other and smaller national cultures, now seen as culturally provincial in relation to the metropolis' (Williams 1981: 84). Indeed, for Matthew Arnold in an earlier period it was precisely the centripetal pull of the centre that made the notion of separate nationhood for the Irish or the Welsh or the Bretons a dangerous illusion:

> Small nationalities inevitably gravitate towards the larger nationalities in their immediate neighbourhood. Their ultimate fusion is so natural and irresistible that even the sentiment of the absorbed race, ceases, with time, to stuggle against it; the Cornishman and the Breton become, at last, in feeling as well as in political fact, an Englishman and a Frenchman.
>
> (Arnold 1859: 71)

The nineteenth-century Swiss writer Rodolphe Töpffer noted with mordant cynicism that consecration from the macro-cosmopolitan viewpoint could only come through the metropolis, whose judgements were then internalized by those on the metropolitan edge:

> Il faut donc de toute nécessité que cet homme, s'il tient à être illustre, transporte dans la capitale sa pacotille de talent, que là il la déballe devant les experts parisiens, qu'il paie l'expertise, et alors on lui confectionne une renommée qui de la capitale est expédiée dans les provinces où elle est acceptée avec empressement.
>
> (Meizoz 1997: 168)

> [It is absolutely necessary that if this man wishes to be famous he must bring his trashy talent to the capital, that there he must lay it out before the Parisian experts, pay for their valuation, and then a reputation is concocted for him which goes from the capital into the provinces where it is accepted with enthusiasm.]

The existence of small countries is justified by their being a kind of pre-cosmopolitan nursery, a warehouse of the mind where cognitive raw materials await the necessary processing and polish of the present and former capitals of empires. If Coulmas is cited *in extenso* it is because he offers in summary form a number of the basic theses of macro-cosmopolitanism, in particular an abiding hostility to political entities that are seen to be primarily defined by notions of national sovereignty or cultural particularism.

Micro-cosmopolitanism

It is possible to oppose to the notion of macro-cosmopolitanism the concept of what we will call *micro-cosmopolitanism*. The concept attempts both to articulate the concerns and intuitions of Held and Hall and to offer a framework for thinking about translation in a progressive, enabling and non-exclusive fashion. Micro-cosmopolitan thought shares a number of macro-cosmopolitan core ideals – such as a concern for freedom, an openness to and tolerance of others, a respect for difference – but it is distinctly different in foregrounding other perspectives, other areas of work and research, and above all in freeing cosmopolitanism from a historical vision and a set of ideological presuppositions that threaten both its survival as a necessary element of human self-understanding and its ability to speak meaningfully to many different translation situations across the planet. Why do we need a micro-cosmopolitan perspective and what does it consist of? We will begin with the necessity for such a perspective.

There are now more nation-states than at any other time in the world's history. In one recent estimate there are around 200 nation-states and approximately 2,000 'nation peoples' who experience varying degrees of displacement, persecution and political uncertainty (Cohen 1997: ix–x). Currently, none of these nations seem particularly keen on abandoning their independence and, in the case of many nation peoples such as the Tibetans or the Chechens, national independence is still very much a live and contentious issue. In this context, it is unlikely that small or new nations, which have often with great difficulty freed themselves from a former colonial presence, will be particularly impressed by being told that the notion of nation is outdated and reactionary and that clinging to such a notion automatically disqualifies them from belonging to the cosmopolitan community.

A dangerous and fatal consequence of this approach is to set up a progressive cosmopolitanism in opposition to a bigoted, essentialist nationalism where the latter has no place for the former. In other words, the inhabitants of smaller or less powerful political units find themselves subject to the 'double bind' famously described by Gregory Bateson (1973: 242–9). Either you abandon any form of national identification, seeing it as associated with the worst forms of irredentist prejudice, and you embrace the cosmopolitan credo or you persist with a claim of national specificity and you place yourself outside the cosmopolitan pale, being by definition incapable of openness to the other. The effects of this double bind are particularly damaging and in intellectual life bring about the paralysis that Bateson noted so clearly in our emotional lives. Extreme nationalists of all hues

take refuge in virulent denunciations of anything construed to represent the cosmopolitan (as has been demonstrated in such a tragic fashion in Europe by the history
of anti-Semitism) while the proponents of macro-cosmopolitanism for their part
are trenchantly hostile to any movement of thought that might appear to harbour
sympathy for nationalist ideology.

Another version of this unhelpful dualism is to be found in certain analyses
of the phenomenon of globalization. Globalization is typically presented by its
opponents as a process of whole-scale standardization (Ritzer 1993). The process
is dominated by large multinational corporations and international organizations
such as the World Bank and the International Monetary Fund, acting at the behest
of the political and economic interests of the world's remaining superpower,
the United States (Klein 2002). This thesis has been challenged by a number
of thinkers such as Roland Robertson, Jonathan Friedman and Manuel Castells
who view globalization as a fragmentary and centrifugal process as much as
a unifying and centripetal one (Robertson 1992; Friedman 1994; Castells 1997).
Their analyses, which would appear to challenge the hegemony of the powerful,
do not in fact offer smaller or less powerful polities a particularly promising role.
Once again these polities are cast in the position of *fidei defensor*, as the touchy
and scrupulous guardians of national difference. Once more there is the trap of
the essentialist conception of national identity, the identity logic criticized by Alain
Finkielkraut in his *La Défaite de la pensée* (1987: 65–106) where political and
cultural differences are reduced to a simplistic and homogenous version of particularism, usually to favour the material and social interests of local elites. In thinking
about translation, the binarism of macro-cosmopolitan approaches, which also
underlies Samuel Huntington's thesis on the clash of civilizations (1993: 22–50)
or Benjamin Barber's vision of 'Jihad vs. McWorld' (1996), is hardly persuasive
and can be deeply disabling both intellectually and politically. Theoreticians and
practitioners of translation, whether from larger or smaller units, should not have
to be condemned to the facile dualism of these macro perspectives.

Micro-cosmopolitan thinking is an approach which does not involve the opposition of smaller political units to larger political units (national or transnational).
It is one which in the general context of the cosmopolitan ideals alluded to
earlier seeks to diversify or complexify the smaller unit. In other words, it is
a cosmopolitanism not from above but from below. Guy Scarpetta in his *Éloge du
cosmopolitisme* is deeply critical of any 'defence of difference' which he believes
leads inevitably to the 'affirmation of a biological inequality between nations'
(1981: 19). The defence of difference is always problematic if the notion is
understood in an essentialist and unitary sense but what we wish to advance here
is a defence of difference not beyond but within the distinct political unit. If we
may modify an idea first put forward in *Across the Lines*, micro-cosmopolitanism
is linked to what we have called *fractal differentialism* (Cronin 2000: 16–21).
This term expresses the notion of a cultural complexity which remains constant
from the micro to the macro scale. That is to say, the same degree of diversity
is to be found at the level of entities judged to be small or insignificant as at the
level of large entities.

ɔf the concept lies in a paper published in 1977 by the French
Benoît Mandelbrot. Mandelbrot asked the following question: 'How
of Britain?' His answer was that there might be no answer because
initely long. Why? He pointed out that an observer from a satellite
ₒuess that would be shorter than that of, say, a travel writer like Paul
ɪ heroux negotiating every inlet, bay and cove on the coast of Britain (Theroux 1984)
and Theroux's guess would be shorter than that of a tiny insect which has to negotiate
every pebble. As James Gleick pointed out, 'Mandelbrot found that as the scale
of measurement becomes smaller, the measured length of a coastline rises without
limit, bays and peninsulas revealing ever smaller subbays and subpeninsulas
at least down to atomic scales' (Gleick 1987: 96). Mandelbrot's discovery was
that the coastline had a characteristic degree of roughness or irregularity and that
this degree remained constant across different scales. Mandelbrot called the new
geometry that he had originated fractal geometry. The shapes or fractals in this
new geometry allowed infinite length to be contained in finite space.

The experience of particular kinds of travellers bears out the discovery of
the mathematician. The traveller on foot becomes aware of the immeasurable
complexity of short distances in a way that is invisible to the traveller behind the
windscreen or looking down from the air. There are many striking examples of
this phenomenon. The English mathematician and cartographer Tim Robinson
in his *Stones of Aran: Labyrinth* (1995) offers a detailed exploration of the 14,000
fields that make up Inismore, a small island off the west coast of Ireland. The French
historian Emmanuel Leroy Ladurie many years earlier offered a similarly fine-
grained history of a small village in southern France in *Montaillou* (1976). On a
somewhat larger scale, Norman Davies and Roger Moorhouse (2002) demonstrate
the immense cultural and historical complexity of just one Polish city, the city
now known as Wroclaw. What Robinson, for instance, clearly demonstrates as
he goes through field after field on this small island is not only the remarkable
richness of these reduced spaces but also the omnipresence of traces of foreignness,
of other languages and cultures, in a place that through the work of John Millington
Synge and others was closely identified with Irish language and culture and
Irish cultural nationalism. The local is honoured in Robinson's work but it is a local
that is informed by diversity and difference.

In a sense, it is the fractal travelling of the intercultural researcher in translation
studies that allows for the elaboration of a concept of the micro-cosmopolitan and
the vital nuancing of cosmopolitan theory as it applies to very different social,
cultural and political realities on the planet. The micro-cosmopolitan dimension
helps thinkers from smaller or less powerful polities to circumvent the terminal
paralysis of identity logic not through a programmatic condemnation of elites
ruling from above but through a patient undermining of conventional thinking from
below. Indeed, if one of the recurrent criticisms of cosmopolitan approaches has
been the charge of cultural, economic and political elitism, then a micro-
cosmopolitan awareness is vital to a proper democratization of inquiry and response.
The micro-cosmopolitan movement, by situating diversity, difference, exchange
at the micro-levels of society, challenges the monopoly (real or imaginary) of a

deracinated elite on cosmopolitan ideals by attempting to show th'
next door, in one's immediate environment, no matter how in'
infinitely large the scale of investigation.

City and country

If there is a place that would seem to offer itself quite readily to the micro-
cosmopolitan approach, it would appear to be the city. In 1961 Lewis Mumford
was already claiming that the 'global city is the world writ small, within its walls
can be found every social class, every people, every language' (Mumford 1991:
620). The cities that have been classed as the great world cities of the past have
included Athens, Alexandria, Rome, Constantinople, Paris, Vienna, London and
New York but now great world cities include, for example, Karachi, Toyko, São
Paolo, Mexico City, Montreal, Beijing and Shanghai. In the opinion of certain
thinkers such as Manuel Castells (1997: 376–428), Saskia Sassen (1991: 195–218)
and Gerard Delanty (2000: 99–102), cities, and in particular the large international
metropolises, are going to become more and more important at the expense of
nation-states. These global metropolises, key nodes in international communication
networks, by bringing together a plethora of different cultures, languages, identities,
are seen as an inexhaustible reservoir for the renewal of the cosmopolitan spirit.
Cities are indeed striking examples of the potential of a micro-cosmopolitan
approach and we will see ample evidence of this in our chapter on immigration.
The work of the translator scholar, Sherry Simon (1999), on the Mile-End district
in Montreal shows that much indeed can be learned from exploring the intercultural
spaces of cities.The fact that by the end of the century more than 80 per cent of the
planet's population will be living in urban centres would seem to be yet another
reason for favouring an exclusively urban focus in research.

The danger, however, is that we end up once again giving new life to a jaded
binary opposition: town or country, progress or reaction. In this view, cosmopolitanism is the proper business of cities and the role of the rural population
(and this includes those living in towns and villages) is to act as guarantors for
the authenticity of the land. It has become a critical commonplace, for example, to
show how the city of Dublin was marginalized in Irish writing for many years
after independence because in the nationalist imaginary the city was a foreign
presence, an alien substance in the Irish body politic (Dublin – city of the Vikings,
seat of British colonial power) (O'Toole 1985: 111–16). The countryside alone was
deemed worthy of interest by many of the post-independence short story writers
(the genre that found particular favour with Irish writers for many decades after
the establishment of the Free State), because it was the countryside that was seen
to be the incarnation of much that was deemed to be specific to Ireland. Needless
to say, in Ireland, it was mainly urban intellectuals – Yeats, Synge, Standish
O'Grady, George Moore – who contributed to the romantic deification of the land
in cultural nationalism (Hutchinson 1987). If the more extreme forms of nationalism
see the city as the polluted well of the cosmopolitan, destroying the manly vigour
of the nation, the ready and too facile identification of the city with cosmopolitanism

in the work of many thinkers on cosmopolitanism itself tends ironically to give succour to the most retrograde forms of nationalism.

One could maintain that instead of arguing by implication and by default for a patriotism of the land, it is more enabling to argue for a cosmopolitanism of the land; in other words, to define specificity through and not against multiplicity. Casual observers of Irish traditional dancing in a pub in rural Ireland might properly feel that they are witnessing a practice which is deeply rooted in a locality but they are also seeing the fruit of the influence of French dancing masters who came to Ireland at the end of the eighteenth century, finding themselves unemployed due to the exile or the untimely demise of their aristocratic patrons (Murphy 1995). More recently, *Riverdance*, for all its egregious excesses and Celticist parody, is a striking synthesis of Irish figure dancing and Hollywood musicals. To stress hybridity in non-urban settings is not to devalue but to revalue. That is to say, to emphasize the multiple origins of a cultural practice, the intercultural dynamic in a micro-cosmopolitanism of the land, is to refuse to give in to a moralizing condemnation of particularisms on the grounds that traditions are always bogus, that the supposedly authentic is an elaborate historical trick and that we all know why the Scots were encouraged to wear kilts.

The withering scepticism about the particular noticeable in the work of Benedict Anderson (1991) and Eric Hobsbawm (1990), and amplified ad nauseam in the commentary of media pundits, is damaging to a genuine openness of cultures and engenders a counter-reaction to a current of cosmopolitan thinking seen as destructive, condescending and hegemonic. A key element of the micro-cosmopolitan argument being advanced here is that diversity enriches a country, a people, a community but that diversity should not be opposed to identity by a dismissive, macro-cosmopolitan moralism. If we have insisted on the necessity of considering cosmopolitanism as a phenomenon that is not the unique preserve of the urban, the underlying concerns are partly ecological. It is unlikely that rampant urbanization of both our societies and our planet is the best way for humanity to proceed. The accelerated drift from the countryside in most parts of the world is a factor that detracts from rather than enhances cultural diversity and represents a significant threat to linguistic diversity, to name but one component of cultural specificity (Abley 2003).

It is important that we track the instances of translation which highlight the micro-cosmopolitan complexity of places and cultures which are often outside the critical purview of the urban metropolis. In this way, in the investigation of the links between culture, place and language from the perspective of the fractal differentialism mentioned earlier it will be possible to develop a reading of, for example, non-metropolitan experience which is not condemned to a wistful *passéisme* but is forward-looking in its restoration of political complexity and cultural dynamism to all areas of territory and memory. Such a move, an integral part of the micro-cosmopolitan project, would both revitalize inquiry into a substantial body of the world's literature, both written and oral, which has the rural as its focus and also have important implications for the development of a progressive approach to translation theory and practice in rural communities throughout the world.

A further argument in favour of a micro-cosmopolitan sensitivity stems from a major potential failing of cosmopolitanism which is its weak conception of solidarity. As Craig Calhoun observes:

> if cosmopolitan democracy is to be more than a good, ethical orientation for those privileged to inhabit the frequent traveller lounges, it must put down roots in the solidarities that organize most people's sense of identity and location in the world. To appeal simply to liberal individualism – even with respect for diversity – is to disempower those who lack substantial personal or organizational resources.
>
> (2002: 108)

Not only do solidarities of various forms, whether based on religion, ethnicity, language, gender or political orientation, help people to make sense of the world but solidarity is also the basis for social and political transformation. Thus, the proximity of macro-cosmopolitanism to rationalist liberal individualism means that cosmopolitanism can find itself disarmed in the face of a neo-liberal onslaught on social achievements, themselves the outcome of struggles based on political solidarity. It is hardly surprising that the first example of usage under 'cosmopolitanism' in the *Oxford English Dictionary* (*OED*) is taken from John Stuart Mill's *Political Economy* in 1848: 'Capital is becoming more and more cosmopolitan'. Similarly, as we shall see in later chapters, to argue for the importance of distinctive language and translation rights as the basis of communal identity is to argue from and on the basis of a notion of solidarity. As Richard Bellamy and Dario Castiglione (1998: 158) point out, 'the proper acknowledgement of "thin" basic rights rests on their being specified and overlaid by a "thicker" web of social obligations.'

In other words, human beings not only have rights and obligations, they also have relationships and commitments. A micro-cosmopolitan perspective admits the importance and complexity of the local as a basis for the formation of solidary relationships but allows for the trans-local spread of those relationships, i.e. for the establishment of solidarities that are not *either* local *or* global but both *local* and *global*. In the words of the Scottish environmentalist, Alastair McIntosh,

> I must start where I stand. As children, we used to be told that if you dug a really deep hole, you'd come out in Australia. I think in some ways this is very true. If any of us dig deep enough where we stand, we will find ourselves connected to all parts of the world.
>
> (2002: 7)

So what are the advantages of this new thinking about the cosmopolitan for the way in which we view translation not only in the contemporary world but at various moments in the history of translation practice? It is possible to extrapolate a set of key notions that makes for the distinctiveness of the new intellectual current with to competing bodies of thought and that point to its relevance for translation First, cosmopolitanism allows us to transcend the nation-state model and *gnizance of new (and old) transnational realities in translation. In addition, the micro version proposed in this work pays due attention to the aspiration to distinctiveness, the functions of solidarity and the existence of complexity across scales. Second, and this point in a sense follows on from the first, cosmopolitan theory permits mediation between the global and the local, a crucial point, as we shall see further on in the chapter, for considering translation in its current state. Third, in its unwillingness to be wholly subject to any fixed, permanent, all-encompassing notion of belonging or being, cosmopolitanism is by definition anti-essentialist, an important consideration for how we defend translation against its critics. Fourth, as we saw above, cosmopolitanism leaves room for complex repertoires of allegiance (cosmopolitanism and multiple subjects); this is crucial in accounting for the multiplicity of factors which can affect translation and translators in any one situation. Fifth, there is the emancipatory thrust of a theory which does not see self as wholly bounded by a community of origin. In other words, just as there is more to the community than self, there is more to the self than community.

This does not mean, however, that the self can only triumph when pitted against community. What Calhoun says about democracy applies equally well to cosmo-politanism: 'it must empower people in the actual conditions of their lives. This means to empower them within communities and traditions, not in spite of them, and as members of groups not only as individuals' (2002: 92). The project of freedom cannot simply be the concern of any one individual but must also take cognizance of a community's capacity for change, if only because tradition itself is a dynamic rather than a static concept. Finally, cosmopolitanism sets itself apart from forms of identity politics whether defined as pluralism, multiculturalism or postmodern relativism. Though identity politics have often been a powerful alibi for the vindication of the translation rights of communities, it is doubtful whether they can ultimately function as an enabling frame for thinking about the porousness and the capacity for dissent of translation and the role it plays in the lives of individuals, communities and larger polities.

Global hybrids

It is crucial in reworking the conceptual basis for translation that we bear in mind the necessity to move beyond conventional divisions or distinctions in human inquiry. One of these distinctions is between the social and the physical or the cultural and the material. John Urry has pointed out that

> most significant phenomena that the so-called social sciences now deal with are in fact hybrids of physical *and* social relations, with no purified sets of the physical or the social. Such hybrids include health, technologies, the environment, the Internet, road traffic, extreme weather and so on.
>
> (2003: 17–18)

In the United States, the Gulbenkian Commission on the Restructuring of the Social Sciences has concluded that former distinctions between the physical and the social are breaking down and that scientific analysis, 'based on the dynamics of non-equilibria, with its emphasis on multiple futures, bifurcation and choice, historical dependence, and . . . intrinsic and inherent uncertainty' (Wallerstein 1996: 63), should now provide the model for the social sciences and so make redundant previous distinctions between humans and nature and between the social and the natural sciences.

In effect, the argument is that many of the disciplines in the social and human sciences are beholden to a paradigm derived directly from a linear, Newtonian, reductionist vision of the world. Thus, typically a society or a translation is broken down into its tiniest constituent parts; once the parts are analysed, they are then reassembled to provide us with an explanation. However, such an approach was not only found wanting to describe complex phenomena in the natural world (Coveney and Highfield 1995) but it also has difficulty in accounting for the operations of non-linear, mobile and interdependent systems which continually hover between order and disorder. Examples of these systems which Urry calls 'global hybrids' are 'informational systems, automobility, global media, world money, the Internet . . . health hazards, worldwide social protest' (Urry 2003: 14). What all of these systems involve is a highly complex interaction between human beings and the technical infrastructure of various kinds, creating what have been called 'material worlds' (ibid., 31). It is significant that in all of the global hybrids cited by Urry translation has a key role to play, from automotive translation in the car industry to the translation of instructions for medical devices. Furthermore, translation as a highly mobile, interdependent activity occurring globally and involving increasingly elaborate engagements with technology is itself an example of a global hybrid or a material world. So in order to account for translation in the contemporary moment, it is necessary to look again at how our changing view of material worlds has consequences for the manner in which we conceptualize and practise the activity.

A Vermont professor, David Zimmer, in Paul Auster's *The Book of Illusions* decides that translation is his preferred form of bereavement counselling after he loses his wife and two sons in a plane crash. Appropriately enough, he chooses François René de Chateaubriand's *Mémoires d'outre-tombe* to translate. Here Zimmer describes the task of the translator as he sees it:

> Translation is a bit like shovelling coal. You scoop it up and toss it into the furnace. Each lump is a word, and each shovelful is another sentence, and if your back is strong enough and you have the stamina to keep at it for eight or ten hours at a stretch, you can keep the fire hot. With close to a million words in front of me, I was prepared to work as long and as hard as necessary, even if it meant burning down the house.
>
> (Auster 2002: 70)

His vision is not untypical, seeing translation as soulless hackwork, a derivative substitute for the unrivalled prestige of the expressive original of Romanticism.

we want to focus on here is not so much the cremation of creative ambition
tting for the task, the house that Zimmer might burn down.

Lefebvre in *The Production of Space* argues that there are two ways in
_____ ...ouse can be viewed. On the one hand, the house can be seen as the epitome
of the rigid, the unmovable, the fixed shape on the horizon that indicates settlement, a degree of permanency. On the other, the house can be presented as an 'image
of a complex of mobilities, a nexus of in and out conduits' (Lefebvre 1991: 93)
which include electricity, gas and water supplies, sewerage facilities, telephone and
information technology connections, radio and TV signals, visitors, deliveries and
so on. In effect, the representative ambiguity (rigid/fluid) of the house parallels
the particle/wave duality of the sub-atomic world that Danah Zohar and Ian Marshall
in *The Quantum Society* (1994) regard as fundamental to our understanding of
the contemporary world. The house exists both as particle (the little house on the
prairie) and as wave (the node of criss-crossing waves of energy, information, goods
and people). Zohar and Marshall argue for the quantum duality of society where
people can be conceived of as both particle (that is, in one spot at one particular
time) and wave (traversed by linguistic, cultural, economic, technological, political
currents of influence). In the micro-cosmopolitan conception of the *particular*
(derived from the substantive 'particle'), it is the wave-like properties of the particle
that connect the global and the local. If we take global hybrids like world financial
markets, the global media or translation, the exchange rate announced on the nightly
news bulletin or the news report from the international press agency or the Estonian
translation of an EU directive on noise at work are instances (particles) of systems
also displaying the wave-like properties of global inputs and outputs. Implicit
in this vision of quantum duality is the necessity for a non-reductionist approach
to global hybrids such as translation. Static theories of society that conceive of
culture as reducible to a finite set of discrete texts and translators operating within
national boundaries isolate the particles but only tell half the epistemic story which
is expressed in the wave-like dimension to human culture and experience.

An area where the particular vision of the particle has been predominant has
been until recently that of history. Due to the close alliance of the discipline in
the nineteenth and twentieth centuries with nation-building, histories when they
were written were largely about specific national territories and peoples and this
was reflected in the disciplinary specializations of university departments where
academics were called upon to teach Japanese, Australian, German, Brazilian
history or whatever. Increasingly, this nationalization of history has been called
into question and a historian such as Christopher Alan Bayly in *The Birth of the
Modern World 1780–1914* argues that 'all local, national, or regional histories must,
in important ways, therefore, be global histories' (2004: 2). It is precisely this
concept of history which foregrounds the quantum duality of cultural experience
that underlies research into translation history and by extension the way we conceive
of translation operating in culture through time.

A transnational history of translation

Gerard Delanty, in his conclusion to *Citizenship in a Glo*
definition of the cosmopolitan moment:

> The cosmopolitan moment occurs when context-bou
> other and undergo transformation as a result. Onl'
> pitfalls of the false universalism of liberalism's univ
> the communitarian retreat into the particular be avoided.

(2000: 14ɔ)

The classic double bind is to be forced to choose between the false universality of a 'world culture' promised by more hegemonic varieties of globalization and the romanticism of the particular. For Delanty, what is indispensable for the emergence of a genuine cosmopolitanism is the encounter between cultures which are both determined by context and also have a capacity for transformation. By way of illustration of the necessary link between the micro-cosmopolitan and the transnational, and the macro-cosmopolitan and the transnational, we will mention briefly the translation history of two very different countries, Ireland and China, which occupy different ends of the scale in terms of territorial size and regional importance. Contrary to earlier practice in the field of translation studies, it is no longer possible to limit histories of translation to literary phenomena within the territorial boundaries of the nation-state; account must be taken of the multiple translation activities of a country's diaspora. It is in this sense that any history of translation must be a 'transnational' history rather than a 'national' history.

In the Irish case, it is possible to identify at least three moments in this transnational translation history. The first moment dating back to the early medieval period sees the involvement of the Irish in the reconstruction of the Carolingian educational system and in particular in the revival of instruction in Latin. The Irish, as speakers of a Celtic language markedly different from Latin, found that they were teaching Latin as a genuinely foreign language. Not only was Latin a foreign language for the Irish teachers, but it had also become a foreign language for many of their continental pupils as a result of the depredations of the invasions by nomadic tribes and the collapse of the Roman empire. The geographical spread of their activities, abetted by the marked nomadism of the Irish monks, meant that their cultural influence was experienced far from their home base in Ireland. Not surprisingly, this religious and pedagogic expansionism has translation consequences. The ninth century will see the emergence of a group of Irish translators – Johannes Scotus Eriugena, Sedulius Scotus and Martinus Hiberniensis – whose Greek–Latin translations will make a significant contribution to the Carolingian renaissance and the revival of neo-Platonism in Europe (Whitelock *et al.* 1982; Mackey 1994; Shiels and Wood 1989; Cronin 1996: 12–15). What is particularly striking in tracing translation activity is the constant traffic in texts, ideas and literary models between Irish monasteries, local powerhouses in a strongly decentralized country, and Irish monastic foundations in Britain and on the European continent.

econd moment in this transnational history occurs in the seventeenth century the religious and political persecution of Irish Catholics leads to the estab- ment of a series of Irish colleges on the European continent. Irish-language anslations are produced in Rome, Prague and Salamanca but it is Saint Anthony's College in Louvain, established in 1603, that becomes the most important site of translation activity. The acquisition of a printing press in 1611 to publish texts in Irish gave an added importance to the translation activity in Louvain as translations were hitherto largely produced and circulated in manuscript form which greatly increased the cost and limited the possibilities of distribution. Not only do the translations themselves demonstrate the engagement of scholars formed by native intellectual traditions with the ideological ferment of the Counter-Reformation but the very language used in them will ultimately influence the linguistic development of modern Irish (Ó Cléirigh 1985).

A third moment in this diasporic history of Irish translation emerges in the twentieth century and is principally the work of Irish modernists in exile such as Joyce, Beckett, Denis Devlin, Brian Coffey and Thomas McGreevy who will make translation an integral part of their specific transnational poetics (Shields 2000: 17–90). Another dimension of this diasporic experience, although much less studied, is the presence of the Irish as missionaries, pedagogues and linguists in colonial and postcolonial West Africa. Irish modernism would be, properly speaking, inconceivable without continued contact with the European continent but similarly the most remote village on the island had a contact either with North America or England/Scotland/Wales through emigration, or with Latin America and West and Southern Africa through the activity of the Church. Literature in the Irish and English languages bears ample witness to the nature and extent of these contacts and it is generally accepted that a territorially exclusivist nationalist historiography has often tended to disregard or minimize the importance of the diasporic. However, what a micro-cosmopolitan transnationalism is arguing for is not that place or identity be dissolved into a rootless geography of free-floating diasporic fragments but rather that we take transnational phenomena like translation in smaller nations such as Ireland to reinvest place with the full complexity of their micro-cosmopolitan connectedness.

Is the quantum duality of cultural experience the exclusive property of the smaller polity? Obviously not, and for an example of the macro-cosmopolitan we want to mention, however briefly, a number of episodes from Chinese translation history. Eugene Chen Eoyang in his *'Borrowed Plumage': Polemical Essays on Translation* warns against overly simplistic views of Chinese language and culture:

> Chinese, despite its apparent monolithic character in the West, is a polylingual and multicultural language, involving elements of Mongol, Turk, Tungusic, Thai and Tibeto-Burman. There are manuscripts in Tun-huang, dating from the fifth to the tenth century, with texts that contain Chinese and Tibetan in interlinear configuration as well as texts in Sogdian, Uighur, and other Central Asian languages.
>
> (2003: 60)

Notwithstanding the complex set of influences on the language, from the first millennium BCE to the early half of the twentieth century Classical Chinese remained the dominant form of written expression. As ideographs were not based on a phonetic script, they were not subject to the laws of phonological evolution, and this allowed the characters to remain largely unchanged through the centuries (Hung and Pollard 1998: 365). However, the relative stability of the language as a formal written medium did not produce cultural closure and it is notable that it is intense and sustained periods of translation contact that allow for the elaboration of a Chinese culture that is as networked outwardly as it is connected inwardly.

The first major example of the transformative impact of translation is the large-scale translation of Buddhist scriptures into Chinese. The enterprise begins around 70 CE and continues for almost nine centuries. The three phases – Eastern Han Dynasty and the Three Kingdoms Period (148–265), Jin Dynasty and the Northern and Southern Dynasties (265–589) and the Sui Dynasty, Tang Dynasty and Northern Song Dynasty (589–1100) – see literally thousands of texts translated, mainly from Sanskrit, into Chinese (Hung and Pollard 1998: 366–68). As Lin Kenan points out, the effect on Chinese culture was profound: 'Because Buddhism was introduced into China through translation, the commingling of and conflict between the exotic Buddhism and the native Confucianism and Taoism have set the foundation of Chinese thought' (2002: 162–3).

A second significant moment in the history of Chinese translation will be the arrival in numbers of Christian missionaries from the West, and in particular of Jesuit missionaries from the late sixteenth century onwards. The missionaries themselves saw the translation of Western texts into Chinese as a way of securing influence over the Chinese administrative elite with a view to eventual religious conversion. Among the keen native supporters of the translation project was Xu Guangqi (1562–1633), a native of Shanghai, a senior court official and Catholic convert (Kenan 2002: 163). It is estimated that over seventy missionary trans-lators were involved in this work at various stages and that they were responsible for the translation of over 300 titles into Chinese. Significantly, a third of these titles related to scientific matters reflecting the growing prestige of the new science of the West (Hung and Pollard 1998: 368–9), with translators like Johann Adam Schall von Bell and Jacobus Rho translating works on astronomy into Chinese which facilitated the reworking of the Chinese calendar by the Ming government.

A third translation movement will be triggered by growing political instability in China due to the incursions of foreign powers around the period of what have become known as the Opium Wars in the 1840s. The interest in translation was prompted by a feeling that the country must either translate or perish. There was no way Western powers could be opposed if you did not understand the science behind their warfare or the politics behind their foreign policy. The establishment of a College of Languages in Beijing in 1862 and the creation of a translation bureau in the Jiangnan Arsenal in Shanghai in 1865 led to a marked increase in the number of scientific translations. Later in the century it was translation of texts from the humanities and the social sciences that was advocated by reformers such as Kang

Youwei and Liang Qichao. One translator, Yan Fu, for example, translated works by T.H. Huxley, John Stuart Mill, Herbert Spencer, Adam Smith, Montesquieu, Edward Jenks and William Stanley Jevons. In Kenan's view, 'this translation movement ideologically paved the way for the 1911 revolution that eventually overthrew the last feudal dynasty of China' (Kenan 2002: 164). These different translation moments in Chinese history can be seen as corresponding to perceived 'gaps' in the culture, whether religious, scientific or political, but the difficulty with the concept of the 'gap' is that it carries with it a notion of the occasional and the provisional ('filling in a gap') and also the sense that once the gap is plugged, cultures can recover a sense of lost wholeness. However, what historical research into translation points to, whether at a macroscopic or a microscopic level, is that in many instances it is the permanent quantum duality of cultural experience that is the norm rather than homogenous national or imperial continuums occasionally disrupted by foreign adventures.

Mutable mobiles

One difficulty with the notion of a cultural continuum is that it can in certain instances shade easily into an overweening universalism. That is to say, what is continuous is seen to be constant and therefore somehow outside the normal operations of place and time, particularly if the culture is a powerful one. Hence the warning repeated by Marc Crépon:

> le péril est de penser qu'en dehors de l'universel, il n'y a que du particulier cloisonné – ou pour le dire autrement, que l'Europe a le privilège de l'universel ou de l'universalisable.
>
> (2004: 44)

> [the danger is to think that outside the universal, there are only closed-off particulars – or to put it another way, that Europe is the privileged bearer of the universal or the universalizable.]

As we noted above, an important source of translation influence for Chinese culture has been Western science and technology and indeed it is the universalist claims of Newtonian science that would provide a powerful underpinning for pretensions to Western cultural superiority (Roberts 2001). However, it is important to examine again how the universalism of technoscience operates, and not solely in terms of well-rehearsed postcolonial critiques of the phenomenon, if only to provide us with a way of discussing translation that is both relevant and enabling.

John Law and AnneMarie Mol note that a conventional way of presenting scientific facts was to insist on their universality. That is to say, once such facts had been discovered, they would apply anywhere:

> The faith in the universality of *well established facts* depended on never asking *where*-questions at all. The universal was, well, universal. Which meant that

universalism didn't figure as a consequence of an attempt to add
between, or otherwise relate various localities, but rather as sc
transcended them.

(Law and Mol 2003: 1; u..

The difficulty, of course, is that '*where*-questions' are crucial. Facts only become
facts when they arrive at their destinations, that is when the exact same conditions
that obtained at the point of discovery are replicated at the point of arrival. If the
conditions are exactly similar but the outcome is not, then the fact is no longer
held to be valid. Indeed, much of the debate around contested scientific experiments
such as cold fusion tends to rest on claims that those who have attempted to verify
results have not created precisely the same conditions as those obtaining during
the original experiment (Mallove 1991). Facts are part of what have been referred
to as 'immutable mobiles', where the configuration of facts and context must be
held stable if they are to arrive safely at their destination and make sense on the
receiving end (Latour 1987). In a similar vein, Portuguese merchant ships on
their way from and to Lisbon and Calicut in the fifteenth and sixteenth centuries
kept their shape because a network was established which remained stable. The
network allowed the ships to move but ensured that when they anchored in the
Indian or Portuguese ports they were to all intents and purposes the same ships.
Law and Mol describe the nature of the network as follows:

It included hulls, spars, sails, winds, oceans, sailors, stores, navigators, stars,
sextants, Ephemerides, guns, Arabs, spices and money – and a lot more besides.
In this way of thinking, then, vessels become invariant and materially hetero-
geneous networks, immutable because the different components hold one
another in place.

(2003: 3)

In contrast to the immutable mobile is the 'mutable mobile' exemplified by the
Zimbabwe bush pump (de Laet and Mol 2000: 225–63). The reason for the success
of this kind of water pump is that it is never quite the same from one village to
the next. Bits break off and other bits are added on, the set-up varies from one
village to the next. In other words, there is no stable network working hard to keep
everything in exactly the same place: the pump changes shape but still remains
recognizable as the Zimbabwe bush pump. So the object moves not because
a particular configuration keeps its shape invariant but because the pump is itself
a fluid object. The version of space through which the object moves is a fluid
one, namely one where the connections holding the object change gradually and
incrementally (bits are added on, bits break off), which means that the object is
both the same (recognizable as the bush pump) and different (configuration changes
from village to village). There are obvious parallels here with translation. As the
anthropologist Aram A. Yengoan puts it, 'the challenge for translation is that it
must convey simultaneously both difference and similarity of meaning' (2003: 41).
What is implicit in the notion of the mutable mobile is Wittgenstein's concept of

family resemblance, where shape constancy does not 'depend on any particular defining feature or relationship, but rather on the existence of many instances which overlap with one another partially' (Law and Mol 2003: 6). In this context, the paradigm of metonymic translation as developed by Maria Tymoczko takes on a new resonance:

> Translators select some elements, some aspects, or some parts of the source text to highlight and preserve; translators prioritize and privilege some parameters and not others; and, thus, translators represent some aspects of the source text partially or fully or others not at all in a translation. . . . By definition, therefore, translation is metonymic: it is a form of representation in which parts or aspects of the source text come to stand for the whole.
>
> (1999: 55)

In the context of mutable mobiles and a fluid spatiality, translation is not only a highly contemporary but also a potentially transformative practice. For example, Law and Mol observe that:

> A topology of fluidity resonates with a world in which shape continuity precisely *demands* gradual change: a world in which invariance is likely to lead to rupture, difference, and distance. In which the attempt to hold relations constant is likely to erode continuity. To lead to death.
>
> (2003: 6; their emphasis)

The perception of translation as a mutable mobile which operates within a topology of fluidity (as one of the global hybrids mentioned earlier) would usefully put paid to the conventional habit of dismissing translation as synonymous with loss, deformation, poor approximation and entropy. This is expressed in any number of conference papers where the default value is that translation is a mutable immobile and two texts are compared to show that certainly the text has moved to another language and culture (it is mobile) but that it has failed to remain immutable (bits have been added on and taken off, it is not the same). More importantly, however, we can begin to isolate enabling projects for translation practice and education which are consistent with the insights implied and which also connect to cosmopolitan visions of translation and the quantum duality of cultural experience. To this end, we want to examine one contemporary debate from the field of localization and then move on to consider aspects of curricular reform and canonical shift in contemporary literature courses.

Bottom-up localization

When we talk about global flows, we mean, of course, not only the physical displacement of human beings and physical objects but also the transfer of information in the virtual world of cyberspace. The migration of information to other sites, where languages other than the language in which the material originated

are used, brings with it the necessity for and the challenge of localiz
Localization indeed is frequently hailed as a means of protecting linguistic spe
ficity and cultural difference. As Detlev Hoppenrath, a German management
consultant puts it, 'Localization is providing the vessel in which cultural content
can be transformed and carried into the world and to the people, allowing them
to participate and keep their own identities at the same time' (2002: 14). The difficulty is, of course, as Richard Ishida has pointed out, that localization may involve
painting the house a different colour but fundamentally the house remains the
same (cited in Schäler 2002a: 9). So cultural content may be carried but it is a
moot point to what extent it is transformed. Thus, while much is made of the need
to change data, time and number formats, colour schemes, pictures and images,
sounds, symbols, historical data, product names and acronyms, the issue remains
as to who are the real beneficiaries of the localization process apart from the
shareholders of corporate giants. Indeed, Reinhard Schäler, a prominent expert
in the localization field, has argued that, 'Around 90% of the overall globalization
effort is . . . invested in the localization of US-developed digital material. In other
words, localization is currently used almost exclusively by large US corporations
as a vehicle to increase their profits' (2002b: 22). A further problem is that
a common localization mantra is the notion of reusability. The aim is to reduce
wherever possible the amount of material which needs to be translated, transformed
or adapted. Hence, 'Designers of global products, of websites aimed at the global
customer, use globally acceptable standards, symbols, and conventions' (ibid., 22).

Schäler pleads for a '"bottom-up localization"' (ibid., 23), rather than the top-
down localization of corporate capital, a form of localization which would seek,
for example, to provide relevant, local digital content in as many languages as
possible. In effect, what Schäler is identifying is the difficulty with a paradigm
of translation which is fundamentally that of the immutable mobile. The localization process ensures that there is a stable network that allows for the mobility
of the material to be translated but the 'US-developed digital material' is the
immutable component. A top-down localization can only conceive of the translation
process as one involving immutable mobiles where the focus of technical effort is
on stabilizing the network and accelerating mobility through the streamlining of
the process. The attraction of translation vendor services (Looby 2002: 10–12),
for example, is that web services connect tools and suppliers without the need for
direct communication. Material to be translated finds its way automatically to the
translator and the basic idea is that '[t]ranslation memory matches will be retrieved
fully automatically from anywhere in the network. And for real-time translation,
the web services architecture will automatically route texts to a machine translation engine' (van der Meer 2002: 9). Behind the development of web services
standards is the familiar logic of profit maximization so that the standards along
with '[w]orkflow automation, e-procurement, supply chain automation and the
arrival of new marketplaces will help to bring transaction costs down' (ibid., 10).
It will cost less to get the virtual vessel from portal to portal but it will still be very
much the same vessel. Aligning Richard Ishida's analogy with Lefebvre's observations on the nature of the house cited earlier (p. 22), the internal rigidity of the

, Built will not be greatly affected by riding the wave of

ulty then in localization is the prevalence of what might be
lticulturalism or a superficial version of pluralism where date/
measurements, colours, abbreviations and so on are changed
herwise can remain strongly marked by the cultural assump-
: of origin (Preston and Kerr 2001: 109–31). The extent of cultural
islation, it turns out, is much greater than the naïve substitutionalism which _ ierlies much corporate thinking about localization. However, more
to the point, 'bottom-up localization' conceives of a translation as a mutable mobile
with a genuine cosmopolitan promise. By this we mean that the provision of many
different forms of digital content from a variety of locations across the planet, using
appropriately deep forms of intercultural engagement with the target languages
and cultures, can encourage the emergence of those cosmopolitan moments 'when
context-bound cultures encounter each other and undergo transformation as a
result' (Delanty 2000: 145). In this way, we avoid the *transcendent universalism*
of the culturally immutable being dispatched from one language to the next at ever
greater speeds, and entertain instead the possibility of an *immanent universalism*,
more properly understood as an 'attempt to add up, make links between, or otherwise relate various localities' (Law and Mol 2003: 1).

It is difficult to see how translation could dispense with a notion of the universal
(if we are not to be condemned to a kind of virtuous monadism of mutual unintel-
ligibility) but it must be one that intuits connections rather than poses absolutes.
However, in order for the properly cosmopolitan project of bottom-up localization
to be realized it needs to be incorporated into an ambitious political programme.
The Multilingual Digital Culture project of the European Union (http://www.
mudicu.org) was a first step but what is necessary is a greater mobilization of
political will on a worldwide scale which would realize the true cultural, political
and social as well as economic importance of localization. If in one of the senses
of cosmopolitanism we alluded to earlier, being a citizen involves an awareness of
connectedness beyond the local and the immediate, then it is important to identify
mobilizing paradigms that can usefully link the local to what lies beyond the local.
One of the ways in which we connect with others from different languages and
cultures is through translation, so commitment to appropriate, culturally sensitive
models of translation would appear to be central to any concept of global citizenship
in the twenty-first century.

Loose canons

Translation is not only a matter, however, of what we do with other languages. It
is, also, pointedly, to do with how we experience and think of our own. An important
consequence of the cultural nationalism of the nineteenth and twentieth centuries
was not only the emergence of national languages as a means of affirming political
sovereignty (Casanova 1999: 69–118) but also the establishment of national
literatures as a suitable subject to be taught in the academy (Eagleton 2004b). The

onus was on educators to draw up a corpus of works that would be seen to express the national genius in literature and thus provide the nation with the cultural alibi of literary excellence. From this perspective, the 'classics' of national literatures were the immutable mobiles that travelled through the space of the imagined community of the nation to remind present-day national audiences of the aesthetic pre-eminence of their forebears.

When national literary curricula came under attack in the Anglophone world in the closing decades of the twentieth century, the principal focus of the 'canon wars' was the exclusion of authors from the national literary canon on the basis of race, class, gender or sexual orientation (Bloom 1987; Nussbaum 1997; Jay 1997). One could argue, however, that there is another form of canonical exclusion which has, remarkably, gone unremarked and that is literature in translation. We are referring here not to 'world literature' (see the discussion in Chapter 3), that is the teaching of foreign authors in translation as part of courses on the literatures of the world, but to the presence of literary translation in mainstream literature courses in different national languages. Michael Hamburger, the translator and critic, made the surprising and somewhat disingenuous comment that 'English poetry is so rich as to have little need or room for additions in the guise of translations' (cited in Tomlinson 2003: 3). The response of another distinguished poet and critic, Charles Tomlinson, was to query this myth of linguistic self-sufficiency:

> One feels obliged to respond to this conclusion by saying that English poetry happens to *be* so rich because of what it managed to incorporate into itself in the 'guise of translations', and that the creative translations of men like Oldham, Dryden, Pope, and in our own century, Pound, helped English shed its provincialisms. Furthermore, these men, whose translation work is a meaningful part of the richness of English poetry, were seldom content to offer merely 'pointers to the original texts'; for the texts they were incorporating into English demanded an extension and enrichment of English itself if they were to be adequately and imaginatively embodied.
>
> (2003: 3; his emphasis)

Tomlinson practises his own form of exclusion through the transformation of an English translation pantheon into a gentlemen's club ('these men') but his observation as to the centrality of translation to the English literary tradition does raise questions about how English-language literature is taught in those countries for which English is one of the national languages.

In other words, rather than considering translation as an issue which only arises when one goes *outside* the national language or the national canon or when one is explicitly embarked on a course in literary translation, is it not time to actively consider translation as a phenomenon *inside* the language, which should therefore properly appear on any undergraduate curriculum that would claim to be a comprehensive or at least a representative reflection of literary achievement in the language? After all, one of the most fundamental insights of the Descriptive Translation Studies scholars is that people who read translations read them as part

from, their experience of other target texts in their own language
The texts may of course signal difference in any manner of ways
ad in the context of the target literary culture. If this was not the
rs would not be looking at them in the first place, they would be
ts in the source languages. In view of the increasingly contested
supremacy of the nation-state as the sole point of political and cultural reference
and the emergence of new forms of cosmopolitan thinking, it is possible to argue
for the reconsideration of literary curricula in national languages at second and
third level. Thus, to take the example of English, it is more helpful to think of the
tradition of writing in the language as a mutable mobile rather than an immutable
mobile from the point of view of a contemporary topology of fluidity. Thus,
integrating translated literature into courses on English literature in English departments or on English literature programmes at second level would involve moving
away from the Romantic notion of an 'original', *sui generis* national genius
which is transported unchanged through time (immutable mobile) to a notion of
literature that is networked beyond national borders through the intrinsic duality
and mutability of translation (mutable mobile). Again, the crucial distinction here
is not to use translated literature in English as a way into other cultures but to
see translated literature as a way into English language and culture itself. The inclusion of, for example, Arthur Golding's translation of Ovid's *Metamorphoses*,
Katherine Philips's translation of *La Mort de Pompée*, Abraham Cowley's
translations of Horace, Eleanor Marx's translation of *Madame Bovary* or Ciaran
Carson's translation of Dante's *Inferno* in an undergraduate English literature
curriculum would not only call into question conventional national presentations
of literary history but would also make available to students as readers the metamorphic energies of literature in translation in their own language. The recovery
of expressive energies from the translation past of a literature also helps to counter-
act the tendency in certain cosmopolitan traditions, both old and new, to see the
past and tradition as baleful nightmares from which the Enlightened Cosmopolitan
seeks to awaken, the long night of prejudice overshadowing the bright day of reason.
   Craig Calhoun notes the

> tendency to treat the West as the site of both capitalist globalization and
> cosmopolitanism, but to approach the non-West through the category of tradi-
> tion. More generally, cultural identities and communal solidarities are treated
> less as creative constructions forged amid globalization than as inheritances
> from an older order.

(2002: 91)

Part of the difficulty is the implicit acceptance of a notion of tradition made current
by Eric Hobsbawm among others (Hobsbawm 1983: 1–14). For Hobsbawm, one
of the preferred tactics of cultural nationalism is to opt for 'invented traditions',
defined as 'a set of practices, normally governed by overtly or tacitly accepted rules
and of a ritual or symbolic nature, which seek to inculcate certain values and norms
of behaviour by repetition, which automatically implies continuity with the past'

(ibid., 1). The difficulty is that all tradition in this view becomes synonymous with invariance, an immutable mobile, one which is largely manipulative and deadening in its effects. Maria Tymoczko and Colin Ireland have strongly contested this tendentious understanding of tradition and argued that

> scholars of folklore, oral literature, music, and so forth are united in acknow-ledging the pervasive presence of variation and change in the domains they study in traditional cultures, and the same is true of, say, high-art literary traditions in non-traditional cultures.
>
> (2003: 13)

To see why this is indeed the case, it is useful to consider what role the past can play in a culture. Éric Méchoulan speaks of the dual composition of present time. One part of the present is ephemeral, it is over before we are even aware of it, and the other part is durational. The durational present is the present which we remember. It is the accumulation of these durational presents that constitute what we like to call our past. What this implies is that each move in the direction of the future, the passage from one ephemeral present to another, modifies our relationship to the sum total of durational elements in the present but in a dynamic, creative rather than reactive and passive sense. So what is new or revealing about our encounter with the present of the future is our changed relationship to the past. As he remarks:

> L'impression d'étonnement vient en fait de ce que mon passé ne semblait justement pas conduire linéairement à ce qui m'arrive; ce qui m'oblige, du coup, à le reconsidérer pour y réunir ce qui en est apparemment tout à fait délié: de là ce frisson frivole de la surprise. Ce n'est pas le futur qui m'étonne dans le présent qui y mène ; c'est le passé qui me surprend dans le futur que je découvre.
>
> (Méchoulan 2003: 14)

> [The impression of astonishment comes from the fact that my past did not seem to lead in a linear fashion to what is happening to me now. As a result this forces me to reconsider the present and bring to it things that appear totally unrelated. What ensues is the frivolous shiver of surprise. It is not the future which surprises me in the present leading to it, it is the past which surprises me in the future I am discovering.]

So the future reform of national literature curricula would almost invariably lead to the surprising discovery of a rich past of translated literature. In this sense, the cosmopolitan moment of connecting up with traditions, cultures and languages from elsewhere would correspond to the most vital element of tradition, its capacity for change.

.n unions

have seen both in the discussion of localization and the consideration of
*.*al curricula, cultures do not remain indifferent to news from elsewhere.
*.*ed, one could argue that the very *raison d'être* of translation studies is based
on this premise. However, this begs the question of how emerging supra-national
structures such as the European Union can give political effect to the versions
of the cosmopolitan articulated in this chapter. In other words, if the local is to
connect up to what lies beyond it, why should this happen in the case of a supra-
national, federal structure and how might it happen? Writing in 1828 on Thomas
Carlyle's translation of an assortment of German texts, Johann Wolfgang von
Goethe made the following plea:

> Die Besonderheiten einer jeden muß man kennen lernen, um sie ihr zu lassen,
> um gerade dadurch mit ihr zu verkehren: denn die Eigenheiten einer Nation
> sind wie ihre Sprache und ihre Münzsorten, sie erleichtern den Verkehr, sie
> machen ihn erst volkommen möglich. Eine wahrhaft allgemeine Duldung wird
> am sichersten erreicht, wenn man das Besondere der einzelnen Menschen und
> Völkerschaften auf sich beruhen läßt, bei der Überzeugung jedoch festhält,
> daß das wahrhaft Verdienstliche sich dadurch auszeichnet, daß es der ganzen
> Menscheit angehört.
>
> (1960: 221)

> [We must get to know the particular characteristics of nations to understand
> them, to be able to have dealings with them. For these idiosyncrasies are like
> language and currency: they not only facilitate dealing among nations, they
> make them possible. The surest way to truly achieve universal tolerance is
> to accept the particular characteristics of individuals and whole peoples, yet
> at the same time to adhere to the conviction that the truly valuable is
> characterized by its being part of all mankind.]
>
> (Robinson 1997: 224–5)

Goethe wrote these lines because of his knowledge of his own indebtedness as
a German writer to the literatures of Europe (Boyle 1992, 2003). Like other regions
of the world, Europe is notable for the extent and variety of the literary traditions
in different languages on which it can draw. For centuries, from the anonymous
Voyage of Saint Brendan in the Middle Ages to Umberto Eco's *The Name of the
Rose* in the twentieth century, European readers have been enriched and influenced
by the literature of their neighbours. The development of poetry, prose and drama
in Europe would be inconceivable without the enormous fertilization that brought,
for example, Cervantes to Britain or Joyce to the Czech Republic or Ibsen to Paris
(Casanova 1999: 241–82). One of the difficulties facing an expanded and expanding
Europe in the twenty-first century is how to ensure that European writers will
continue to be read in Europe and elsewhere and also to make sure that those writers
represent the full linguistic and cultural diversity of the European continent.

It is a commonplace of political commentary on the European Union to claim that European integration lacks a cultural dimension similar to that of the individual nation-states which make up the Union. As Gerard Delanty points out:

> Europe lacks the core components of national culture: language, a shared history, religion, an educational system and a press or media. Language is the main stumbling block. With some few exceptions, language has been the key dimension to the formation of national culture from the late nineteenth century onwards. Since the decline of Latin in the Middle Ages, there is no common European language.
>
> (2000: 114)

The absence of a cultural dimension is often pointed to by critics of the European project who see it as primarily economic and technocratic in nature and share former President Jacques Delors's sentiment that, 'You don't fall in love with a common market: you need something else' (Grant 1994: 221). The nature of what that 'something else' might be is indicated in Article 128 of the Treaty on European Union (2002) where it is stated that: 'the Community shall contribute to the flowering of the cultures of the member States, while respecting their national and regional diversity and at the same time bringing the common cultural heritage to the fore' (Treaty on European Union 2004).

The Article states clearly the commitment of the European Union to the principle of cultural diversity and envisages a role for the Union in the promotion of that diversity. The difficulty in relation to cultural matters is that aspiration can often become a substitute for action and although the principle of diversity might be accepted, there is no clear vision of how diversity might be protected and promoted in practice.

In seeking to give practical effect to the aspirations of the European Union in the cultural domain there are any number of cultural activities which might be targeted but in this section of the chapter we will argue that literature has a very specific role to play in the development of linguistic and cultural diversity in Europe, a role which is in part dictated by the very nature of the literary object itself. A means of exploring the specificity of that object is to ask the question as to what kind of rationale might be advanced to place literature and translation at the heart of any future European cultural policy or indeed of the policy of any similar large, federal political structure. The rationale can be considered under a number of headings: language; history; the economy; politics.

Language

The world is currently facing a threat of unprecedented proportions to its linguistic diversity and some commentators believe that as many as 90 per cent of the world's existing languages may be extinct by the end of this century (Maffi 2001: 1–50; Abley 2003). Given that more than three-quarters of the world's economic production is accounted for by the speakers of six languages (English, French,

German, Spanish, Chinese and Japanese), then increasingly market-driven economies will further threaten linguistic pluralism (Cronin 2003: 138–72). Against
this observation is the credible contention that the different literatures of Europe
derive their strength and specificity from the languages in which they are written.
Furthermore, an important element of the continued vitality of any language is the
production of literature in that language so that in literate societies, literary creation
and linguistic elaboration are closely related in maintaining and developing the
expressive resources of a language and culture. It would seem perverse to devote
considerable public funds to the upkeep of the material heritage of different EU
member states in the form of historic buildings, parks and so on if the priceless
treasures of different European literatures and languages with their connections to
story, myth, history, specific ways of seeing, living and being in the world were
to be neglected. Promoting literatures in different languages is thus, by association,
a way of promoting the languages themselves and conserving the ecology of cultural
diversity necessary to avoid monocultures of the mind (Shiva 1993) which can only
be to the detriment of all those living within the European Union and without.

  In the context of linguistic diversity it is worth bearing in mind the very significant
disparity between the number of translated titles published in the UK, which is
as low as 2 per cent, and the figures for translated titles in other EU countries
and accession states, which are 25 per cent and higher (European Booksellers'
Federation 2004). There is clearly a translation imbalance in terms of a privileged
source language (English) which does not engage in a relationship of reciprocity
in the area of literary translation. It is important to note that literature occupies
a relationship to translation which is both defining and expansive. The definitional
dimension of translation relates to the manner in which throughout European
history, translation has acted as a means of establishing and enriching vernacular
language and culture, whether in Elizabethan England, Romantic Germany or
Classical France (Matthiessen 1931; Zuber 1968; Berman 1984). In each of these
periods, the translation of literature led to the development and consolidation of
national vernacular languages and cultures. Indeed, translation has been specifically
identified in polysystemic theories of literature as part of the programme of national
self-construction, particularly at the point of national self-origination and/or cultural
crisis (Gentzler 2001).

  On the other hand, translation also functions as a way of establishing transnational networks which are expansive in their ambition and reach. That is to say,
it is translation which prevents national literatures from cultivating a myth of pure
autonomy or essentialist autogenesis. Translation can contribute to movements
of linguistic or cultural independence but only on condition that the state of independence is one of interdependence. As translation by definition involves a form
of dependency on the source language and culture, the translational relationship
is an interdependent one but is a form of dependency which is potentially enabling
rather than confining or disabling. The development of symmetrical literary
translation relationships across Europe therefore allows for a dual national and
-nal dynamic in cultural development.

History

The literatures of Europe have been variously influenced by each other over the centuries and indeed periods of intense cultural fervour and creativity (the Renaissance/the Enlightenment/Modernism) have been characterized by increased traffic between the literatures of different European countries (Casanova 1999). Policy interventions in the present would thus not only be able to draw on historical precedents but would also allow for the emergence of a *transnational archaeology of literature*. By this we mean that highlighting and encouraging links between different national literatures in the present leads almost inevitably to a greater interest in exploring relationships which existed in earlier historical periods, relationships which were marginalized or downplayed in the construction of separate national literary canons in the nineteenth and twentieth centuries. Timely interventions in the literary arena would not only allow the European Union to build on a distinguished history of European cultural exchange but would also enable the EU to reconfigure the aesthetic self-representation of the supra-national entity and its constituent parts.

The economy

A certain fastidiousness can accompany discussions of literature in an economic context as if literature were, by definition, hostile to the instrumental short termism of market logic. The notion of literature as a disinterested haven of spiritual refuge in the raging seas of acquisitive materialism may flatter a romantic theology of the outcast and the outsider but the reality is that through publishing, translation and media-related activities literature is part of a significant economic sector in Europe. Publishing is a major cultural industry and in 2002 alone there were over 3,320,000 indivdual titles available from book and journal publishers in the European Union. The three most important member states in terms of number of titles were the United Kingdom (944,000), Germany (900,000) and France (450,000) (Gill 2003). The European Union currently has 25,000 people employed in bookselling and a further 54,000 people are engaged in writing and translating (European Booksellers' Federation 2004). Thus, stimulating activity in the area has tangible economic spin-offs in terms of increased sales for publishers, greater incomes for writers and translators and wider audiences for literature-based activities such as readings, performances and festivals.

There is a less immediate but more far-reaching dimension to the economic resonance of literary publishing and translation in Europe which is linked to the changing nature of economic activity in the developed world. The British sociologists Scott Lash and John Urry have argued that the objects created in the post-industrial world are progressively emptied of their material content. The result is the proliferation of signs rather than material objects and these signs are of two types:

> Either they have a primarily cognitive content and are post-industrial or informational goods. Or they have primarily an aesthetic content and are what

can be termed postmodern goods. The development of the latter can be seen not only in the proliferation of objects which possess a substantial aesthetic component (such as pop music, cinema, leisure, magazines, video and so on), but also in the increasing component of sign-value or image embodied *in* material objects. This aestheticization takes place in the production, the circulation or the consumption of such goods.

(Lash and Urry 1994: 4)

The aestheticization referred to explains the prodigious rise in advertising budgets in the last three decades of the twentieth century and the strong emphasis on value-added design intensity in the production of clothes, shoes, cars, electronic goods, software and so on in late modernity. If the economic future of Europe is increasingly in the area of the production of goods and the provision of services with high added value as a result of the incorporation of a significant cultural and informational component then it makes sense to develop the significant cultural assets represented by the vast array of contemporary literatures in Europe.

The Lisbon strategy for the European Union presented in March 2000 seeks to make the EU the world's most dynamic and competitive economy and crucially this strategy is founded on the pre-eminence of the knowledge society and the production of the post-industrial and postmodern goods referred to by Lash and Urry. The new information and knowledge society envisaged for the EU would only seem to benefit then from the rich cognitive and aesthetic environment offered by the literatures of Europe. The importance of advancing an economic rationale lies not only in changed economic circumstances but in the necessity to avoid the marginalization of literature, and cultural policy more generally, in political debate through a combination of misguided market pragmatism and self-congratulatory aesthetic sanctimoniousness.

Politics

Citizens of different member states are often justifiably proud of their national literatures. If the EU is seen to be actively promoting these literatures, this can only strengthen identification with the Union as a body which is committed to protecting diversity rather than imposing homogeneity. This function of literary promotion is important in the context of debates around the centrifugal and centripetal nature of contemporary globalization. Pieterse, for example, contrasts the vocabulary of globalization-as-homogenization (imperialism, dependence, hegemony, modernization, Westernization) with the lexicon of globalization-as-diversification (interdependence, interpenetration, hybridity, syncretism, creolization, crossover) (1995: 45–67). Friedman, for his part, argues that 'Ethnic and cultural fragmentation and modernist homogenization are not two arguments, two opposing views of what is happening in the world today, but two constitutive trends of global reality' (1994: 102). If the EU is publicly identified with one constitutive trend, namely modernist homogenization, then the risk is that the Union will be politically undermined by the other constitutive trend, the forces of ethnic and cultural fragmentation. To this end, support for literature and by extension for literary and cultural diversity is a means of harnessing centrifugal energies for the greater European project of supra-national connectedness.

Politics and literature further interact at the level of imaginative empathy. In the Explanatory Statement accompanying the Report on Cultural Industries to the European Parliament the following arguments are advanced:

> European cultural identity is closely linked to the historical memory of European citizens, their social consciousness and political attitudes. The political entity and efficiency of the European Union presupposes a European cultural identity and expression. A value like 'unity in diversity' can emerge only through the participation of European citizens in European civil society, where culture plays a central role. It is obvious, then, that such a cultural identity must be closely linked to the democratic participation of European citizens in the vision of a common European destiny.
>
> (Committee on Culture, Youth, Education, Media and Sport 2003: 2)

It is difficult to see any of these aims being realized if the different peoples of the Union are largely ignorant of each other's histories and cultures. Literature is often a highly effective way of allowing people from different countries to understand the history, way of life and outlook of citizens from other member states.

One explanation for its effectiveness relates to the relationship between time and depth or between temporal investment and strength of commitment in the construction of cultural relationships. A difficulty for human beings as political citizens and cultural agents is that they are subject to what the cultural commentator Geoff Mulgan has termed the 'economics of attachment'. As he observes, 'All attachments and memberships take time. We cannot be members of an infinite number of groups in the same way because attachments require not just "quality time" but also quantities of time, to learn about the people involved, their motivations and idiosyncrasies' (Mulgan 1998: 98). Humans cannot be members of an infinite number of cultures or speak an infinite number of languages. To engage with a language or culture in a way that is both effective and meaningful for a person entails the surrender of considerable 'quantities of time' to acquiring the language and immersing oneself in the culture. So the economics of translating militate against the more facile versions of networking possibilities offered by Anglophone monoglossia. In other words, the general decline in foreign-language learning in the English-speaking world in recent years can be attributed in part to the ready identification of English as the sole language of globalization but also to the desire to maintain the benefits of connectedness without the pain of connection (Holborow 1999). The tendency indeed in a world of space–time compression is to favour first-order exchanges over second-order exchanges, i.e. rapid transactions limited in time and involving limited contact over longer-term, multidimensional, complex engagements.

The network underpinned by information technology brings Anglophone messages and images from all over the globe in minutes and seconds leading to a reticular cosmopolitanism of near-instantaneity. This cosmopolitanism is partly generated by translators who work to make information available in the dominant language of the market. However, what is devalued or ignored in the cyberhype of global communities is the effort, the difficulty and, above all else, the time required to establish and maintain linguistic (and by definition, cultural) connections. Conversely, however, the time invested in literature leads to a privileging of first-order relationships in the context of an economics of attachment and therefore is likely to constitute a more enduring basis for cooperation and understanding than more superficial, second-order forms of contact. Thus, literature can arguably act as an influential agent in cultivating both diversity and mutual understanding in the European Union and generate a greater enthusiasm among citizens of the Union for the European project. For this to happen, of course, due cognizance must be taken of the principle of subsidiarity and the cooperation that can take place at the subnational or regional level in the European Union. It is generally understood and accepted in the cultural domain that the European Union should not seek to replicate activities that are already being carried out at national level. The focus, therefore, should be on those activities where coordinated action at a European level can generate significant added value above and beyond what could be achieved at the purely national or regional level.

In discussing the rationale for the promotion of literature at a European level it is necessary to consider more general arguments relating to language, culture and translation which are not the sole remit or preserve of the European Union. We have already seen in the case of localization that the linguistic diversity of the planet drives the translation enterprise. Translators are kept busy as companies globalize and time–space compression means that more goods go to more and more places, more and more frequently. Given the size of the planet and the number of languages and the many millions outside the charmed circle of Western consumption, the translation potential of the global seems infinite. However, mathematicians are not the only group made uncomfortable by the infinite; accountants too prefer closure. Translation costs money and takes time and in contemporary society these are deemed to be interchangeable. Localization may indeed be an intermediary stage in the progression to a different scenario for the new millennium.

One sketch of the possible future is a global caste system based on language where a monoglot elite speaking a global language has a direct interface with new technology – the credit card advertisements tell us in English, 'Wherever you go, it speaks your language' – and wields the economic power of the international service class. The subordinate class will be those unable to speak the global language and dependent on the largess of localization. In other words, one group performing an act of *self-translation* or *autonomous translation* (Caliban learning the language of the master) will be pitted against another group who find themselves in a situation of *heteronymous* or *dependent translation*, where they rely on the translations of others. The paradox for the latter group is that independence (of language) is grounded on (translation) dependence. Consumerism also believes in independence, the autonomy of choice, the freedom of 'direct' access, 'direct' choice. 'Direct' has indeed become one of the most popular corporate adjectives of our age with its promise of originary fulfilment. As the message is spread by the new missionary orders of global conglomerates – advertising firms – prestige becomes increasingly a matter of unmediated access to the original product. The assertion of 'autonomy' is being able to deal directly with the masters of the universe in their own language. The pressure, then, is only set to increase on heteronymous forms of translation as translators are seen as unnecessary go-betweens, obstacles on the road to autonomy and to direct dialogue with those bodies of vested economic power who rule the world from cyberspace. Active advocacy of the foundational multilingualism of the European Union and the positioning of literature as a core element of European cultural policy would help to generate an alternative translation logic in the contemporary world by demonstrating that independence can be realized through interdependence, that heteronymous modes of translation are there as a different route from that implied by the cultural self-annihilation of autonomous translation.

In giving policy effect to the various linguistic, political and cultural imperatives for the active promotion of literature as a key element in the European project a number of elements must be borne in mind. First, there is a need to clearly identify and champion literature as a cultural industry. Revenues from book and learned journal publishing were worth €19 billion in 2000, €6 billion more than the European music industry with revenues of €13 billion (Gill 2003), demonstrating that literature is clearly one of the foremost cultural industries in Europe alongside music and cinema. Second, the enlargement of the European Union from fifteen to twenty-seven member states has meant a historic opportunity to allow the citizens of Europe access to the greatly expanded literary and cultural riches of this grouping. Finally, the policy of the European Union in this area has much wider ramifications in terms of contemporary debates about the relationship between culture and globalization and the possibility of new forms of cosmopolitan practice.

There is an increasing awareness at international level that countries and bodies must act to protect cultural diversity from the homogenizing influences of market monopolies and unequal flows of texts and ideas. Article 1 of the UNESCO Universal Declaration on Cultural Diversity, adopted unanimously by the 185 member states represented at the thirty-first session of the General Conference in 2001, states that:

> As a source of exchange, innovation and creativity, cultural diversity is as necessary for humankind as biodiversity is for nature. In this sense, it is the common heritage of humanity and should be recognised and affirmed for future generations.
>
> (UNESCO 2004)

The challenge is twofold. First, how does the European Union or any other regional political grouping on the planet deal with the economies of scale that are generated by the involvement of media giants in the area of publishing such as AOL Time Warner with its turnover of more than €40 billion a year and workforce of more than 80,000 employees? The dissemination of cheap product largely sourced in one language does little to advance the cause of cultural diversity. Second, if there is not an active policy at the supra-national level to promote cultural diversity, the desire for cultural distinctness will not go away but find refuge in various forms of fundamentalism which in the name of cultural difference will promote not interaction and understanding but separation and segregation. In this context, translation must obviously be to the fore in the search for humanizing forms of globalization. In the next chapter, we will consider the role of translation not so much in the movement of goods, information and texts but in that area which also grabbed the imagination of Herodotus, the movement of people themselves.

2   Translation and migration

In 1949 Warren Weaver drew up a memorandum presenting his vision of speech-to-speech translation based on the use of machines. His mind is on Babel but his images are those of the high-rise developments which would come to house countless numbers of immigrants in postwar Europe:

> Think, by analogy, of individuals living in a series of tall closed towers, all erected over a common foundation. When they try to communicate with one another they shout back and forth, each from his own closed tower. . . . But when an individual goes down his tower, he finds himself in a great open basement, common to all the towers. Here he establishes easy and useful communication with the persons who have also descended from their towers. Thus it may be true that the way to translate from Chinese to Arabic, or from Russian to Portuguese, is not to attempt the direct route, shouting from tower to tower. Perhaps the way is to descend, from each language, down to the common base of human communication – the real but as yet undiscovered universal language – and then re-emerge by whatever particular route is convenient.
>
> (cited in Silberman 2000: 226)

Down in the Adamic basement, communication is a fluent feast of talk, no one excluded from the easy embrace of universal language. The speakers in Weaver's tall, closed towers have different language backgrounds (Chinese, Arabic, Russian, Portuguese) but in the universal underground the shouting dies down (foreigners everywhere being notoriously hard of hearing) and 'useful' exchanges are the norm.

What the pioneer of machine translation deftly echoes in his utopian memo is the biblical connection between translation and migration. The impulse to build the tower and the city on the plain in the land of Shinar is after all the desire to resist the endless onward march of migration: 'let us make us a name, lest we be scattered abroad upon the face of the whole earth' (Genesis 11: 4). The moment of linguistic confusion, when the city builders are forced up from the basement level of 'one language' and 'one speech' to the new reality of translation, is also the moment of forced departure, the journeying once again to the uncertain and the unknown:

'Therefore is the name of it [the city] called Babel; because the LORD did there confound the language of all the earth: and from thence did the LORD scatter them abroad upon the face of all the earth' (Genesis 11: 9).

Different migratory paths bring Weaver's apartment dwellers to their hermetically sealed towers and it is only by descending to the underworld of the great open basement that they can undo the original scattering. In this chapter we would like to explore the consequences of that scattering (linguistic and physical) and ask what forms the relationship between translation, migration and identity takes in a contemporary setting. For the sake of specific illustration we will look at the example of recent developments in Ireland and elsewhere but this will be with a view to examining the broader implications for translation theory of population movements in the modern world.

Migration

In 2002 the United Nations Population Division reported that over 175 million people were residing in a country other than the one in which they had been born. In the period between 1975 and 2002 the number of migrants living in the world had more than doubled. The majority of migrants were living in Europe (56 million), Asia (50 million) and North America (41 million) (United Nations Population Division 2003). In the developed regions of the world, one person in every ten was a migrant while in the developing regions, one person in every seventy fell into this category. Over the period 1995–2000 the world's more developed regions gained an estimated 12 million migrants. In 2000–5, in twenty-eight countries net immigration either prevented population decline or at least doubled the contribution of natural increase (births minus deaths) to population growth. Among the countries concerned were Austria, Canada, Croatia, Denmark, Germany, Italy, Portugal, Qatar, Singapore, Spain, Sweden, United Arab Emirates and the United Kingdom (United Nations Population Division 2005). In 2005, the UN Population Division projected that in the period 2005–50 the net number of international migrants to more developed regions would be around 98 million. The projections for the major net receivers of international migrants were the United States (1.1 million annually), Germany (204,000), Canada (201,000), the United Kingdom (133,000), Italy (120,000) and Australia (100,000). The major countries of net emigration were projected to be China (–333,000 annually), Mexico (–304,000), India (–245,000), Philippines (–180,000), Pakistan (–173,000) and Indonesia (–168,000) (United Nations Population Division 2005).

A significant factor in current and future migration is the demographic disparity at global level, with the population of the developed countries projected to remain more or less unchanged between 2005 and 2050 at around 1.2 billion and the population of the fifty least developed countries predicted to double. Over the same period the population in the rest of the developed world is set to grow from 4.5 billion to 6.1 billion (United Nations Population Division 2005). Immigration does not only directly affect the economic fortunes of the immigrants themselves but it has an important collateral effect in the form of workers' remittances. In 2000, for

example, remittances from abroad augmented Gross Domestic Product (GDP) t
more than 10 per cent for countries such as El Salvador, Eritrea, Jamaica, Jordar
Nicaragua and Yemen (United Nations Population Division 2002). As a major
source of foreign exchange earnings, remittances can be used to import capital
goods and add to household income and savings, or be used for the purchase of
goods and services. Alternatively, they can provide investment funds for entre-
preneurs in the immigrant's country of origin. Migrants themselves can be what
Bauman (1998) calls 'global nomads', who migrate to find opportunities equal
to their skills and opportunities, or they can be what King (1995) terms 'post-
industrial migrants', who are available to work anywhere at low rates of pay. In
addition, there are those who migrate as the result of civil strife, war or persecution.

Implicit in this movement of peoples in a multilingual world is a shift between
languages and cultures. If monolingualism has never been a default condition for
humanity (Edwards 1995), the fiction that it is or might be is even more difficult
to sustain as the languages of new immigrants complicate the monophone pieties
of the unilingual, unitary nation-state. The condition of the migrant is the condition
of the translated being. He or she moves from a source language and culture to
a target language and culture so that *translation* takes place both in the physical
sense of movement or displacement and in the symbolic sense of the shift from
one way of speaking, writing about and interpreting the world to another. As Anne
Malena notes:

> Migrants are translated beings in countless ways. They remove themselves
> from their familiar source environment and move towards a target culture
> which can be totally unknown or more or less familiar, depending on factors
> such as class and education as well as reasons for migrating; they most
> likely will have to learn or perfect their skills in another language in order to
> function in their new environment; their individual and collective identities
> will experience a series of transformations as they adjust to the loss of their
> place of birth and attempt to turn it into a gain.
>
> (2003: 9)

Translation is thus not a matter of idle theoretical speculation or a hidebound
classroom exercise destined to excite the jaded appetites of pedants but is a question
of real, immediate and urgent seriousness. The ability to translate (autonomous
practices) or be translated (heteronymous practices) can in some instances indeed
be a matter of life and death.

Alexander Bischoff and Louis Loutan list the poor health outcomes for patients
who have no access to effective interpreting services. These include the fact that
allophone (foreign language-speaking) patients are less likely to be given appointments for medical follow-up visits, less likely to return for follow-up consultations
and less likely to comply with prescriptions. The absence of interpreting has also
been linked to a higher use of diagnostic investigation, lower uptake of preventive
services such as breast examinations, lower adherence to monitoring of blood
glucose and lower patient satisfaction (Bischoff and Loutan 2004: 183; Sarver

and Baker 2000: 256–64; Pitkin and Baker 2000: 76–91; David and Rhee 1998: 393–7; Hampers *et al*. 1999: 1253–6; Woloshin *et al*. 1997: 472–7; Karter *et al*. 2000: 477–83; Carasquillo *et al*. 1999: 82–7). In the case of those migrants seeking refugee or asylum status the role of translation in determining their fate is particularly stark. As Sonja Pöllabauer observes in her study of asylum hearings in Graz (Austria):

> People who have fled their home countries in fear of their lives or seeking a better life elsewhere need interpreters for their voices to be heard. In many cases, interpreters hold the key to these people's future. Misunderstandings are more than a breakdown in communication, as they can potentially lead to deportation. The consequences of misunderstandings here are thus not merely damage to the asylum seeker's personal image, misleading information or a financial loss, as in many other fields of community interpreting but, in the worst case scenario, are tantamount to a death sentence.
>
> (2004: 143–4)

So the question of translation is at the centre of one of the most important and highly contested social, cultural, political and economic phenomena on the planet, migration. Moreover, this is a phenomenon that is certain to remain centre stage by virtue of overall demographic trends, continued income inequalities and regional political strife which shows no signs of abating. Given the importance, then, of translation for the experience and prospects of migrants, what are the issues that must be addressed if translation studies is to make an effective contribution to debates on a topic which is both very much of our time and often deeply and dangerously divisive?

Culture

Terry Eagleton has noted how for particular versions of postmodernism, hostility to any kind of foundational thinking produced a new candidate for foundationalism: 'It seems, however, that anti-theorists like Fish and Rorty may simply have replaced one kind of anchoring with another. It is now culture, not God or Nature, which is the foundation of the world' (Eagleton 2004a: 58). The promotion of culture as a primary concept is indeed implied in translation studies itself in the 'cultural turn' the discipline took in the late 1970s and 1980s. Where the use of 'culture' becomes problematic is not so much in whether we intend the term in an anthropological (what humans do in their daily lives) or an aesthetic sense (what humans do in the realm of creative expression) but in how cultures have come to understand culture.

Titley points out that 'in our societies, ideas of culture as the more or able and bounded ways of life of racialised and ethnic national groups)4: 9). So the notion of a culture as the essentialized way of life of a generally linked to a geopolitical territory, continues. At a meta-level, civilizations' notion (civilizations as supercultures) 'has been critiqued as being of such import primarily because dramatic dichotomies grounded in cultural fundamentalism are appealing in a geopolitically complex world' (ibid., 11). Singular Culture, then, is what all humans beings have in common as cultural beings or language animals (in this sense culture can be presented as foundational) but pluralized Cultures are what makes us different. Culture allows us to translate and Cultures make us translate. In a world of extensive flows of images, information, people and commodities, the difficulty is that ideas of bounded, immutable cultures are increasingly difficult to sustain. Mike Featherstone and Scott Lash highlight the fragility of static notions of culture and identity in the contemporary world:

> Culture which was assumed to possess a coherence and order, to enable it to act as the grounds for the formation of stable identities, no longer seems to be able to perform the task adequately. The linkages between culture and identity have become more problematic as the sources of cultural production and dissemination increase, and the possibilities of inhabiting a shared cultural world in which cultural meanings function in a common sense taken-for-granted manner recedes. In effect, both inside and outside the academy, we are all asked to do more cultural work today.
>
> (1999: 1)

Part of that cultural work would naturally appear to involve language. If different speech communities arrive in a country, then at the very fundamental level of human communication and language contact, it is no longer possible linguistically and by extension culturally to operate in 'a common sense taken-for-granted manner'.

However, there are different ways of reacting to difference and how we conceptualize difference has significant consequences for how we might respond to it and the policies we might adopt on translation, among other things. As Brah notes:

> the way in which these differences are understood is what shapes the social outcome. It depends on whether such differences are experienced simply as unproblematic ways of doing things differently or are invested with valuations and emotions of hierarchy and unacceptability, in other words, seen as a threat to one's way of life.
>
> (2004: 36)

A feature of political radicalism in the late twentieth century was a concern with minorities in societies and with the legitimacy of their aspirations to affirm their different cultural practices which included the right to speak their language. From the language activism of subnational, regional groups in France to the defence of the tribal customs and rights of indigenous peoples in the Amazonian jungle, the standardizing cultural imperative of unitary citizenship of the nation-state or assimilation into the regionally dominant culture was called into question (Branchadell and West 2005). It was increasingly claimed that equality without difference was merely inequality with a difference and that the right to be equally different was a substantially different proposition from the obligation to be equally like the dominant group in a given society. Iris Marion Young argued that 'groups cannot be socially equal unless their specific experience, cultural and social contributions are publicly affirmed and recognised' (Young 1990: 37). So education within one's cultural traditions, the inclusion of one's language in the state educational system, support for one's faith community and minority group-centred public service provision are part of the set of policy responses to the acceptance of the legitimacy of minority cultural rights.

This practice is variously described as 'multiculturalism' or giving effect to a notion of multicultural citizenship (Kymlicka 1995). The provision of translation and interpreting services to immigrant communities in a society is at one level a classic example of multiculturalism at work in the body politic, and the demand for and provision of such services are part of the albeit reluctant embrace of multiculturalism in mainstream politics. However, multiculturalism, in the eyes of its critics, can find itself subject to the same charge as culture itself. Colm Ó Cinnéide argues that, 'This form of "difference multiculturalism" is seen as defining ethnic minorities as unchanging cultural communities, based on a static notion of culture that ignores the constant flux and changing nature of social groups' (2004: 49). Rather than promoting an understanding of cultural difference, multiculturalism can merely aggravate cultural indifference as groups retreat behind the pale of identity politics and coexist in a plurality of predetermined and mutually exclusive cultural frameworks. Furthermore, a potential danger is that multicultural theory can serve to reinforce notions of group difference and cultural autonomy which tend to be part of the staple of racist and anti-immigrant groups (Malik 1996). Immigrant groups can now be attacked not because they are 'racially' inferior but because they are 'culturally' different. In the disingenuous benevolence of differentialist racism, immigrants properly belong to their culture of origin and all translation in the form of migration is a mistranslation.

In contradistinction to the philosophy of multiculturalism, interculturalism is an approach in which policy 'promotes interaction, understanding and integration among and between different cultures, with a focus of attention on the interaction between the dominant and minority ethnic communities' (Ging and Malcolm 2004: 127). The term 'intercultural', like culture itself, means many different things, of course, to different people and Iben Jensen distinguishes two strands in the research literature on intercultural communication. On the one hand, there is the functionalist approach which tries to predict how culture affects communication and focuses on identifying culture as a barrier against more effective communication. Thus, in certain cultures, if you remove your shoes inside the house, do not offer chrysanthemums when invited to dinner and remember that the left hand is better kept in the pocket than proffered for a handshake, cultural difference will be neutralized and everyone will have a pleasant evening. On the other hand, post-structural approaches look at intercultural communication 'in relation to questions of power, political discourse, constructions of "the other" and so forth' (Jensen 2004: 83). For the functionalist, culture is largely a matter of essences, for the post-structuralist it is mainly a matter of relations though the former may be more productive of easily assimilated recipes for 'appropriate' behaviour than the latter.

Though the multiculturalists and the interculturalists will differ on the degree of exchange implied by their respective terms and the functionalists and the post-structuralists will appear to differ on the question of power, it is the very focus on culture itself which troubles some analysts of multiracial or multi-ethnic societies. Alana Lentin, for example, claims that:

> Many theorists, artists, musicians and writers have emphasised the fluidity of cultural identities. But without challenging the underlying reasons for why culture dominates our understandings it is unlikely that this will have a significant impact in the realm of politics and policy making. Thinking culturally about difference is the default for not talking about 'race', thereby avoiding the charge of racism. But the need for such a substitute obscures precisely the fact that the hierarchy put in place by racism has been maintained.
>
> (2004: 99)

The danger is that culture is simply perceived as politics without the pain. It is easier, in other words, to promote upbeat images of cultural diversity and deal with racial violence on a piecemeal basis than to address the structuring effects of racism on national societies.

The emergence of multiculturalism, interculturalism and cultural diversity as issues for many societies in recent decades is to do with the increased scale of migration attendant on economic and political developments and demographic changes but the prevalence of debate on these topics is also linked to the implications of living in a world of global connectedness. John Tomlinson, for example, argues that the 'impact of globalisation is to change the very texture of locality' and that it is more useful to look at the way in which the effects of globalization are felt within a particular locality than to apply the macro perspective of globality in a top-down, indiscriminate fashion (Tomlinson 2004: 26). In other words, everyone who sits down to eat in a McDonald's in Moscow is not necessarily an uncritical groupie of transnational capital. Tomlinson's argument which echoes at some level our plea for a micro-cosmopolitan perspective in the previous chapter needs to be put into the context of two tendencies in local responses to global changes.

On the one hand, as Mary Kaldor (1999) has pointed out, the more globalization comes to impact on a society or group the more intense can be the local or specific identification as a way of countering forces that are perceived, rightly or wrongly, as inimical to difference. On the other, the notion of 'deterritorialization' means that the 'natural' relation of culture to geographical and social territories is gradually fading. As Tomlinson observes, 'Deterritorialisation, then, means that the significance of the geographical location of a culture – not only the physical, environmental and climactic location, but all the self-definitions, clear ethnic boundaries and delimiting practices that have accrued around this – is eroding' (2004: 26). The English language as the specific cultural expression of an island people shaped by geography and history has now become 'deterritorialized' as a global language and though it still bares the multiple traces of its territorial origins, its evolution is no longer beholden to the accidents of British geography.

The two responses are linked of course in that a reaction to deterritorialization in a society can be an anxious reassertion of essentialist and particular difference as an attempt to 'reterritorialize' place or community. For example, Gerard Delanty (2000) noted with respect to rising levels of anti-immigrant sentiment in Europe in recent years that part of this antipathy is linked to the declining role of the nation-state in the new global order and that immigrants are designated as both culturally other (modes of dress, marital arrangements, gender roles, place of religion) and socially undesirable (as competitors for welfare provision). Thus, the response to the transnational neo-liberal assault on the public provision of goods and services translates into a particularist welfare nationalism that uses cultural difference to identify migrants as the putative cause of social and economic dislocation and fragmentation. The co-option of culture into a politics of exclusion begs questions, as we saw above, as to how cultures are constructed or said to exist. A related question is how individual identity is believed to emerge and whether identities are viewed as primarily to do with separation and autonomy or are seen as 'dialectical constructs, intrinsically relational, and shaped by otherness' (Bagnoli 2004: 58). Though the notion of the autonomous self has been largely privileged in Western thought (MacIntyre 1999) it is difficult to see how we can define ourselves except in relationship to what we are not. If everything is the same, there is no difference and if there is no difference, there is no identity. Consequently, difference is essential to the construction of identity. The 'dialogical self' (Hermans 2001: 243–81) is a processual self who needs a continuous dialogue with others (who can of course be imaginary as well as real) in order to get a distinct sense of who he or she is and this process of endless recalibration can of course last a lifetime. Thus, at the level of both self and culture, open-ended interdependency is a more credible candidate than essentialist autonomy for thinking about forms of living in interconnectedness.

Locale

In order to explore the relationship of migration to identity, culture and translation we want to enlist Tomlinson's call (see p. 49 above) for more local examination of the effects of globalization, and look at the translation consequences of a dramatic shift in migration patterns for one specific locale, Ireland. Ireland for many centuries was less of a destination than a memory. Indeed, it was said that the Irish boomerang differed from its Australian counterpart in one important respect. When you threw it, it never came back – it only sang about coming back. Ireland remained a country of marked net outward migration for most of the twentieth century and, notwithstanding independence in 1922, the country continued to lose large numbers of young people to foreign labour markets (Lee 1989). The situation was so critical in the 1950s that a popular book of the period had as its title, *The Vanishing Irish* (O'Brien 1954). Though the situation improved somewhat with economic reforms and a move away from protectionist policies in the 1960s, Ireland emerged from the severe economic slump of the late 1970s and 1980s as the country with the highest net emigration rate in the European Union (Clinch *et al.* 2002: 24–42).

By the 1990s, however, there had been a dramatic change in the country's migratory fortunes. Between 1996 and 2002 over a quarter of a million people came to live in Ireland and over half of these were foreign nationals. Work permits issued to EU nationals rose from 5,750 in 1999 to 40,504 in 2002 so that by the end of 2002 Ireland had become the country with the highest net immigration rate in the European Union (Ruhs 2003: 3). The new immigrants were largely made up of Irish nationals returning from abroad and economic migrants, with political refugees and asylum seekers accounting for 10 per cent of net migration to Ireland since 1995 (Ward 2002: 27). In 2005 immigrant workers represented around 6 per cent of the overall population of the Republic of Ireland and this was projected to rise to 10 per cent by 2020. The projected need for immigrant workers for the same period was in the region of 45,000 per year in order to satisfy the needs of a growing economy (Lally 2005: 11).

The influx of immigrants to Ireland has led to a radical change in the Irish linguistic landscape and though no comprehensive statistics are available on the topic of language ability (in languages other than English and Irish Gaelic) it is possible to get an idea of the scale of the changes through collating figures from different sources. Tanya Ward in a study on the language and literacy needs of adult asylum seekers in the Dublin area established that there were seventy-eight different nationalities living in the area covered by the Eastern Regional Health Authority. In a survey on a representative sample from the asylum-seeker population she determined that there were sixty-three different mother tongues among the respondents. The dominant minority linguistic group was Romanian, with 28 per cent of respondents speaking it as their first language. Bantu languages from Africa's main linguistic family, Niger Congo, represented 13 per cent of respondents and of these approximately 11 per cent were Yoruba speakers, while 2 per cent spoke Ibo/Igbo (Ward 2002: 32). Other languages spoken included Russian (8 per cent), Arabic (7 per cent), French (5 per cent), English (4 per cent), Polish (3 per cent) and Albanian (2 per cent), and fifty-three other languages accounted for 26 per cent of the respondents. The majority of Russian speakers came from Russia, Azerbaijan, Ukraine, Chechnya and Tajikistan. The mother-tongue French speakers originated from former French or Belgian colonies such as the Democratic Republic of Congo, Côte d'Ivoire and Cameroon, and French was also spoken as a second language by nationals from Romania and Rwanda.

If we examine economic migration between 1999 and 2003, workers came to Ireland from 152 countries, but of these countries ten provided more than 50 per cent. The top five countries were Latvia, Lithuania, the Philippines, Poland and Romania (Ruhs 2003: 5). If we look to immigrants from other European Union countries it is significant that in the 2002 census, the largest national groups from non-Anglophone countries were Germans (8,770) and French (6,794) (Cullen 2003: 3). The extent of the change in the linguistic make-up of Irish society can also be gauged from the claim by the Eastern Regional Health Authority that it is dealing with over 130 languages and from the stated commitment by the Irish Courts Service to provide translation and interpreting services in 210 languages. In 2000, the national broadcaster Radió Teilifís Éireann (RTE) launched its Radio One World service broadcasting on medium wave on weekdays with programmes in a dozen languages. The year 2000 also saw the commencement of *Bilten Zajednice*, a weekly broadcast on the Dublin station Phoenix 105.2FM in Bosnian to the 1,000-strong Bosnian community, mainly living in the Blanchardstown, Castleknock and Clonsilla areas of Dublin. In 2001 Anna Livia FM began the broadcast of a half-hour radio show in Mandarin called *Dodo Time* presented by Hou Wan Ling, known as 'Dodo', and Oliver Wang.

What then are the translation consequences of this significant change in migratory flows and what can translation tell us about a situation which is by no means unique to Ireland? Considering how immigrants themselves respond to their new linguistic situation, we can say that there are two strategies: one might be termed *translational assimilation*, where they seek to translate themselves into the dominant language of the community, and the second is what might be called *translational accommodation*, where translation is used as a means of maintaining their languages of origin though this does not rule out limited or indeed extensive acquisition of the host-country language. These two strategies are not mutually exclusive and in different domains, at different times, an immigrant might elect to use either of the strategies.

Translational assimilation

The Austrian artist Rainer Ganahl points to the market value of language learning and the close fit between knowing a language and knowing your rights: 'a migrant worker's poor language skills in the dominant language of the host country result in and supposedly justify his or her miserable living and working conditions' (Ganahl 2001: 30). Ward notes the particular vulnerability of asylum seekers who are unable to handle the dominant language of day-to-day institutional interaction: 'Asylum seekers without communication skills in English will experience difficulties trying to carry out very basic actions, for example, providing a medical history to a doctor, filling out forms and dealing with officials' (Ward 2002: 72). Awareness of the primacy of communicative competence as a means of economic integration and social survival is the rationale behind the organization of language classes for immigrants and the stress on the acquisition of the dominant language as the key to successful integration.

The extent to which the translational promise is realized is partly related to a socio-economic context which can frequently be an obstacle to the linguistic co-option envisaged by translational assimilation. In *Alien Winds* (1989), a study of Indochinese refugees who had been invited to settle in the United States, Tollefson describes the limits to the notion that the refugees could acquire basic, functional English and through work gain greater proficiency in the English language. The theory was that language would help to integrate refugees into American society and through integration they would improve their language, helped by their American co-workers to learn English. However, this happened but rarely. The refugees found labour-intensive and unskilled jobs with few opportunities to associate with Anglophone Americans. In addition, they had to work long hours to support their families as their wages were almost invariably low. The Indochinese refugees thus had great difficulty integrating into American society as their material circumstances often militated against language contact with speakers of English.

Translating oneself into the language of the host community is not only a way of understanding how that community thinks and functions but also a way of allowing oneself to become a fuller and more active member of it. Meryam Shirinzade from Azerbaijan sees this act of translation as a way of countering the malign rise of racism:

> In Dublin some people seem to be distant from foreigners, but I am worried about the possibility of open hostility that might come sooner or later. I think it will disappear only when this city will become really cosmopolitan and when all the immigrants who live here will be able to communicate in English.
>
> (2001: 20)

It is important to note here, of course, that the cosmopolitanism the Azeri commentator mentions involves not simply speaking to the locals but also speaking to the newly arrived locals from other language groups. Mahin Sefidvafh, an Iranian woman who was persecuted for her belief in the Baha'i faith, sees language as pivotal to her acceptance in Ireland, as related in an article on her experiences: 'She did not encounter any racism when she first settled here. She believes that this was because she integrated well into the community. She learned the English language easily and this helped her to communicate with people' (McCarthy 2000: 14).

The fact that Mahin Sefidvafh was involved in a pilot programme *Zena* in 1998 which sought to integrate Bosnian women into the community through English language classes is not incidental. There is a significant gender dimension to translational assimilation as women in certain immigrant communities find access to the public sphere particularly problematic because of poor or insufficient knowledge of the host language. This is the difficulty highlighted by Gundara in *Interculturalism, Education and Inclusion*:

> The men tend to become bilingual, and operate within different skills and knowledge levels. But in many underclass communities women and girls remain monolingual, unskilled, and only able to do traditional tasks. As the children grow up they learn different languages and skills, and operate in different knowledge systems. This leads to underperformance by children in schools, and total isolation of women, with ensuing social and psychological problems.
>
> (2000: 72)

The failure to be translated becomes cruelly confining and the women find themselves dependent on either bilingual males or their bilingual children to provide them with lifelines to the outside world. Hence the right to exercise autonomous forms of translation (the immigrant woman herself in control of the translation situation) as opposed to heteronymous forms (others controlling the translation exchange) is seen as a crucial element in the emancipation of immigrant women and an important factor in their social and psychological well-being.

A question that arises for immigrants in a community is what exactly is the target language of this personal translational practice. In other words, does the language of the host community actually correspond to the pedagogic ideal of the language class? This question is particularly acute for immigrants arriving in a country where the dominant language is a major international language such as English. The basic imperative underlying translational assimilation is that language provides privileged access to the community. Language itself becomes a metonymic representation of the culture as a whole. To truly understand the language is to fully know the culture. This viewpoint is articulated most clearly by a Swedish interior designer based in Ireland, Petra Berntsson, in her advice to immigrants thinking of setting up business in Ireland. She argues that they must pay particular attention to learning the language and its subtleties: 'It takes a long time to tune into the everyday language and slang but it is very important for understanding the Irish way of doing things' (Lebedeva 2001: 12). Berntsson makes a distinction here which is of capital importance to apprentice English speakers in Ireland: she refers specifically to 'everyday language and slang'. The success of English as a global language can in fact be a handicap to the comprehension efforts of those who come to Ireland knowing some or a lot of English.

The access promised by knowledge promises to be more elusive than anticipated because accent, lexical variety and the metacommunicative framing of statements suddenly render the meaning opaque. The seamlessly global becomes the mystifying local. As Glowena Actub Batutay, a Filipino nurse in St James's Hospital in Dublin, confessed, 'Irish accent and slang are too hard for me. I keep on re-asking people what they mean just to get clearer information. Back home I speak English, our second national language' (Onyejelem 2001b: 2). Malebo Kebabonye, a medical student from Botswana studying in Ireland, tracks the shifting definitions of bilingualism: 'In my country I speak Setswana but I learned English as an official language. Two types of English are spoken in Ireland – one is street – the other is classroom. Irish street English is difficult to understand' (Onyejelem 2001a: 17). If language is a gateway into the culture then what is challenged in many immigrant accounts is a notion of instrumental transparency, that the language can somehow be mastered as a pragmatic global lingua franca involving little or no specific local acculturation. English in a manner of speaking becomes a special way to know the Irish. Conversely, the Irish do things to English that complicate more pessimistic views of English as a single, transferable idiom levelling all before it.

Appropriate, target-oriented translation practices do not so much involve conforming to the dominant, metropolitan varieties of the global language, though this obviously obtains in certain domains; rather, they demand a dual translation process: native language → global language; and global language → local variety of global language. The translation effort involved in this dual process points to the manner in which immigrant communities serve to highlight and in many senses reinforce specificity and local identities in much the same way that translation from continental European languages into English was used by the architects of the Irish literary renaissance to forge a new literary language out of Hiberno-English (Cronin 1996: 138–43). The rendering of foreign materials into the target language intensifies the sense of its difference as difference engenders more difference. This is the aesthetic intuition of Joyce who in *Finnegans Wake* saturates the text with languages in order to make more manifest the particularities and peculiarities of Dublin language and speech.

The Chinese translation theorist Eugene Chen Eoyang, for his part, argues that what unites early Republican Rome, early Tang China, Elizabethan England and Meiji Japan is a tendency to borrow heavily from other cultures which, rather than diminishing, heightened the linguistic and cultural self-awareness of these very different polities (2003: 17–26). But Joyce reminds us also that in the act of reception which is translation, there is also transformation, 'The babbelers with their thangas vain have been (confusium hold them!) they were and went; thigging thugs were and houhnyhymn songtoms were and comely norgels were and polly-fool fiansees' (1939: 15). The Latin, Danish, Irish Gaelic and French languages which alter the surface structure of Joyce's English suggest the metamorphic potential of translational assimilation as the speakers of other languages enter the space of the host language bearing their own particular gifts of insight and expression.

So what will be the impact of Nigerian English, Filipino English, Romanian English on Hiberno-English? What kind of language, in other words, will emerge from the mixing and crossing over of idiom, particularly in the translation zones of the large population centres on the island? It is in a sense too early to tell but, as Maria Tymoczko has argued, translation is not a substitutive, metaphorical process of wholesale replacement of one language or culture by another (or the complete surrender of one language or culture to another) but is rather a metonymical process of contiguity and connection. As she observes:

> Critics will, of course, differ in their norms, but translation-as-substitution breeds a discourse about translation that is dualistic, polarized, either/or, right/wrong. A metonymic approach to translation is more flexible, resulting in a discourse of both/and which recognizes varying hierarchies of privilege, overlapping and partially corresponding elements, coexisting values, and the like.
>
> (Tymoczko 1999: 282)

It is the subtle metamorphosis of the metonymic rather than the absolutist expropriation of the metaphorical which will give rise to a different idiom with its multiple translation traces where the 'overlapping and the partially corresponding' will tilt the language in new directions.

Another possible scenario for translational assimilation when the target language is English relates to the migrant status of English itself. We have already spoken of the 'deterritorialized' status of contemporary global English. The Canadian travel writer Mark Abley, for his part, speaks of the particularly predatory and expansionist nature of English in his account of travels to territories with endangered languages: 'it struck me that modern English is the Wal-Mart of languages: convenient, huge, hard to avoid, superficially friendly, and devouring all rivals in its eagerness to expand' (Abley 2003: 56). Expansion implies movement and displacement and in a sense, of course, English as a global language has become a 'new sort of transit language, a mobile language' (Ganahl 2001: 29). Not only is English the language that in theory allows immigrants to integrate in Anglophone countries but the language itself is a kind of perpetual migrant both in terms of its historical spread and in relation to its contemporary pre-eminence in the audiovisual and cyber spheres. As the result of the globalization of cultural products such as certain US television series and specific US urban sub-cultures, the process of language acquisition for younger immigrants or first-generation immigrants into Irish culture may in future be less the mastery of a specifically Irish variety of the language and more an accented version of a mobile global English or what one French commentator has called *le globish* (Nerrière 2004). The native speakers of English are increasingly speakers of a displaced language which, in a sense, displaces them so that translation becomes the common condition of all who speak the transit language, natives and newcomers alike.

Translational accommodation

The question which must be asked by all immigrant communities at some stage is their attitude to translation. In other words, is all the translation to be unidirectional and assimilationist or is there a moment when the refusal to be translated into the dominant language or the demand for translation into the immigrant's language becomes a conscious form of resistance, a desire to assert language rights, namely those relating to the maintenance of the mother tongue? Elizabeth Povinelli in her editor's note to a special issue of the journal *Public Culture* on translation in a global market argues that when we talk about the circulation of cultural goods, texts and meaning, we must not make the automatic assumption that more is better and that ease of access is commensurate with the value of access:

> For equally ubiquitous to the notion of cultural flows is the notion that for a social practice, text, or aspiration to reach an audience, incite a public, garner critical attention, and thus reshape public culture, it must move, and widely with a form of openness that allows for maximal identifications. Scale and value are thus commonsensically related in a straightforward one-to-one way in liberal and capital cultures. But this is not a universal way of relating scale and value. Many cultural forms accrue value by their radical locality, their restricted market.
>
> (Povinelli 2001: x)

Translational accommodation is intimately bound up with the assertion of a radical locality in ways which counter the perception of the activity of translation as a form of universalist *laissez-faire*. The forms this resistance takes are various. To use the example of the Bosnian community, around 770 Bosnian refugees arrived in Ireland in the early 1990s and the majority have elected to stay rather than return to their homeland. Not only is there, as noted earlier, a weekly radio broadcast in Bosnian but there are also regular Bosnian language classes for children in the Bosnian Community Development Centre. The Irish Islamic Association founded in 2001 to cater for the spiritual and cultural needs of the 20,000 Muslims living on the island of Ireland has as a specific objective the teaching of Arabic to Muslim children. There is a Society for Russian Speakers in Ireland (Sorussi) and, as has already been pointed out, there are broadcasts in many different languages on local and national radio stations. There are now regular publications in Russian, Tagalog and Chinese in Dublin. The Information Officer for the Bosnian Community Development Centre was explicit in expressing his fear that Bosnian children will end up 'assimilating instead of integrating' into Irish society, hence the efforts devoted to teaching Bosnian language and culture (Peters 2001: 4). In addition to fears of cultural and linguistic assimilation and a consequent suspicion of total translation, there are other factors related to translation and language maintenance, namely interpreting, documentary translation and the role of religion.

Anar Odon, a Mongolian national, spent thirteen months in Clover Hill prison in Dublin awaiting a trial on serious charges. The jury was directed by the judge at the Dublin Circuit Criminal Court to find the defendant not guilty as it transpired that Odon, who had only the most basic English, was not informed of his rights by the interpreter when taken to the police station for questioning. This was in breach of Article 5.2 of the European Convention on Human Rights which provides that those arrested must be informed of their rights in a language they can understand. Nor was there any way of checking the accuracy of the translation of his statement which was riddled with mistakes in English and whose contents were not communicated to him before he was formally charged (Coulter 2003a). In another case, a Chinese national accused of two murders turned out to be dating the interpreter who took his witness statement in the police station. He had initially got her number from the police (Coulter 2003b). In July 2003, Dr Philip Crowley, director of the Irish College of General Practitioners General Practice in a Multicultural Society Project, claimed that GPs identified 'lack of interpreters as the biggest single barrier to offering quality medical care to ethnic minority patients' and demanded a proper face-to-face interpreting service in the large population centres (Houston 2003). Particularly acute problems arose in cases where family members, often children because of their English-language schooling, were brought in to interpret in cases involving domestic violence, child abuse, mental health difficulties or gynaecological problems.

Moves are being made to reform the situation, with a number of initiatives from the Health Service, the Garda Síochána (police service) and the Courts Service and the launch of the first graduate diploma course in Community Interpreting in Dublin City University in September 2004. The scale of the interpreting task can be gauged by figures from 2001 when the Office of the Refugee Application Commissioner conducted 12,100 interviews and the Refugee Appeals Tribunal held 3,428 oral hearings with approximately 60 per cent of applicants coming from non-English speaking countries (Office of Refugee Application Commissioner 2004). What is implicit in the practice of community interpreting is that speakers of languages other than English are entitled to access to state services that puts them on an equal footing from a rights perspective with speakers of English and Irish, even though the historical experience of Irish Gaelic speakers has shown how difficult it has often been to have those rights vindicated in practice (Ní Dhonnchadha 2000). In community interpreting translating becomes a means to consolidate or maintain native language usage rather than a practice to eliminate it.

Allied to the provision of properly trained community interpreters is the provision of documentation in different languages. Writing about English-language instruction in Ireland, Ward notes,

> Embracing difference involves dealing with and accepting language diversity. It was discovered in the present research very few providers had actually translated promotional materials and basic information on courses. With a client population with limited reading skills in English, ensuring documentation is translated into key languages is extremely important.
>
> (2002: 88)

Ward is making a plea based on a point of principle (language rights) and a practical necessity (no point in communicating information that is not understood). Responses have been forthcoming with, for example, the Northern Area Health Board producing a video entitled *Your Health is Important to Us* in four different languages, English, French, Romanian and Russian (Uzomah 2001: vi). For its part, the Racial and Intercultural Office of the Irish police now produces booklets in English, French, Arabic, Romanian, Serbo-Croat and Russian. Thus, whereas classically translation demand is often construed as based on the relationship between one country and language and other countries and languages or between the historical languages of a multilingual nation-state, we now have a situation where translation pressures are endogenous rather than exogenous and are increasingly dictated by the highly volatile nature of migratory flows. In other words, translation scholars will have to look at complex, internal translation relationships metonymically linked to global flows rather than focusing exclusively on what happens to languages and cultures beyond the borders of the nation-state.

As Stuart Hall, among others, keeps reminding us, the globe has been around for a long time and human beings have always been on the move (1991: 20). When talking about translation and immigration it is worthwhile therefore to consider how our translation present relates to our translation past. Evidence of this revisiting of Ireland's multilingual past in the context of an altered present and an uncertain future can be found in two publications, *The Languages of Ireland* co-edited by the author of the present work and Cormac Ó Cuilleanáin and the volume edited by Maria Tymoczko and Colin Ireland entitled the *Language and Tradition in Ireland* (Cronin and Ó Cuilleanáin 2003; Tymoczko and Ireland 2003). Tymoczko and Ireland stress the flexible, adaptable and inventive nature of tradition which they contrast with the tendentious reduction of the term by Hobsbawm and others, as we saw in Chapter 1, to essentialist, timeless immobility, and they go on to trace the outlines of a history of linguistic mixing for Ireland which is explored in detail for a number of languages in *The Languages of Ireland*:

> From the pre-Celtic languages and the various dialects of the Celtic invaders to the integration of Latin after the conversion of the Irish to Christianity by British clerics, from the linguistic diversity encountered by Irish missionaries abroad to the integration of Scandinavian dialects introduced by the Vikings, the early history of Ireland is rich in multilingualism. The Anglo-Norman conquest brought still other languages to Ireland at the end of the twelfth century, with armies and settlers speaking more than one dialect of French, Occitan, Welsh, Flemish, and English.
>
> (Tymoczko and Ireland 2003: 1)

An effect of the marked increase in multilingualism since the mid-1990s has been to make visible elements of the Irish multilingual past so that language change is presented less as a threat to the founding languages of the nation (to borrow a Canadian term) and more as part of an Irish multilingual tradition which has been largely though not exclusively overshadowed by the rivalry between English and Irish. Developments in the present then are likely in the future increasingly to foreground the particular variety and richness of Ireland's multilingual past. As part of the events to mark Ireland's presidency of the European Union in 2004, the European Commission building in Brussels hosted an exhibition curated by the poet and critic Peter Sirr which had as its theme the multilingual heritage of the island of Ireland.

Tymoczko and Ireland call Ireland the 'translational island' (ibid., 20) where two cultural traditions, the English-language and the Irish-language, once separate, have now become blended and hybridized. In this sense, Ireland is part of a more generalized, global condition where migratory forces are bringing any number of languages and cultures into closer contact. Robert Welch argued over a decade ago that, 'in questions of culture and tradition everything comes back to language. Whenever there is a crisis, of something vital being transacted, the words a person uses, in speech or in writing, become crucial' (1993: 32). Something vital has been transacted in Ireland, and identity, translation and immigration are at the heart of the transaction though it often only appears in public accounts in a fragmented, indirect way. The transaction takes two forms.

The first is the country's incorporation into the turbomarket of the English language. As the Austrian artist and critic Rainer Ganahl has pointed out, languages are 'not just products of exchange; they also encourage the exchange and commodification of most other things' (2001: 27). Whether scientific, technical or commercial discourse is produced in English, German, French or Yoruba 'has an impact on university studies, research, corporate investments, and decision and definition making of all kinds' (ibid., 28). A recent report which indicated that US investment in Ireland in 2003 was 2.5 times greater than total US investment in China pointed out that a 'large, English-speaking labour force' was a decisive factor influencing the investment decisions of US technology firms (O'Clery 2004). It is remarkable that in all of the debates around Ireland and its relationship to Europe and North America so little attention is devoted to the linguistic dimension of Ireland's relationships with the rest of the world. One effect of the turbomarket has been, for example, to reduce interest in foreign language acquisition at third level so that as the European Union expands, Irish interest in European languages diminishes.

The second form of engagement is ironically linked to the positive economic fallout of the first, and this is the linguistic complexification of the Republic. The relative health of the economy has brought the citizens of Babel to the Irish door-step. And one view of this situation is not to see language (singular) as a barrier but rather to see languages (plural) as cultural and aesthetic resources. The Scottish poet Kenneth White speaks of the geopoetic adventure: physical journeying as travelling through the conspicuous wealth of the world's languages and cultures (White 1978). This geopoetic adventure now begins at home where Irish and English, the official languages of the Republic, enter into a new phase in their linguistic coexistence. But this adventure will not be without its tensions and its dramas. It is Pietro Bachi, the slighted translator in Matthew Pearl's *The Dante Club*, who articulates the painful scepticism of the immigrant:

> What freedom here in America? You happily send us away to your factories, your wars, to waste into oblivion. You watch our culture trampled, our languages squelched, your dress become ours. Then with smiling faces you rob our literature from our shelves.
>
> (Pearl 2003: 315–16)

If immigration is not to become an inferno of linguistic expropriation and cultural theft then translation theorists must indicate the particular, convenient routes away from the tall, closed towers of ethnic and linguistic egotisms. In order to do this, it is worth both relating the Irish experience to that of more established migrant communities elsewhere and relating these experiences to the theoretical questions with which we opened this chapter.

Almost 400,000 immigrants settled in metropolitan Vancouver in Canada in the 1990s. In contrast to conventional assumptions about immigrant settlement (inner-city neighbourhoods as opposed to suburbs) many immigrants settled in suburban areas to the extent that the suburban municipalities of Richmond became associated with Chinese Canadians; Surrey with Indo-Canadians; and North Vancouver with immigrants from Iran (Hiebert 2002: 214–15). David Hiebert, in reporting the research findings of a study into how the processes of immigration settlement and integration differed in five distinct neighbourhoods in the Greater Vancouver area, noted that in the initial phase of immigrant settlement, 'social interaction between immigrants and people outside their cultural community is minimal, and is mainly confined to the mechanics of finding work and shelter'.

Most of the immigrants are not English speakers and 'this creates major obstacles inhibiting everyday interaction' (ibid., 215). In focus groups and interviews, immigrants identified this period of isolation from mainstream society as particularly stressful.

In keeping, then, with observations on the Irish experience, acquisition of the dominant language of the host community is perceived as both necessary and desirable but this move towards a translation of self into the language of other is complicated by other equally telling factors. A valuable source of initial support for a newly arrived immigrant is the already existing immigrant communities which can provide shelter, sustenance and advice. They most importantly speak the language of the immigrant and can 'translate' the realities of the new place into an idiom that he or she can understand. In Vancouver, where the Chinese-origin community numbers more than 300,000, the enclaves for larger cultural groups can be substantial in size. Thus, in terms of movement towards the target language and culture, the immigrant community can help initiate the dialogue through the provision of a support structure and the initial translation framing of the host society, but the research project showed that the community can also be a hindrance and a disincentive to linguistic integration, with certain Chinese speakers electing to spend their whole lives within the Chinese-speaking community. This is partly to do with employment realities: difficulty in securing employment meant that many immigrants were forced to rely on their ethnic community to source work of any kind (ibid., 217).

Another factor which comes into play is the increasing importance of trans-national networks in a globalized world. Transnationalism is the fact of being attached to or experiencing two places simultaneously (Glick-Schiller *et al.* 1992) and is obviously a process that is facilitated by modern mass travel, broadcast and print media and new technology (the web, e-mail, texting). Ayse Caglar, for example, in her study of the Turkish community in Germany notes that around

> 70 per cent of German Turks have satellite dishes with which to receive the numerous commercial channels from Turkey – like the *ATV*, *Kanal D* and *Star* – and more than 85 per cent of all Turkish households in Germany can receive the Turkish state broadcasting channel TRT-INT, which has already gone transnational.
>
> (2002: 181)

Whether the movement between source and target culture is physical, as in the search for work or return visits to family and friends, or symbolic, through frequent contact with cultural products from the source culture, transnationalism both strengthens the bonds of association and familiarity with the source language and, arguably, makes migrants even more aware of the fact that they are, in a sense, living in translation. That is to say, whereas in earlier centuries many migrants were certain never again to see their homeland, such were the financial and logistical difficulties involved in return, this is less often the case in the contemporary world but in a somewhat different sense. Though for many migrants, travel itself is still an unaffordable luxury, it is possible to 'see' and hear the homeland on the satellite channel or in the internet café.

In a transnational age, then, it is of course possible, but less easy for immigrants to 'lose' themselves in translation as they have not only the support network of increasingly transnationalized ethnic communities but also, as a result of modern technology, a readily available cultural infrastructure which constantly keeps the source language and culture in view. Thus, in a sense, implicit in the transnational – to paraphrase Mike Featherstone and Scott Lash cited earlier – is that today the immigrant is asked to do more translation work as the process becomes a much more explicit and ongoing one for a subject who is attached to or experiences two different language-spaces simultaneously. For this reason, it is hardly surprising that conventional assumptions about the translational assimilation of immigrants are beginning to break down. Hiebert comments that many of the children in the study, though fully integrated into the Canadian educational system from an early age, were increasingly attracted to their language and culture of origin as they progressed into adulthood rather than forsaking this identity in the classic melting pot. A quote from one focus group interviewee is eloquent in this respect:

> During my elementary and high school, I could say that I almost never spoke Chinese other than inside of my home and I could almost say that I didn't have any Chinese friends. But I notice that besides myself, I see a lot of Chinese people as they reach adulthood or when they enter university there is a big change in their life. They start to look for their roots. That happened with me. Even first-year university I spoke all English, but now if you look at my friends, most of my friends are Chinese now. A lot of times I speak Chinese now.
>
> (Hiebert 2002: 221)

Increased transnationalism, the arrival of new immigrants and entry into a crucial phase in a life cycle, all acted as triggers for cultural self-reflexivity. In effect, if the children of immigrants were tending in the direction of translational assimilation at one stage in their lives, they were signalling a move towards translational accommodation at a later stage. Again, what is apparent is that the desire to 'look for roots' involves the foregrounding of the translational nature of the experience of the immigrant child moving from the source language of home to the target language of school and back again. What this new cultural self-consciousness or awareness implies is the wish not to make translation invisible but rather to make it more visible, to acknowledge that there are two languages, two cultures (each with its own internal complexity), which come to determine or influence the dialogical self of the immigrant subject and his or her dependants. Diego Herrera Aragon in his account of the experiences of Moroccan children in the school system in Barcelona points out that 'most Moroccan parents encourage their sons and daughters to become proficient in the skills of the dominant culture while also counselling them to remain loyal to their cultural origins' (2004: 73). The research data showed that many of the children did in fact follow the precepts of their parents in practising a form of accommodation without assimilation, along the lines of the policy advocated by the Information Officer for the Bosnian Community Development Centre in Ireland cited on p. 57. In addition, research elsewhere in Europe shows that there is no necessary correlation between high academic performance and unconditional adhesion to the dominant culture (Suarez-Orozco 1991; Crul 2000; Lindo 2000; van Niekerk 2000). In other words, to be in a permanent state of translation is not a fact to be bemoaned or deplored in favour of a solution that would see an end to translation with the full assimilation of the immigrant subject into the host language as the only desirable outcome. It is significant that in the Vancouver survey, immigrants described the provision of translating and interpreting services by regional and national government as a factor which facilitated the development of a more cosmopolitan outlook and encouraged greater interaction with the host society (Hiebert 2002: 216–17).

Articulation

One could argue that the demand for translation and interpreting expressed in these examples and elsewhere is a variation on Stuart Hall's notion of 'articulation': he argues that things are connected as much by their difference as by their similarity. Using the concept of articulation, he advances the claim that 'an effective suturing of the subject to subject-position requires, not only that the subject is "hailed", but that the subject invests in the position' (Hall and du Gay 1996: 6). That is to say, the interest or commitment of humans must be solicited on the basis of what makes them different as their difference is what constitutes them as separate subjects with an identity. The most successful kind of politics, Hall argues, tends not to be one that tells everyone to believe and behave like the party leader but one that addresses people in their different situations and different needs. Whether this differential solicitude is sincere or not is less important than the fundamental intuition that you are unlikely to do or believe something if you do not feel at some level individually concerned or 'hailed'. Difference from this perspective, then, is something which binds rather than divides. If, as Seyla Benhabib argues, 'Democratic citizenship requires commitment; commitment requires accountability and a deepening of attachments' (2002: 183), then both commitment and accountability are likely to be strengthened by the binding force of difference understood in this sense. Thus, from the immigrants' standpoint, the inclusion of translation and interpreting services among the public services constitutes a form of articulation. They are literally being addressed or hailed in their (language) difference and it is arguably easier to invest in the subject-position of intercultural contact if the host society is addressing you as a subject with a specific identity than if you are treated as a generic other whose language and cultural difference are simply ignored. The services of the translator and the interpreter can be subsumed under this more general heading of articulation which as a concept expresses precisely that dynamic relationship between similarity and difference which is central to the core definitions of translation itself.

It is not only public service providers who sense that respecting difference through translation has a legitimate pay-off. The private sector is also beginning to acknowledge that internationalization and localization begin at home and that transnational networks mean that a product description in Mandarin Chinese on a website is as likely to be read by a neighbour in Toronto as by a potential customer in Shanghai. Ayse Caglar notes the results of a highly influential survey on the consumption habits of German Turks carried out in the 1990s which showed that around 97 per cent of the annual net income of the 1.85 million Turks living in Germany was spent in Germany itself. In addition, it was found that German Turks tended to spend more on quality products and designer goods. This gives the lie to the stereotype of the immigrant as invariably opting for the cheap purchase (Caglar 2002: 182). As the Turkish population was significantly younger than the rest of the German population – 82 per cent of German Turks fall into the 14–49 age group compared with 56 per cent of the German population – they were particularly attractive to advertisers as consumer preferences and brand loyalties are established earlier rather than later in life. There was, as a result, a concerted effort by many major companies to provide advertising, promotional literature, customer service facilities in Turkish, which involved a mixture of direct provision in the Turkish language and translation of German materials into Turkish (ibid., 182–4).

The relationship between immigrant income and projected social mobility is also made explicit in the decision in 2005 by the Bank of Ireland to diversify its language offerings in a bid to assist immigrants to access its services. The decision was not, of course, motivated by a high-minded commitment to the virtues of multilingualism in the new century but was dictated by a clear perception of economic self-interest. This view was expressed succinctly by Brendan Nevin, the Bank of Ireland's retail strategy and marketing director:

> We find that migrant workers have an above-average distribution of third-level qualifications and in many cases, are working below their qualification level. But over time, this will change as more people open up businesses of their own. They will be the business people of tomorrow, so potentially, it is a very lucrative market for us.
>
> (Lally 2005: 11)

As in some branches immigrants accounted for 70 per cent of new account holders, the Bank had hired five staff who were fluent in one of Mandarin, Russian and Polish. In addition, (translated) in-branch literature in Mandarin, Russian and Polish were made available in the 287 branches of the Bank from August 2005 onwards. It was ironically around the same period that the major Irish trade union SIPTU began advertising for union officials who were proficient in Russian and Polish to protect immigrant workers from exploitation and ill-treatment.

Extrinsic and intrinsic translation

Both the German and the Irish instances point again to the shift from *extrinsic* to *intrinsic* translation, from translation as an operation taking place beyond the borders of the company's main base of operations (extrinsic) to translation as an activity practised within its borders (intrinsic). Migration means that translation can no longer be seen as simply an aspect of the 'foreign' operations of the firm but is increasingly present on the 'domestic' front. What we have in effect is the deterritorialization of translation itself where translation is no longer a practice identified with a 'foreign' territory and deemed unnecessary on home ground. On the contrary, the presence of translation through migration, in both the private and the public sectors, makes problematic any ready identification between specific national territory and a particular national idiom. It might be objected, of course, that many societies are always already in a state of translation because of de facto or *de jure* multilingualism and that immigration does not dramatically alter the situation. However, even in those societies where foundational multilingualism is part of the constituent make-up of the body politic, the translation demands of migration are not always readily understood or appreciated.

Bischoff and Loutan, for example, note that even in a multilingual country such as Switzerland, language difference is problematic and the need for professional language mediation is only reluctantly acknowledged. They offer the following explanation for this seeming paradox:

> Most Swiss people speak several languages and succeed fairly well in basic communication in the Swiss languages. This, combined with the fact that most immigrant languages were essentially Romance languages (Italian, Spanish, Portuguese), may account for the minimal awareness of language barriers in the past. Over the last 20 years, however, with the arrival of different immigrant groups, this mode has proved unsuccessful, as the many new languages, most of them unrelated to Western European languages, have made communications difficult.
>
> (Bischoff and Loutan 2004: 191)

In their nationwide survey of interpreter services in Swiss hospitals they found that the languages most frequently cited as requiring interpreters were, in order of importance, Albanian, South Slavic (Serbian, Croatian, Bosnian, Slovenian, Macedonian, Bulgarian), Turkish, Tamil, Kurdish, Arabic, Russian, Spanish and Portuguese (ibid., 191). If we compare this spread of languages with that cited in the Irish case, then it is clear that in neither instance is there much scope for overlap resulting from cognate languages and assumed familiarity along the lines suggested by Bischoff and Loutan with respect to the use of Romance languages by previous generations of immigrant workers in Switzerland. The accelerated linguistic diversity of societies which are migrant destinations carries with it a number of implications for the way in which translation is set to figure in key political and educational debates in the coming decades.

The first point to note is that whatever accommodations might have been made with linguistic neighbours, the arrival of speakers of radically dissimilar languages into a culture means that translation becomes an immediate and therefore more prominent issue. It is hardly a coincidence that the marked rise in interest in community interpreting also coincides with a notable increase in migration across the planet, as we saw in the figures from the United Nations Population Division (p. 44). The global reach and diversity of migratory flows mean that languages from far afield come into contact with languages near at home and if communication is to happen it is no longer feasible to dispense with language intermediaries.

Second, radical linguistic dissimilarity can potentially feed into the 'grim essentialism of identity politics' (Kundnani 2004: 105) as utter difference mutates into utter indifference. To put this into context it is worth considering what Richard Sennett has to say about the impact of new forms of economic practice on the kinds of urban environments people come to live in. Sennett perceives a direct connection between flexibilization and indifference and sees cities and the communities that come to live in them as reflecting new forms of economic organization. Part of the institutional revolution of modern capitalism is that,

> There are high degrees of risk taking in which you do not know what the outcomes will be, groups of workers feeling comfortable about working short term with unknown and unknowable colleagues whom they are only going to work with on that task.
>
> (Sennett 2002: 45)

Important in this revolutionary upheaval is that any sense of identification, whether with fellow workers or with a physical space, must become provisional and contingent. The project will last for a fixed period, then it is on to a different project in a different place with different colleagues. Excessive attachment to place or colleagues will ultimately lead to heartbreak, redundancy or both. Not only must the flexibilized offices of the neo-liberal economy not excite too much affection in their users but they must equally be resistant to any idiosyncratic differentiation on the part of their owners.

As buildings are readily tradable on the global property market and you can buy a 1,000 square feet of office space in London from Singapore, it is important that the 1,000 square feet of office space can be understood by someone in Singapore or Sydney or Warsaw: 'in other words, you create the flexibilization of work, where you have impermanent residents in a spot with a market in impermanent office space. Flexibilization leads to standardization' (ibid., 46). The standardized environment that results is manifest not only in the physical buildings that inhabit it but in a socio-economic context that tends to devalue long-term attachments and favours strategic indifference. The potential outcome is a 'regime of indifferences that are non-interactive' (ibid., 47). That is to say, if long-term engagement with others is discouraged in flexibilized work practices, the danger is that these relational patterns extend to the spaces in which people live. Thus, the form of deep or long-term engagement implied by getting to know the markedly different language or culture of another, it could be argued, is inimical to an ideology of flexibilized short-termism.

If we take Sennett's distinction between difference and alterity – 'The distinction between difference and alterity has to do with the possibility of classifying strangers in terms of difference versus the possibility of the unknown other' (ibid., 43) – then it is possible to chart two possible responses to the translation challenge of migrant linguistic diversity. One response is the 'difference multiculturalism' mentioned earlier (p. 48), where the main focus is on identifying differences and classifying migrants into different language groups. Difference is accepted, managed through the provision of appropriate translation services and, in certain instances, celebrated as evidence of 'cultural diversity'. In political terms, such an approach is predicated on the belief that, as Seyla Benhabib puts it, 'Language differences ought to be no bar to democratic participation' (2002: 148). The danger, however, in the era of flexibilized short-termism is, in Sennett's words, that, 'You get a regime of geographical, educational, even to some extent leisure, segregation in which class, race and ethnic differences are managed in the city by principles of non-interaction' (2002: 47).

Another response is to regard language difference as part of an 'unknown other' which in turn results in two forms of alterity, negative alterity and positive alterity. Positive alterity can be said to exist where the 'unknown' becomes an invitation to discover, to engage with, the otherness of the immigrant's language, even if there is always the attendant risk of exoticization. Here the subject either translates from or is translated into the language of the other and there is not simply a recognition of difference but an active engagement with it in the spirit of Muneo Yoshikawa's 'double-swing model', a model of communication as an infinite process where both parties change in the course of the communicative or translational exchange (Yoshikawa 1987). Negative alterity is the ready association of the unknown with the unwanted, a threat rather than a promise. This negative construction views the linguistic opacity of the other as threatening, as carrying with it the potential menace of all situations of non-communication; any number of paranoid fantasies can be projected on to those who 'lack national linguistic qualifications' (Jensen 2004: 88). The incomprehensible language of others becomes a further sign, along with dress or food habits or manners of socializing, of their fundamental undesirability. Indeed, in certain instances, the 'lack' of a comprehensible language is interpreted as a lack of humanity itself and the other is rendered inhuman.

Descartes in his *Discours de la méthode* (1637), F. Max Müller in *Lectures on the Science of Language* (1861), Claude Hagège in *L'Homme de paroles* (1986) and Chomsky (1965) in his discussion of discontinuity theory, all see language as defining *homo sapiens*. If language differentiates the animal from the human, then denying the utterances of others the status of language-that-can-be-translated is to reduce them to the condition of animals. Charles Darwin made the following observation on the language of the Fuegians:

> The language of these people, according to our notions, scarcely deserves to be called articulate. Captain Cook has compared it to a man clearing his throat, but certainly no European ever cleared his throat with so many hoarse, guttural, and clicking sounds.
>
> (Darwin 1986: 17)

Edward Tylor in *Primitive Culture: Researches into the Development of Mythology, Philosophy, Religion, Language, Art and Custom* (1871) noted that the hunting down and killing of indigenous peoples of Tasmania was possible because colonists heard the languages of the aboriginal peoples as grunts and squeals. Deprived of language and therefore of culture, the Tasmanians were dehumanized and treated as prey for imperial hunters. It is partly, of course, because immigrants are aware of the pressure of negative alterity that they frequently report, as we have seen above, the necessity to acquire host-country language skills.

A more positive construction is to see linguistic otherness as an area of genuine possibility, bringing with it new perspectives, energies, traditions and forms of expression into a society. This, of course, begs the question as to how this positive view of alterity might be realized in view of the sheer language diversity of contemporary migration. Again, translation has a crucial role to play here and this can be articulated briefly in two domains, urban planning and education. Sennett claims that the major problem for urbanists committed to a cosmopolitan perspective is 'how do you intensify rather than localize social interaction' (2002: 47). One way of doing this is to see multilingual, multi-ethnic urban space as first and foremost a *translation space*. In other words, if translation is primarily about a form of interaction with another language and culture (which in turn modify one's own), then it is surely to translation that we must look if we want to think about how global neighbourhoods are to become something other than the site of non-interactive indifference decried by Sennett. Everything, from small local theatres presenting translations of plays from different migrant languages to new voice recognition and speech synthesis technology producing discreet translations in wireless environments to systematic client education for community interpreting to translation workshops as part of diversity management courses in the workplace, could begin to contribute to a reformulation of public space in migrant societies as primarily a translation space. Urbanists have not been known to talk to translation scholars and vice versa but in the context of the challenges posed by ongoing migration, neither party can afford to avoid a dialogue.

An area where there is a tradition of engagement, on the other hand, is education (Tennent 2005). Whereas traditionally translation was viewed as an adjunct to language learning, whether of the classical or the modern languages, in more recent times much effort, not surprisingly, has focused on the most appropriate and effective way in which to impart skills to students of professional translation. Another question, however, is raised by the changing linguistic profile of many host societies as a result of migration: what kinds of languages are students going to be taught to translate and how will they be taught these languages? In many English-speaking countries languages that typically feature on translator training programmes have been Western European languages such as French, German, Italian, Spanish and so on. The focus here is primarily on extrinsic translation and they feature on the curriculum for a mixture of reasons to do with history, culture, politics, trade and tourism. If we view the curriculum from the point of view of intrinsic translation, however, and the increasing de-differentiation of 'foreign' and 'domestic' languages, then obviously the number of languages needed to open up translation spaces in

many Anglophone societies will have to be much greater. Indeed, translator education as a conscious part of a strategy to create translation spaces in contemporary
places of residence and work would need to actively embrace a much expanded
range of languages if such a strategy were to have any chance of succeeding.

One way of ensuring this happens is to use the paradigm of transnationalism at
work in migration as a model for the delivery of different migrant languages. That
is to say, the university in the host society should work closely with universities
from the countries of origin of migrants in the provision of multilingual translator
education. Enabling web-based technologies can greatly assist in the realization
of this process. In a sense, the challenge is to move from a notion of the university
or the institute of higher education as primarily a *national* institution to one of the
university as a *transnational* institution. It could indeed be argued at a fundamental
level that if we are to have any meaningful sense of the 'dialogical self' in migrant
societies then translation is not only desirable, it is vital. In other words, dialogue
with others will not get you very far if you do not know what they are saying.
In these circumstances, the dialogical self is hardly likely to flourish if there is
nobody to talk with rather than talk at. So whether others translate themselves into
a language the self can understand or whether the self translates himself or herself
into a language others can understand or whether there is recourse to language
mediators in the form of translators or interpreters, translation has to be present
in the construction of the dialogical self in the context of migration. Thus, from
the point of view of migration, there is a continuum from the concept of translation
space in urban settings to the redefinition of universities as transnational institutions
to the incorporation of translation into any viable notion of a dialogical self.

We noted earlier (p. 48) that a major element in a post-structuralist critique
of functionalist interculturalism is that issues of power are ignored or marginalized.
Already in 2002 the United Nations noted that over 40 per cent of countries
had policies aimed at reducing immigration levels and although these policies were
more often to be found in developed countries, developing countries were also
moving in that direction (United Nations Population Division 2002). Therefore,
although much is made of the movement of goods, services and information in the
era of globalization, the movement of people is infinitely more problematic. Political
developments in Australia, Denmark, France, the Netherlands, Austria, to name
but a few countries, point to the strength of anti-immigrant feeling which finds
political expression in parties which articulate or manipulate anxieties around
immigration. One response to the antipathy to migration has been to instrumentalize
the process and individualize the selection of migrants. Thus, 'migrants are seen
as desirable or undesirable according to criteria based on individual attributes,
mainly governed by economic rationale' (Lentin 2004: 102). Will Kymlicka, for
his part, argues that one of the reasons for the relative success of multiculturalism
in Canada is that immigrants are perceived as net contributors to the Canadian
economy and this for specific reasons:

> Whether immigrants are perceived as net contributors or net burdens depends
> on a number of factors. In the Canadian case, the perception that they are

contributors is largely the result of the pro-active system of recruiting immigrants based on their education, skills and experience. Since immigrants are chosen precisely for their employability, it is not surprising that they tend to have relatively high rates of employment.

(Kymlicka 2005: 84)

The difficulty with this approach, as even Kymlicka himself concedes, is that it leads to the instrumental short-termism of the 'guest worker' which is as undesirable as it is ultimately unmanageable.

Societies may want workers, but they get human beings. The process of settling into a new country and culture takes time and involves varying levels of language acquisition. More importantly, from the point of view of the present study, migrant workers are already being shaped by their new experiences so that they are in a sense on their way to becoming 'translated beings'. They can no longer have the same attitude towards their country of origin, irrespective of whether they wish to return to it or not, because distance in and of itself leads to a reframing of past experiences. Inviting workers to a country and then attempting to dispense with them once their services are no longer required is, in a sense, an attempt to annul the process of translation that has been described so eloquently by Eva Hoffman (1991) among others. What the relevant authorities fail to recognize is that migrant workers are not so much lost in as lost to translation. The workers cannot easily undo the daily traces of the hermeneutic work involved in living in another country, in many cases with a different language and culture. What is revealed in fact is how momentous and life-altering the process of translation is. To treat it lightly or to ignore it as it impinges on the lives of migrants is to brutally abbreviate the human capacity for constructive empathy.

Citizenship

There is another level at which immigration and economic instrumentalism do not make for wholly satisfactory bedfellows and it relates to the very definition of citizenship in a liberal democracy, a definition that has implications for the role and formulation of translation in immigration contexts. Seyla Benhabib argues that citizenship and humanity are indissociable:

> For moderns, the moral equality of individuals qua human beings and their equality as citizens are imbricated in each other. The modern social contract of the nation-state bases its legitimacy on the principle that the consociates of the nation are entitled to equal treatment as rights-bearing persons precisely because they are human beings; citizenship rights rest on this more fundamental moral equality, which individuals enjoy as persons.

(2002: 175)

The rights of citizens are based primarily on their human rights, on their rights as members of the human race. As Benhabib observes, however, "'We, the people'",

is an inherently conflictual formula, containing in its very articulation the constitutive dilemmas of universal respect for human rights and particularistic
sovereignty claims' (ibid., 177). Implicit in this conflict are the limits to economistic
instrumentalism. In other words, liberal democracies cannot look solely at questions
of economic well-being within the framework of 'particularistic sovereignty
claims'; they must also consider a commitment to and a respect for fundamental
human rights because to fail to do so is to radically undermine the basis on which
citizenship is justified in the first place.

Furthermore, economic developments themselves, whether in the areas of
global restructuring, the exponential growth of international financial markets, the
continued expansion of tourism worldwide and acute labour shortages, make it
'implausible today to proceed from the counterfactual Rawlsian assumption that
"a democratic society can be viewed as a complete and closed social system".
A theory of political justice must necessarily include a theory of international
justice' (Benhabib 2002: 168). If the right to exit a society is viewed to be the fundamental right of the citizen of a liberal democracy, as distinct from the restrictions
on travel of totalitarian states, then that implies a reciprocal recognition of entry
to the society. In other words, the (physical) translatability of human beings
implies their (symbolic) translatability – their right to exit and enter languages is
in a sense implicit in their right to enter and exit territories. If a democratic society
in the era of globalization can no longer be conceived of as a complete and closed
social system, then the language or languages of that society cannot be presented
as complete and closed symbolic systems (not that they ever were, of course, except
in the minds of self-deluding purists). Therefore, a theory of political justice
not only requires a theory of international justice but also demands a theory of
translation.

This demand stems from the recurring tension between the recognition of the
universal rights of humans and the attachments of humans to particular places
and forms of expression. As a practice and a way of thinking about the practice
which shifts between the universal and the particular, translation is at the heart of
this constitutive dilemma of the modern liberal democracy. In linking humans
to what is beyond their own locality or medium of expression, it is an integral part
of that universalist impulse that provides the basis for a notion of the citizen as
a rights-bearing person. But in reminding humans of what is valuable about their
own particular form of culture and mode of language through translational accommodation, it ensures that access, participation and justice are realized through rather
than despite plurality.

In taking translation as a central paradigm of political thinking and practice it is
possible to go beyond the cultural holism of identity politics (cultures as unified,
hermetically sealed wholes) and the cultural hegemony of universalist idealism (we
are all the same so differences do not matter). There is a further utopian dimension
to this perspective in that just as the translation realities of the immigrant present
in Ireland have led to altered and novel interpretations of past understandings
of history and culture on the island, so too in terms of immigrant contributions to
society through language and culture is it important to emphasize the creative

newness of translation. As Homi Bhabha observes, 'the borderline work of culture demands an encounter with "newness" that is not part of a continuum of past and present. It creates a sense of the new as an insurgent act of cultural translation' (1994: 70).

Not only does translation allow for the possibility of something new or different to emerge but the possibility of translation itself is the possibility of dialogue across difference which is vital if societies are to survive the predatory divisiveness of identity-based terrorism and repressive responses to it. That is to say, to posit that societies are made up of different groups, or of Them (immigrants, refugees) and Us (natives), whose ways of thinking and speaking are fundamentally irreconcilable, is to imply a state of radical incommensurability or radical untranslatability where we cannot ever hope to understand what another person says or means because our conceptual frameworks or our genres of discourse are so hopelessly different. Benhabib underlines, however, the incoherence of this position:

> Radical incommensurability and radical untranslatability are incoherent notions, for in order to be able to identify a pattern of thought, a language – and, we may add, a culture – as the complex meaningful human systems of action and signification that they are, we must first at least have recognized that concepts, words, rituals, and symbols in these other systems have a meaning and a reference that we can select and describe in a manner intelligible to us – as being concepts at all, for example, rather than mere exclamations. If radical untranslatability were true, we would not even recognise the other set of utterances as part of a language, as, that is, a practice that is more or less rule-governed and shared in fairly predictable ways.
>
> (2002: 30)

Spatial and symbolic translatability, then, is not a salient characteristic of societies in a global age but translatability is a crucial principle of dynamic inner coherence in societies if the body politic is not to degenerate into a warring federation of mutually antagonistic cultural enclaves sustained by a false rhetoric of untranslatability or incommensurability, or equally if the only unifying mechanism is to be the imperium of a dominant language imposing order through exclusion.

We have already alluded to the increased importance of language mediators as the result of the increased presence of structurally various and dissimilar languages in host societies to immigration. What then of the status of these language mediators and in what sense does increased migration mean a shift in the power configuration of translation and immigration? Cecilia Wadensjö notes that,

> In an interpreter-mediated conversation, the progression and the substance of talk, the distribution of responsibility for this among co-interlocutors, and what, as a result of interaction, becomes mutual and shared understanding – all will to some extent depend on the interpreter's words and deeds.
>
> (1998: 195)

Pöllabauer claims that certain traits were common to all tʰ
she studied and these included:

> Neither the officers nor the asylum-seekers seem ᶠ
> as 'invisible' neutral mediators. Their behaviour an
> highly visible and – in most cases – equal particiᵛ
> shorten and paraphrase statements, provide explanaᵤ.
> – and if possible, also the other participants' – face and intervᵥ.
> it necessary.

(2004: 175)

The comments by Wadensjö and Pöllabauer highlight the centrality of the interpreter in language-mediated exchanges and, as increased migration brings with it the demand for the greater availability of community interpreting services, the interpreter is in consequence inevitably going to feature more prominently in migratory phenomena.

It is possible to argue that in the setting of migration we need to pay more attention to the notion of the translator's *audibility* and *inaudibility* rather than confining ourselves to the sole use of the visual and the textual implied in the notion of visibility and invisibility. What counts in the Swiss hospital or the Austrian asylum seeker interview is primarily (though not only, of course) the audibility rather than the visibility of the interpreter. Visibility is not what makes the difference, it is audibility. In other words, if interpreters simply sat there and said nothing, they would indeed be visible but they would not be translating in any sense of the word. By extension, in immigrants' engagement with the wider language community their difference is as much (if not more) heard as seen. That is to say, as immigrants, for example, attempt to translate themselves into the language of the host community, their accent can carry with it traces of their language or languages of origin. This is the phenomenon of the *translator's audibility* where the practice of translation is audible in the mouth and language of the newcomer as translator. It is this audibility which can of course lead to ready identification of the immigrant (who 'sounds' different) and in certain instances render him or her vulnerable to discrimination, abuse or worse.

Conversely, the translator's *inaudibility* is not only the relative marginalization of translation in debates around immigration, the failure to hear the voices of the translators, whether the children of migrants or interpreters working in less than satisfactory conditions in the courts. It also refers to the manner in which the translation labour of the immigrant is rendered inaudible through a zealous pursuit of translational assimilation. The more successful the product of assimilation, the less audible the process. To insist on the translator's audibility, then, is not only to emphasize the crucial importance of orality, the spoken word, in the form of interpreting in any discussion around translation and immigration. It is also to draw attention to the fact that the dominant language reality of the multilingual community is aural. Therefore contending with the aural realities of the community and the concomitant oral response to this aurality will give both natives and

...ers their most persistent and immediate experience of the task of the ...tor. Given the enormity of what is at stake in current debates around immi-...on, it is high time that translators were not merely seen but heard. In the next ...apter, we are going to consider more particularly what happens to those translators who are both heard and not heard in situations of conflict and where identity comes at a very high price.

3   Interpreting identity

Listening to a lecture was a serious business for Plutarch. For this Greek thinker living under the Roman empire, mind and body were one in the commitment to truth. Slackness of jaw and slackness of spirit were one and the same. In his educational treatise *On Listening to Lectures*, Plutarch reminds students that they must:

> Sit in an upright position without lounging or sprawling; look directly at the speaker; maintain a pose of active attention; with a clear expression on the face, without sign not merely of insolence or bad temper, but also of other thoughts or pastimes. . . . Not only are frowning, a sour face, a roving glance, twisting the body, crossing the legs, unseemly behaviour, but also nodding, whispering to another, smiling, sleepy yawns, lowering the head, and everything like this, are accountable and need much care to be avoided.
>
> (cited in Goldhill 2004: 188)

The proper behaviour of the listener was important not so much as an enforced tribute to teacherly vanity as because the body of the citizen in the ancient world had its part to play 'as a speaking subject within the city of words' (ibid., 179). Being demonstrably attentive to the teaching of the philosopher, the speech of the orator or the recital of the poet was instrumental to being a worthy member of the community. In this sense, for the ancient world 'literature' cannot be termed a primarily aesthetic category. This category did not exist and, as Goldhill points out, 'what is taken as ancient "literary criticism" is aimed not at a discrete body of textual material, but rather at the formation of a good citizen' (ibid., 177).

What Plutarch's dutiful student is demonstrating and what translation studies can tend to neglect is the overwhelmingly oral nature of humanity's encounter with the expressive arts, the fact that human beings have bodies as well as minds and *embodiment* that there is an inescapably political dimension to the subject's engagement with culture. If we consider James Foley's contention that using the calendar as a model of human history, writing only emerges on the last stroke of midnight, 31 December (1984: 2591), then any study of intercultural contact in translation studies must consider not only the historical record of the oral practice of interpreting but also how the eloquent speech that is seen to be the fit subject of study for Plutarch's student has had far-reaching implications for the manner in which translation has been implicated in the more violent moments of people's contacts with other cultures.

Unlike translation, interpreting is an oral activity but, except in special circumstances, it does not leave written records. Indeed, the oral dimension to the activity has often been used as a convenient reason for ignoring it altogether. As in oral cultures generally, then, any historical work must use the documentary evidence of the *scripta* to reconstruct the importance of the *verba*. Given that humans throughout history have come into contact with speakers of foreign languages both while staying put and while on the move, there is no gainsaying the importance of the manipulators of *verba* in more than one language. In exploring aspects of identity in the practice of interpreting through the centuries, this chapter investigates a number of notions, namely the idea of embodied agency, the relative ethics of fidelity, the autonomy–heteronymy shift and the representative dynamic of interpreting encounters.

Embodied agency

A text that has come to haunt translation scholars is Brian Friel's play, *Translations*. It is a text that is frequently invoked in discussions of translation and politics. However, in a sense, from a translation point of view, what is misleading about the play is not the account of the motives of those working for the Ordnance Survey but the title. *Translations* is arguably not about translation at all but about interpreting. The tragedy in the play comes not from incorrect orthography or the clumsy paraphrase of transliteration but from the physical presence of the interpreter, just as the Anglophone Yolland's lexical duet with the Gaelophone Maire Chatach is not a failed attempt at translation but an impossible exercise in interpreting.

In the play, from the outset, the status of Owen, the native returnee, is uncertain. When he first arrives in Ballybeg with the Ordnance Survey team, his brother Manus asks him incredulously whether he has enlisted as a British soldier. Owen's answer is swift if not altogether convincing: 'Me a soldier? I'm employed as a part-time, underpaid, civilian interpreter. My job is to translate the quaint, archaic tongue you people persist in speaking into the King's good English' (Friel 1981: 29).

Already, the interpreter has begun to interpret the language context. The asymmetrical situation of languages and their temporal positioning are made clear. The 'quaint, archaic tongue' is opposed to 'good English', one the language of the past, the other the idiom of the present and the future, one the expression of nostalgic resistance ('persist'), the other the instrument of utilitarian rectitude. Owen as interpreter is better placed than most in the play to understand the new linguistic dispensation that he is partly responsible for bringing into being. He is an amphibian figure, straddling two cultures and two languages, adulated on his return to his home village of Ballybeg by his father and yet actively distrusted by his brother.

Interpreters are frequently what we might term *prodigal* figures in cultures. By this, we mean that they will often leave (voluntarily or through force) their native place, learn the language of another, then return to their place of origin where, in colonial history, they frequently act as the agent of the other. The return of the native is of course unsettling and the situation in *Translations* has distinct biblical echoes, presenting Owen as the both the Prodigal and the Prodigious Son (his consummate mastery of two languages). Fêted by the father, resented by the brother, Owen's linguistic doubleness makes him a useful tool of empire but a dangerous insider for the guardians of native language and culture. Owen's dilemma, and it is the recurring dilemma of interpreters in history generally, is that the consequences of oral agency are often inescapable in a way that is not the case with the textual agency. To illustrate this point, we want to look briefly at an interpreter in another context before returning to Friel.

When Primo Levi arrives in Auschwitz, the descent into hell involves among other things a deprivation of familiar language. In *Se questo è un uomo* he describes the arrival of the SS officer who asks if anyone speaks German. A man named Flesch steps forward and is asked to interpret into Italian the rules of the camp. The officer takes particular pleasure in humiliating the interpreter by asking him to translate words she knows to be derogatory or offensive. When her superior enters, the attitude is no different:

> Parla breve, l'interprete traduce. 'Il maresciallo dice che dovete fare silenzio, perché questa non è una scuola rabbinica.' Si vedono le parole non sue, le parole cattive, torcergli la bocca uscendo, come se sputasse un boccone dis-gustoso. Lo preghiamo di chiedergli che cosa aspettiamo, quanto tempo ancora staremo qui, delle nostre donne, tutto: ma lui dice che no, che non vuol chiedere. Questo Flesch, chi si adatta molto a malincuore a tradurre in italiano frasi tedesche piene di gelo, e rifiuta di volgere in tedesco le nostre domande perché sa che è inutile, è un ebreo tedesco sulla cinquantina.
>
> (Levi 1958: 21)

> [He speaks briefly, the interpreter translates, 'The Officer says you should be quiet because this is not a rabbinical school.' The words are not his, bad words, making his mouth writhe in disgust as if he was spitting out a horrible drink. We request him to ask what to expect, how long will we be here, about our wives, everything; but he says no, he does not want to ask. This Flesch, who very reluctantly translates into Italian German sentences full of ice and refuses to translate our questions into German because he knows it is useless, is a German Jew around fifty years old.]

The interpreter is German, not Italian. He is interpreting into his foreign language not his native language. When his fellow inmates ask him to interpret into his mother tongue, he refuses. German, in this instance, is a language not of requests but of orders. Flesch's own language has disowned him in a way that perhaps only Levi understands. The Italian writer is struck by the physical toll of the translation task on the interpreter. Flesch is used as an instrument, a mouthpiece, but the mouth that utters the words also expresses its revulsion, the expressive and alimentary functions of the same organ combining to articulate the distress of the interpreter who becomes a hostage to his own skills.

The philosopher Charles Taylor talks of the specific boundedness and vulnerability of human inquiry in a way which is particularly relevant to interpreting as an intercultural practice throughout history. He contrasts the picture of the human thinking agent as disengaged, as a person who is disincarnate, who speaks from nowhere in particular, with twentieth-century attempts to rethink the nature of the agent. Taylor sees both Heidegger and Wittgenstein as struggling in different ways 'to recover an understanding of the agent as engaged, as embedded in a culture, a form of life, a "world of involvements", ultimately to understand the agent as embodied' (Taylor 1995: 61–2). When Taylor speaks of 'engaged agency' he understands this to mean the way our thinking about the world is shaped by our body, culture, form of life (ibid., 63).

The fact of Flesch having a body situated in place and time not only means that his body will give expression, voluntarily or involuntarily, to his world-view. His embodied agency also means that he is immediately aware of the consequences of his interpreting activity. Not only as a speaking body is he affecting the bodies of the other deportees but as an embodied agent he is uniquely vulnerable to torture and worse should he fail to discharge his duties to the satisfaction of his superiors. Similarly, the tragic implications of what is happening to Owen in *Translations* become apparent to him not when he reflects on the approximations of translation in toponymy but when he is brought face to face with his own irreducibly embodied state as interpreter. When the British officer Yolland goes missing having being kidnapped by local rebels, and his fellow officer Lancey announces a campaign of reprisals, Owen is made starkly aware of both his divided loyalties and his own vulnerability:

LANCEY: Commencing twenty-four hours from now we will shoot all livestock in Ballybeg.

[*Owen* stares at *Lancey*]

At once.

OWEN: Beginning this time tomorrow they'll kill every animal in Baile Beag – unless they're told where George is.

LANCEY: If that doesn't bear results, commencing forty-eight hours from now we will embark on a series of evictions and levelling of abode in the following selected areas –

OWEN: You're not – !

LANCEY: Do your job. Translate.

(Friel 1981: 61)

In a sense, Owen's job would be easier if he did follow Lancey's instructions and just 'translated' but he is not a translator, he is an interpreter. As such, there is no appreciable time-lag between the act of translation and the moment of reception. Message and messenger are co-terminous in time so that they are easily conflated.

Although translation has a long list of martyrs and victims from Étienne Dolet and William Tyndale to the Italian and Japanese translators of Salman Rushdie, textual translation does always potentially provide the possibility of anonymity and the point of textual production is almost invariably remote in time and space from the point of textual reception. The applications of modern technology in the form of video-interpreting and telephone interpreting have freed the occupation from spatial constraints but for much of the history of humanity and indeed throughout much of the world to this day, interpreting is an exercise in bodily proximity. This is why the conditions and context of utterance are always of real and primordial concern to interpreters and are inseparable from the contents of the utterance. Owen, as Lancey reminds him, is not free to say what he likes.

The interpreter's testimony

Interpreters in history are not always, however, fallen angels, hopelessly compromised by circumstances. Depending on the narrative perspective, the monopoly of the scarce resource of language can confer on the interpreter a prestige and authority normally reserved for myth and majesty. This elevated status is apparent in one of the most important works in French to be produced in Ireland, the long verse chronicle commonly known as *The Song of Dermot and the Earl*.

The chronicle was composed around the year 1200 and eulogizes the exploits of the Irish king Dermot mac Murrough and his Norman allies. The text was given the title *The Song of Dermot and the Earl* by William Orpen, who was responsible for editing it in 1892. The beginning of the chronicle has been lost and the surviving text begins with a reference to the person who is the main informant for the story of Dermot's activities:

> Par soen demeine latimer
> Que moi conta de lui l'estorie
> Dunt faz ici la memorie.
> Morice Regan iert celui,
> Buche a buche parla a lui
> Ki cest jest endita.
> L'estorie de lui me mostra.
> Icil Morice iert latimer
> Al rei Dermot, ke moult l'out cher.
> Ici lirrai del bacheler,
> Del rei Dermod vus voil conter.
> (l.1–11)

> [By his own personal interpreter
> who related to me the account of him
> which I record here.
> This was Maurice Regan,
> who face to face spoke to him,

and related this tale.
He taught me the history of him.
This Maurice was the interpreter
of King Dermot who held him dear.
Here, I shall quit talking about the squire
for I wish to tell you about King Dermot.]

The word *latimer* originates in the Latin word *latimarius* < *latinarius*. The substantive derives from the Latin verb *latinare*, meaning to translate into Latin. As Jean-Michel Picard notes, 'By 1086, when the forms *latinarius* and *latimarius* appear in the *Domesday Book*, the latimer was a professional secretary and interpreter, translating and writing down in Latin the speeches and letters dictated to him in various languages' (2003: 71).

Maurice Regan, a native Irish speaker from southern Ireland, is clearly designated as enjoying the close friendship of the Irish king, 'ke moult l'out cher'. We are told that he is entrusted with the important mission of going to Wales to recruit soldiers and knights to fight for Dermot in Ireland. Regan is also dispatched to enter into negotiations with the Norman notable Raymond Le Gros, to whom Dermot offers his sister in exchange for Raymond's support:

Dunc fit le conte passer
Un son demeyn latimer,
Al gros Reymund fist nuncier
Qu'i tost a lui venist parler,
Si li durreit a uxor
Le gentil conte sa sorur.

(l.2994–9)

[So the earl sent across the sea
his own personal interpreter
to communicate to Raymond Le Gros
that he should come and talk to him
and that he would give him as a wife
his sister – the sister of the noble earl.]

The language used in the negotiations is not mentioned but it is presumably either French or Latin. Regan's activities are not confined to Hiberno-Norman tractations, as is indicated in l.1626–61, where he is involved in negotiating the surrender of the people of Dublin at the siege of 1170. The Scandinavian king is named as Esculf Mac Turkil and talks would have been conducted in Irish, a language spoken by both Regan and Mac Turkil.

The interpreter in the chronicle is not an anonymous, shadowy figure. He is explicitly named and his central role in what were important historical events in Irish history is made abundantly clear. In a sense, Regan plays on his role as *informant* not to jeopardize but to enhance his reputation. In *Translations* the suspicion that Owen is not simply an innocent functionary but an active informant for the imperial authorities sours the relationship between him and his brother. The perception of the interpreter as spy, potential betrayer of secrets, is a powerful source of suspicion and indeed, in the case of certain historical figures like Cortés's interpreter, la Malinche, active hostility (Mirandé and Enríquez 1979: 24). However, in *The Song of Dermot and the Earl* it is the interpreter who is presented as inform-ing the narrative so that he is in a sense able to emphasize his own centrality to the events that he describes.

His role as informer is thus not tainted with the opprobrium of double-dealing but, on the contrary, for the chronicler it is the interpreter's role which makes him credible as a witness. In addition, it is worth noting that the narrator of the *Song* emphasizes the dual function of orality in the case of Maurice Regan. We are told, after all, that: 'Morice Regan iert celui,/*Buche a buche parla a lui*/Ki cest jest endita' (my emphasis). The most obvious function is, of course, interpreting itself which is defined by its constitutive orality. But the intrinsic orality of interpreting leads us to the second function which is the *testimonial* function. Because the interpreter is obliged by the nature of his practice to be physically present at the important moments of mediation in the history recounted in the chronicle, he is particularly important as a source of historical information. Here, it is the intrinsic orality of interpreting which will confer authority on the literacy of the textual account.

The authors of the chapter 'Interpreters and the Making of History', in *Translators through History*, make the following observation:

> The spoken word is evanescent. Our knowledge of the past performance of interpreters tends to be derived from such sources as letters, diaries, memoirs and biographies of interpreters themselves, along with a variety of other documents, many of which were only marginally or incidentally concerned with interpreting.
>
> (Delisle and Woodsworth 1995: 245)

This assertion is self-evidently true of *The Song of Dermot and the Earl*. We know about Maurice Regan's activities through the text of the chronicle. On the other hand, it would be mistaken to establish a hierarchy of precedence where the oral is seen as invariably subordinate to the textual, its transience depriving it of lasting value.

What is highlighted by the thirteenth-century text is that Regan's influence as a historical figure relies precisely on the oral nature of his work, which brings him into direct contact with the main protagonists of late twelfth-century Ireland, the Irish, the Scandinavians and the Anglo-Normans. It is the oral engagement of the interpreter rather than the textual traces of the chronicle which significantly determines the outcome of events. It is not despite the fact but because Regan is an interpreter that his influence is enduring. His embodied agency which makes him uniquely susceptible to physical containment or destruction also accounts for his particular power in directly using languages to effect change at a crucial point in Irish history. It is ironic, then, in commentaries on a text such as *Translations* which presents us with the image of an interpreter at a moment of historical change that the oral dimension, the defining feature of interpreting, is almost wholly ignored in favour of discussions that privilege the textual problems of written translation (Peacock 1993; Dantanus 1988).

Diplomats, spies and officials

If Regan's knowledge of Latin confers status upon him, knowledge of the same language makes interpreting a more problematic activity in Tudor Ireland. In a letter to the Gaelic chieftain O'Carroll, Lord Deputy Bellingham intimates his unease at the use of Latin as a medium of communication between English and Irish speakers:

> And where you would have answwher in latyn, remember you lyve under a englyshe kyng, which requirythe in so gret a cyrcut of countrey as you occupy to have sum honest man whom you myght trust to wryte your letters in englyshe, and I lykewhyse trust to expounde myn sent unto you.
>
> (cited in Jackson 1973: 21)

Latin was suspect not so much because of the intrinsic nature of the language itself – it would after all remain a staple ingredient of English public school and university education – but because its most able practitioners were Catholic priests whose loyalty to Reformation England could not be counted upon. The difficulty with an 'answwher in latyn' is that it might fall into the hands of someone who was not an 'honest man', most probably a priest, and therefore likely to be hostile to the Crown interest. Bellingham's suspicions were not, of course, wholly un-justified. Access to education and sojourns on the European continent meant that the Irish Catholic clergy of the sixteenth and seventeenth centuries would find themselves to be important language mediators in times of conflict. The conflicts themselves ranged from minor administrative difficulties to important affairs of state.

One such figure was Hugh McCaghwell, a Franciscan priest who was appointed archbishop of Armagh on 27 April 1626 but who died unexpectedly on 22 September of the same year while still in Rome, awaiting his departure to Ireland. As a theologian of some distinction and a lecturer in theology at the Ara Caeli, the principal Franciscan house in Rome, his knowledge of Latin was extensive (Giblin 1995: 64). Born in County Down in 1571 into an Irish-speaking family, he was author of *Scáthán Shacramuinte na hAithridhe* ['Mirror of the Sacrament of Penance'], one of the Irish texts to be printed in 1618 by the Franciscan press in Louvain in the Spanish Netherlands. As tutor to the two sons of the Irish Gaelic leader Hugh O'Neill, McCaghwell became a close confidant of the earl of Tyrone and was sent as a legate on O'Neill's behalf to Spain with O'Neill's son, Hugh, in 1599. They settled in Salamanca where McCaghwell attended lectures and during this period acquired Spanish.

It was in Salamanca that he decided to enter the Franciscan Order (Ó Cléirigh 1985: 48). In 1610 he was appointed Guardian of St Anthony's College in Louvain, succeeding Donagh Mooney (McCaghwell had arrived in Louvain in June 1607). McCaghwell's command of English is evident from the fact that as early as 1609 he was trying to negotiate terms with the English government and king on behalf of the earl of Tyrone. On 3 July 1614, a letter from Whitehall written by Robert, earl of Somerset, urges the English representative in Brussels, William Trumbull, to have no further dealings with McCaghwell:

> It is his majesty's pleasure that you forbear from further treaty with the friar or any other touching Tyrone, in expectation of being received to his majesty's grace upon those terms of restitution to his dignity and lands in Ireland, because that would disjoint the whole course which his majesty hath been so careful to settle in that country.
>
> (Jennings 1964: 354)

McCaghwell's linguistic abilities meant that while he was negotiating with the English, he was also giving an account of Irish affairs to Guido Bentivoglio, the papal nuncio to Flanders, and supplying information to the Spanish court. Bentivoglio in a letter to Cardinal Borghese, dated 3 May 1608, refers in passing to his valuable informant:

> Per quanto ho inteso a quest'hora il Conte di Tirone deve esser in Roma. . . . So senz'altro, ch'egli è partito forzato da gli Stati del Re. E lo so dalle cose passate tra qual Franciscano e me come più volte significai pienamente a Vostra S. illustrissima.
>
> (cited in Giblin 1995: 84)

> [As far as I know at this time the Earl of Tyrone should be in Rome. . . . I know for certain that he was forced to leave the King's States. And I know of the things that happened through this Franciscan as I fully indicated several times to your Holiness.]

Though the memoranda of Bentivoglio's conversations with McCaghwell went from Flanders to the Holy See in Italian, it would appear that they conversed in both Spanish and Latin. When McCaghwell, along with Eugene Matthews, archbishop of Dublin, and Christopher Cusack, president of the Irish College at Douai, presented Bentivoglio in 1613 with a document which included details on the military needs of the native Irish, the document was drawn up in Latin (ibid., 304–7). In the fraught world of the early seventeenth-century Irish diaspora McCaghwell is *interpreter* in the richly ambiguous sense of the term, his role both linguistic and hermeneutic. He not only brings information, perceptions, sentiments across the Irish, Latin, English and Spanish (and later in Rome, Italian) languages but he also interprets the meanings of events and plans for Trumbull, Bentivoglio, O'Neill, his contacts in the Spanish court and for all who fall within the ambit of his multilingual activism.

It is noteworthy, however, that McCaghwell's interpreting activities are not confined to the destinies of nations but that he exercised his skills in a variety of domains. When the Spanish Infanta sent her confessor to Louvain in 1610 with the intention of moving the English Augustinian Canonesses Regular of the Lateran from their house and replacing them with another order of nuns, McCaghwell was appointed as the confessor's interpreter. The English nuns were distraught at their likely fate and pleaded with the confessor through McCaghwell that they be allowed to stay. McCaghwell reassured the religious that he would ensure that the confessor did intercede on their behalf with the Infanta and it was the Irish interpreter who eventually brought them the welcome news that they would be permitted to remain in the house (Hamilton 1904: 75). McCaghwell was also involved in persuading the town council of Douai on 18 February 1616 that the planned foundation of English Franciscans in the town would not place any extra burden on the inhabitants of Douai and its environs (Lepreux 1875: 266–8; 270–1).

In both instances, McCaghwell is to the fore in promoting the interests of his English co-religionists, so clearly in his work as interpreter/mediator religious loyalties transcend ethnic or linguistic differences. McCaghwell's role as interpreter cannot be seen as purely a matter of linguistic dexterity. To function as interpreter at the level he did, he needed to have a thorough understanding of the politics and culture of the different parties to the Irish conflict. His sympathy for and understanding of native Irish culture are borne out not only by his writings in Irish but also by his support for the scholarly activities of his Louvain colleagues who would in part help to refashion the Irish language itself through their publishing activities (Cronin 1996: 59–65). This is why his Irish sobriquet appears in the title of Tomás Ó Cléirigh's 1935 work *Aodh Mac Aingil agus an Scoil Nua-Ghaeilge i Lobháin* ['Aodh Mac Aingil and the School of Modern Irish in Louvain'].

McCaghwell's knowledge of English politics is alluded to in the strange episode of George Ligonius, an alumnus of the English College in Rome. In 1615 Ligonius moved to Louvain where he resided with the Jesuits. He then decided to write a book to demonstrate to King James I the harm he was doing to English Catholics. Before Ligonius set sail for England armed with his opus, the Jesuits, fearful of the damage he might cause, had him arrested and his book confiscated. Ligonius appealed to the internuncio in Brussels and the Holy See, asking that a prominent theologian be allowed to inspect the contents of his book. The theologian he named was Hugh McCaghwell who he claimed was a man of notable piety, a famous professor of theology and a man exceptionally well versed in English affairs (Giblin 1995: 90). That a relative outsider like Ligonius should have had such a favourable view of McCaghwell's familiarity with English political life meant that it was not only Trumbull who viewed McCaghwell as a worthy mediator with whom he could do business.

The strategic value of interpreting to the colonization process in sixteenth- and seventeenth-century Ireland is evident in the succession of named interpreters who are in the employ of both colonizers and the soon to be colonized. Given that only a small fraction of the Irish population spoke English when the reconquest of

Ireland began in earnest under the Tudors, it was inevitable that Ireland would become the theatre for a very real war of words. Submission, for example, was meaningless unless it was intelligible. In 1567, therefore, we have an account of a visit by O'Connor Sligo to Elizabeth I in London:

> and there in his Irish tongue, by an interpreter, declared to her Majesty that the chief cause of his coming was to see and speak to the illustrious and powerful Princess, whom he recognised to be his sovereign Lady, acknowledging that both he and his ancestors had long lived in an uncivil, rude and barbarous fashion, destitute of the true knowledge of God, and ignorant of their duty to the Imperial Crown of England.
>
> (cited in Jackson 1973: 22)

If it was symbolically expedient to understand those willing to accept the new dispensation, it was even more important to understand those who were not. As the Gaelic Irish leaders naturally dealt with their followers in Irish, it was necessary to engage the services of interpreters/informants who would practise, in somewhat less exalted circumstances than McCaghwell, the antique trade of spying or intelligence gathering. It is interesting to note that ethnic intermarriage has a particular role to play in the evolution of interpreting networks. For example, in a letter of 1580 Lord Deputy Sidney urges his successor Grey de Wilton to spare no expense in the recruitment of spies. He mentions three informants as particularly valuable, Thomas Masterson, Robert Pipho and Robert Hartpole, all of whom were English speakers who had married Irish-speaking women (Egerton 1847: 71).

An English-speaking male who married an Irish-speaking woman could use the language skills of his spouse to help him acquire information on the political or military activities of the native Irish. This is what we have termed elsewhere in the present work (pp. 40–1) a heteronymous interpreting strategy, where the colonizers have recourse to the services of the natives to interpret for them. Alternatively, the Anglophone male could have recourse to an autonomous interpreting strategy where he learns Irish from his spouse and puts the language to use in espionage. In this instance, it is the colonist himself who acquires the language of the native through a relationship with the natives. The recurrent danger with the heteronymous strategy was, of course, that the native's loyalties would revert back to the native. As William Jones observed in his *Grammar of the Persian Language* (1771), for British officials, 'It was found highly dangerous to employ the natives as interpreters, upon whose fidelity they could not depend' (cited in Niranjana 1992: 16). An Elizabethan adventurer Captain Thomas Lee would have agreed with Jones, though in Lee's case the infidelity was closer to home. Lee had the ambition of establishing a 'principality' for himself on the borders of the two Irish counties of Kildare and Wicklow. He married the Irish-speaking daughter of a local landholder in the area and then set about extending his own holdings through the ousting or elimination of both his English and Irish rivals in the area. As Donald Jackson notes, Lee's exploitation of his wife's interpreting abilities had an unforeseen outcome:

> He [Lee] employed his Irish-speaking wife as an intermediary in a plot to dispose of one of the most dangerous of the local Irish rebels. Unfortunately, it turned out her sympathies were with the rebel, to whom she betrayed the plan.
>
> (Jackson 1973: 24)

For interpreters in situations of conflict, as Lee would discover to his cost, fidelity is a relative rather than an absolute notion.

One way of maintaining loyalty is to regularize the situation of interpreters and give the activity some form of public recognition. This was the tactic adopted by the Spanish Crown in Latin America where, according to the *Recopilacíon de Leyes de las Indias* ['Compendium of the Laws of the Indies'], between 1529 and 1630 there were fifteen laws governing the activities of interpreters. The 1529 law gives the *lenguas* (tongues) the formal status of auxiliaries of 'Governors' and 'Justice' and, by 1563, the laws recognize a professional hierarchy of interpreters, establish specific compensation for particular language tasks and enunciate a general set of ethical principles. In return for this new-found status, interpreters were forbidden to request or receive jewels, clothes or food from the native peoples (Delisle and Woodsworth 1995: 262–3). There was an incipient professionalization in the Irish situation with the creation in the mid-sixteenth century of an official post of Interpreter of the Irish Tongue, attached to the establishment of the Lord Deputy in Dublin. William Dunne held the position in the early period of Elizabeth's reign and he is explicitly mentioned as an interpreter in a document from 1570 where an Irish saying is described as having been 'interpreted by Christopher Bodkin, the Archbishop of Tuam, and Mr. Dunne' (Hughes 1960: 24). Thomas Cahill would occupy the same position in 1588.

The difficulty, of course, is that the long-term survival of a cadre of official interpreters depended on the languages on the island of Ireland being accorded equal status and this did not happen. Though there were inconsistencies in English language policies in Ireland and a tension between the evangelical commitment of Protestantism to the vernacular and the cultural wars of the Crown, Irish was effectively removed from the official, public life of the country by the end of the seventeenth century (Cronin 1996: 47–90). In these circumstances, although interpreters would still be employed, as we shall see, in the law courts, there would be no retention of interpreters in the new Ascendancy administration. Interpreters who were to prove so useful in furthering the aims of conquest through intelligence operations and negotiations would in a paradoxical way become victims of their own success. Once the regime was fully in place, to have a body of official interpreters would be to offer recognition to a language which was seen as indissociable from sedition and disloyalty. Indeed, when official interpreters emerged once more in Ireland, it would be as a measure to give Irish comparable official status to English though, by this stage, it was English, not Irish, that was the majority language of the country (Daltún 1983: 12–14).

As Jean Delisle notes in his preface to Ruth A. Roland's *Interpreters as Diplomats*, 'language has always been more than a simple communication tool: it has also been a mark of national prestige, and interpreters have brought this prestige to the international arena' (Delisle 1999: 2). The presence of an interpreter is not simply a matter of expediency, it confers a particular status on a language and suggests a symmetrical dimension to political relationships. This dimension was particularly relevant in Tudor Ireland where conquest involved not only territorial acquisition and military supremacy but the progressive acculturation of the native Irish (Canny 2001). The practice of interpreting both facilitates communication by removing the obstacle of language and also, through the person of the interpreter, establishes the *distance of difference*. In other words, the use of an interpreter by the Irish Gaelic leader Hugh O'Neill in his dealings with Elizabeth I (even though he himself spoke English) was a way of initiating dialogue that nonetheless marked the cultural and political distance and difference between the two parties, thereby constructing interpreting as an activity of both interaction and resistance. Crucially, the change from the seventeenth- to the eighteenth-century interpreting practices in Ireland was marked by a shift in what R. Bruce W. Anderson calls the 'arena of interaction' (1976: 209). If the political and legal arenas of interaction are present in the interpreting situation in Ireland in the sixteenth and seventeenth centuries, the greater part of the eighteenth century would see the exclusion of interpreting from the political arena of interaction. Thus, though interpreters would still be used in the courts, their absence from the public sphere of politics signalled a decisive change in the fortunes of Irish, the uncoupling of the language from structures of power and prestige which would have such damaging long-term consequences for it.

Metonymic presence

The re-entry of interpreting into a politico-military arena of interaction in Ireland at the end of the eighteenth century was the result of dramatically changed political conditions. French support for the armed insurrection of the United Irishmen in 1798 would materialize most memorably in the landing of French troops at Killala, County Mayo, under the leadership of General Humbert. A problem which had been anticipated by the French in their preparations for the Irish expedition was that of language. Humbert, in particular, was persuaded of the urgent necessity of recruiting an interpreter who had mastered both French and Irish and knew some English. He was eventually introduced to an Irish-speaking officer in the French army, Henry O'Kane, initially referred to as 'MacKeon' (Bertaud 1990: 225).

The officer in question was, in fact, a Mayo-born priest who had emigrated to France and in 1788 had become a curate in the parish of Saint Hermand, near Nantes in Brittany. O'Kane was obviously attracted to the radical new ideas that were current in late eighteenth-century France as he became a member of an Irish Freemason lodge there known as *Les Irlandais du soleil levant* (Keogh 1993: 182; Hayes 1945: 48). On Humbert's instructions, O'Kane was commissioned as staff officer and official interpreter to the French expedition to Ireland. O'Kane proved to be a brave soldier and able interpreter during the Connacht campaign and 'le citoyen Henry O'Keane' was praised by Humbert in a letter from 1800 as having shown commendable bravura and intelligence in 1798 (Beiner 2001). When the insurrection was finally put down by the Crown forces, O'Kane was taken to Castlebar and court-martialled on a charge of high treason. He was sentenced to death but unlike many of his compatriots, he was fortunate in receiving a reprieve and he returned to France where he served with distinction in the Republican and Napoleonic Wars. He was subsequently awarded the Legion of Honour and retired in 1815.

Like Maurice Regan, Henry O'Kane is an interpreter who appears in verse, this time in the lyrics of a song that was especially well known in the western county of Mayo in the nineteenth and twentieth centuries. Guy Beiner has transcribed and translated what may be the only surviving full version of the song (ibid., 2001). The first stanza goes:

> Tá na Franncaig 'teacht thar saile
> fada a gcabhair ó Clanna Ghaedheal
> Tógaidh suas bhur gcroidhe 's bhur n-aigneach
> 's suibhliadh amach le Corporéal Caen.

> [The French are coming over the sea
> Long has been their help from *Clanna Gael*
> Raise up your heart and your mind
> And step out with Corporal Kane.]

It was most probably a rallying song aimed at encouraging local men in Mayo and further afield to join the Franco-Irish army (Hayes 1979: 243). It is notable, again, as we saw with *The Song of Dermot and the Earl*, that the interpreter occupies a prominent position, is indeed the main subject of the song. It is not General Humbert but his interpreter who comes to be the incarnation of the cause of the United Irishmen for the anonymous author of the verses, just as Maurice Regan was closely identified with the victory of the Anglo-Normans. One could argue that interpreters in periods of conflict are always potentially open to *metonymic* as distinct from *metaphorical appropriation*. That is to say, whereas women, for example, have featured in figurative representations of Irish resistance to conquest and occupation down the centuries, they have done so primarily in a metaphorical mode. Granuaile, Banba and Cathleen have been images of both tragic plight and rebellious hope (McPeake 2001).

In the case of interpreters, however, it is their active engagement as a party to conflict which makes them representative figures. They thus occupy a metonymical relationship to the cause they serve and come to embody (in every sense of the word). But the intrinsic duality of the interpreter's task, mediating between more than one language and culture, complicates any simple-minded or closed sense of allegiance. This dimension is apparent in the responses of O'Kane's political enemies as detailed in their accounts of the events of 1798. The staunchly pro-Crown Sir Richard Musgrave, for example, noted that *O'Keon*, as he called the Mayo interpreter, 'was humane, having on all occasions, opposed the bloodthirsty disposition of the popish multitude'. Musgrave further remarked that O'Kane was 'free from the sanguinary spirit which actuated the common herd' and that 'more than once he prevented rebels from murdering the Protestant prisoners' (Musgrave 1995: 546–7, 560–1, 565).

The Protestant Bishop Stock claimed with reference to O'Kane that 'his language breathed nothing but mildness and liberality' and he too noted O'Kane's key role in preventing the ill-treatment of local Protestant loyalists (Freyer 1982: 58–60). If O'Kane's enemies found his presence reassuring, his putative allies, the Gaelic Irish, were less sure. Dominick McDonnell of Muingrevagh in County Mayo, recounting local 1798 folklore, claimed that O'Kane was remembered as a 'brave soldier' and a 'great talker' and that no one 'could handle a crowd like him'. However, he was also feared because of his involvement in recruitment efforts, which sometimes involved violent intimidation. As McDonnell put it, 'A lot of people hid themselves away, for there was terror on them' and he gave the example of fifty men hiding in the house of Honor McNulty of Knockboha where during the course of the search of the house O'Kane shot the dog (Hayes 1979: 219).

In view of the treatment meted out to them by the British military and yeomen, the reluctance of the native Irish to get involved in the conflict was understand-able. Whereas captured French soldiers and officers were treated according to normal conventions of warfare, the Irish soldiers were summarily executed as traitors (O'Donnell 1998). O'Kane's knowledge of his native language made him well qualified to be a 'great talker', an essential attribute of the effective interpreter, and reputed skill with crowds is testimony to his communicative efficacy. This skill must have delighted Humbert with his choice of O'Kane as official French inter-preter in Ireland. But it was precisely this ability which produced ambivalent responses to O'Kane in local folklore. On the one hand, he is the subject of song, praise, admiration. On the other, O'Kane's ability to speak the local language along with the strong-arm tactics used when persuasion failed meant that he was a much more disruptive presence in a local community than a French officer, say, with little Irish. O'Kane's knowledge of Irish made the Gaelic Irish much more vulnerable. If some of them tried to physically hide in a house, it was because there was no hiding from what O'Kane was saying. He spoke their language. They knew exactly what he meant. And the consequences terrified them. In this way, the interpreter in song, folklore and local history comes to represent the very real human dilemmas of a population who find themselves caught up in violent conflict or war.

Judging interpreters

As we mentioned earlier, though interpreters were excluded from the political arena of interaction after the collapse of the Gaelic order, they did continue to function in the legal system (Ní Dhonnchadha 2000). In a society where even at the beginning of the ninteenth century the majority of the population was Irish-speaking, it was neither practicable nor desirable to try people in a language they did not understand, though this, of course, did sometimes happen. A persistent theme in representations of interpreting practice, whether in literature or legal folklore, is the interventionist nature of the interpreter. The modern notion of the court interpreter as an impartial, self-effacing conduit for the business of the court is noticeably absent.

A typical example is an anecdote relating to the Irish lawyer and statesman Daniel O'Connell attending the Assizes in the south of the country in the first half of the nineteenth century. An old man beseeches O'Connell in Irish to defend his only son who is on trial and offers him his life savings, ten guineas, to take the case. O'Connell refuses, explaining that his arrangements with his colleagues and his professional code of conduct would not allow him to renege on other commitments, but recommended giving the ten guineas to his colleague James Lyons. O'Connell claimed that Lyons would be just as effective as he in defending the son of the poor farmer:

> At that, the old man burst into tears and joined a despondent group that had watched the interview. When the court rose and O'Connell left the building, he saw across the road a delighted crowd around a handsome youth. Most prominent in the crowd was the old man he had met that morning. The great advocate strode up and held out his hand.
> 'The boy is free?'
> 'He is, thank God.'
> 'Well, you took my advice then and gave your ten guineas to James Lyons.'
> 'Oh Christ no! I didn't waste it – I gave it to the interpreter.'
>
> (McArdle 1995: 55)

The clear implication is that the interpreter was not only willing to take a bribe but that he (women interpreters only appear in Irish courts in the late twentieth century) would exploit his knowledge of the two languages and the linguistic ignorance of the magistrates to achieve specific outcomes.

In Gerald Griffin's highly successful nineteenth-century novel *The Collegians* (1834), it is the irascible Dan Dawley, sworn in as court interpreter when the Irish-speaking court secretary Mr Houlahan professes not to know Irish, who intervenes directly in the court exchanges. In this instance, though, the interpreter's outburst favours the prosecution. When Dawley asks a certain Philip Naughten whether he was acquainted with the deceased Eily O'Connor, Naughten conveniently answers a question he was never asked. This is too much for Dan Dawley:

> 'He says', continued the interpreter, 'that when he was a young man he rented a small farm from Mr. O'Connor of Crag-beg, near Tralee. He has as much tricks in him, plase your honour, as a rabbit. I'd as lieve be brakin' stones to a paviour as putting questions to a rogue of this kind.'
>
> (Griffin 1944: 379)

In the absence of transcripts of the Irish spoken by witnesses or defendants in nineteenth-century court cases, it is not possible to substantiate or invalidate allegations of interpreter bias. However, one can ask why the image of the interventionist or indeed manipulative interpreter persisted in the Irish legal system. It is possible to advance two reasons, one relating to language and power, and the other connected to literacy/orality tensions.

The use of legal instruments to further land expropriation in the seventeenth century and the existence of discriminatory legislation directed against the majority population in the eighteenth were not designed to inspire Irish Catholic confidence in the British legal system in Ireland. Thus, though the courts might be used to seek redress, they would generally be viewed with suspicion. In what would be perceived to be a strongly asymmetrical situation from the standpoint of the dispossessed, language was a potential point of weakness, a way of tilting the balance in favour of those who were disadvantaged not only in the legal but in many other realms of Irish public life of the period. Thus, in such a situation, which has been replicated in colonial encounters throughout the world, interpreters are potentially power-brokers for the powerless. The adverb is deliberately chosen: 'potentially' because the interpreter may indeed view his or her status as a sign of election and to curry favour with the master may either collaborate in his designs or exact a high price (ten guineas) for his or her pliancy.

The repeated references to the wily interpreter or the devious defendant who insists on having an interpreter while being able to understand and speak English make interpreters and interpreting suggestive metaphors of politico-linguistic anxieties in nineteenth-century Ireland. As the Irish-speaking population gradually translates itself into English throughout the century (whether at home or abroad), anxieties on the part of defendants or witnesses about the 'fidelity' of interpreters and knowledge of English appear to reflect wider concerns about political discipline and control in post-Union Ireland. The court interpreter was, in a sense, an uneasy reminder that areas of Irish life and experience were still outside the Anglophone purview. Moreover, the necessity for interpreting would inevitably be an object of continual suspicion as it acts as an index of anglicization. The very need to be interpreted shows the limits to the process of linguistic assimilation but it is the motives of the clients (duplicitous natives) rather than the paymasters of interpreting which are continually called into question.

In a much-cited incident from a court case at the beginning of the twentieth century, a Clare barrister, Michael McNamara, who also acted as court interpreter in Irish, administered the oath in the following manner to a defendant who was up on a charge of unpaid debts:

> the Counsellor addressed him in Irish: 'Listen carefully now to the terms of the oath, and repeat after me – "If I do not tell the truth in this case – "
> '"If I do not tell the truth in this case – "'
> '"May a murrain seize my cattle – "'
> 'What's that, Counsellor? Sure that's not in the oath?'
> 'Go on and repeat your oath: "May a murrain seize my cattle – "'
> 'Oh! Glory be to God! "May a murrain seize my cattle – "'
> '"May all my sheep be clifted – " [i.e. fall over a cliff].'
> 'Yerra, Counsellor, what oath is that your [*sic*] trying to get me to take? Sure I never heard an oath like that before!'

> 'Go on, sir; don't argue with me; repeat your oath: "May all my sheep be clifted – "'
>
> 'Oh! God help us all! "May all my sheep – " yerra, Counsellor, are you sure that's in the oath?'
>
> 'Go on, sir!'
>
> 'Oh! God! "May all my sheep be clifted – "'
>
> '"May my children get the falling sickness – "'
>
> 'Arrah, Counsellor, tell his Honour that I admit the debt, and I only want a little time to pay!'
>
> (Healy 1939: 152–3)

Leaving aside the somewhat unorthodox practice of the prosecuting lawyer doubling up as interpreter, the humour of the episode lies partly in the inappropriate use of particular kinds of language in a formal or legal setting. The ritual curse which McNamara puts into the mouth of the unfortunate defendant is taken from the oral culture with which the defendant is familiar. McNamara, 'who had a great dread the defendant would swear himself out of the debt by barefaced perjury', knows the curse of the defendant's unwritten, oral culture to be considerably more potent than the formal oath of the court's literate culture.

Interpreting, unlike written translation, is by definition an oral encounter so differences between an orality overdetermined by literacy and an orality that retains many of the features of primary oral culture will be strongly marked. It is a general failure to recognize this which must explain in part the notion of the dissembling native in nineteenth- and early twentieth-century interpreting stories. In listing characteristics of orally based thought and expression Walter J. Ong mentions the redundant or 'copious' nature of oral discourse. In writing, the mind can concentrate on moving ahead in a linear fashion because the written text is there to remind it of what has already been said. In oral discourse, the situation is different because there is nothing to refer to outside the mind, the oral utterance vanishing as soon as it has been uttered. Therefore, in primary orality, 'the mind must move ahead more slowly, keeping close to the focus of attention much of what it has already dealt with. Redundancy, repetition of the just-said, keeps both speaker and hearer surely on track' (Ong 1982: 40). In addition, acoustic problems in addressing large audiences where it is necessary to repeat what has been said so that everyone gets a chance to hear it, and dealing with the fatal threat of hesitation in oral delivery by repeating more or less the same thing while thinking of something else to say, mean that, 'Oral culture encourages fluency, fulsomeness, volubility.' The copiousness of speech is evident in the Clare interpreting story: the curse is repeated in a number of different formulations and could be extended indefinitely were it not for the panic-stricken admission of guilt.

To those in a position of authority, where authority itself is invested with the legitimacy of literacy through laws, decrees, legal instruments, the speech of those from primarily oral backgrounds with no access to literacy in their own language will appear when interpreted as 'blarney' or 'blather', a wordy, whimsical subterfuge. The assumption readily made by literates is that 'fulsomeness' and 'volubility' are suspect deviations from plain speech. Interpreters, then, by remaining *faithful* to the *copia* of their clients in Irish, would paradoxically present them as somehow being *unfaithful* to the truth. In a way, what is asked of interpreters in these situations is to make a dual translation, from oral mode to literate mode and from one language to the other.

Owen does this in reverse order in *Translations* when events silence banter and he interprets the highly formal or literate register of Lancey's threats into a more colloquial register, albeit within the same language for the purposes of the play. Interpreters are faced with a double bind. If they do not make the oral–literate mode switch, the recurrent difficulty arises of a systematic misrepresentation of the motives and nature of speakers of a language coming from a predominantly oral culture. Conversely, if they do make the switch, the risk is another form of infidelity, a failure to adequately represent the epistemic wholeness of an oral world-view (Sturge 1997: 21–38). Thus, the intercultural dilemma is twofold: on the one hand, the carrying across of information and sentiment from one language to another; on the other, the mediation between a culture of primary or secondary orality and a culture of high literacy.

It would be a mistake, however, to see high literacy as being inimical to a concern with orality and, as we noted from the outset, the concern of Plutarch in his writings was with the foundational importance of eloquence and its reception in the shaping of the fit subject of empire. Part of the task of translation studies is to show that translation questions arise often when they are least expected and that a translational and intercultural perspective on canonical texts, for example, can lead to new readings, not least those which highlight the vital connection between translation, identity and power. In an ambitious survey of the history of the English language, the novelist Melvyn Bragg does not steer clear of hyperbole when recruiting Shakespeare to the seraphim of the language's elect:

> He is not only thought to be the greatest writer the world has seen but the most written-about writer the world has ever known for his chroniclers and commentators spill over global tongues, German, Italian, Spanish, French, Dutch, Russian, Japanese, Hindi: unroll the map. He is in more than fifty languages. He was not for an age but for all time, was the boast and the prophecy, and so far it has been fulfilled.

> (Bragg 2003: 141)

Bragg's comment can be seen at one level as a rather excitable proof of the Derridean intuition in 'Des Tours de Babel' that originals owe their prestige to the existence of translations (Derrida 1985: 165–248). As Derrida argued, an elegant paradox of literature is that it is those authors who are famously 'untranslatable' (Joyce, Proust, Shakespeare and so on) who attract the most assiduous translation attention, their very untranslatability a prime motive for their translatability. However, our concern in this chapter will not be what happens to a canonical author like Shakespeare in translation but what happens to translation in Shakespeare.

More specifically, we will be tracking an intra-textual translation presence to show how Shakespearean drama through the conduit of translation articulates English and more broadly European concerns with language, power, identity, metamorphosis, proximity and control in the context of intercultural contact. The question of translation will be bound up with the way in which the 'unique' island of Britain will translate itself around the globe, its translatability both articulated and foreshadowed in the work of the world's most translated dramatist.

A context for the exploration of these issues will be the practices of translation and interpreting in sixteenth- and early seventeenth-century England and Ireland and their role in the political and military conflicts opposing the two islands in the period. We will begin by sketching out the background to Classical and Renaissance theories of eloquence and then proceed to examine the relationship between translation and English nationalism and imperialism as it emerges in different plays by Shakespeare. The dual purpose of this examination is to show that identity issues in translation, as we have already seen in this chapter in the case of interpreting, have a long history and did not suddenly emerge at the end of the twentieth century; and that discussions around literary translation need to consider as much what happens within as between texts. An ahistorical or partial understanding of the phenomenon of translation leads inevitably to a narrowing of the discipline and a foreshortening of perspectives.

Eloquence

An abiding preoccupation of the European Renaissance was the notion of civility. It was civility that admitted one to the community of the civilized and made one a worthy citizen of the *polis* (Bryson 1998). Not surprisingly, a great deal of polemical and pedagogical energy would go into defining what exactly constituted civility, who had it and what was the best way of passing it on to the next generation. Few commentators disagreed, however, about the centrality of language to the construction and representation of civility. The consensus lay in the perceived link between language and eloquence. Eloquence not only took place in the world but had the power to change the world. Thus an essential part of the transformative vision of the Renaissance resided in the belief that words properly ordered possessed a power which changed the minds, habits and dispositions of those who heard them.

An illustrative example of this credo can be found in Pier Paolo Vergerio's *De ingenuis moribus et liberalibus adulescentiae* ('The Character and Studies Befitting a Free-Born Youth') (1402–3). Vergerio lists those objects of study most likely to promote the cultivation of civility in a young man of means and social standing. He advocates the study of history and moral philosophy but to these subjects he adds a third, eloquence:

> Per philosophiam quidem possumus recte sentire quod est in omni re primum; per eloquentiam graviter ornatque dicere qua una re maxime conciliantur multitudinis animi.

> (Vergerio 2002: 40)

[Through philosophy we can acquire correct views, which is of first importance in everything; through eloquence we can speak with weight and polish, which is the one skill that most effectively wins over the minds of the masses.]

Vergerio is not innovating here but drawing on the models from antiquity which would animate so much of Renaissance thinking. Cicero in his *De inventione* presents a scene of what might be described as primal colonization where the rude and uncouth savage is converted to civility through eloquence. In his *De optimo genere oratorum* he makes explicit the connection between using language and winning friends and influencing people:

> The supreme orator, then, is one whose speech instructs, delights and moves the minds of his audience. . . . For as eloquence consists of language and thought, we must manage while keeping our diction faultless and pure – that is in good Latin – to achieve a choice of words both proper and figurative. Of 'proper words' we should choose the most elegant, and in the case of figurative language we should be modest in our use of metaphors and careful to avoid far-fetched comparisons.
>
> (Cicero 1997: 7–8)

Underlying Cicero's pedagogy is the Classical tradition of topical rhetoric. Arguments are won when the speaker takes hold of the *topos*, the place of argument. The successful orator becomes sole owner and all others are driven from that place which is no longer rightfully theirs and which they have forfeited through defective eloquence. Eloquence in this sense is agonistic and proprietorial. It is Quintilian who will ask what the resources are that the orator might draw on and who establishes a link between translation and eloquence:

> For the Greek authors excel in copiousness of matter, and have introduced a vast deal of art into the study of eloquence; and, in translating them, we may use the very best words, for all that we use may be our own. As to [verbal] figures, by which language is principally ornamented we may be under the necessity of inventing a great number and variety of them, because the Roman tongue differs greatly from that of the Greeks.
>
> (Quintilian 1997: 20)

If eloquence is related to the exercise of power, then translation is related to power in that it is a mechanism that allows politically stronger cultures to appropriate the 'copiousness of matter' that is to be found in cultures annexed by or subordinate to empire. For Quintilian, the power of the eloquent orator lies not in the proud isolation of imperial autonomy but in the careful exploitation of translation heteronymy whereby 'all that we use may be our own'. Classical antecedents and Renaissance reappropriation make of the eloquent orator one of the most significant voices of authority in the Western tradition. Those who speak well not only move their audiences to action but also move others out of places previously occupied and expropriation through eloquence further enhances the power and position of the speaker.

In tracing the crucial connection between translation, eloquence and empire in Shakespeare's drama it is necessary to consider first an internal shift in his history plays. Jean-Marc Chadelat in his discussion of Shakespeare's history plays describes the key transition from the world of *Richard II* to that of *Henry V, Julius Caesar* and *Coriolanus*,

> A l'espace clos et défensif des sociétés passéistes correspond par une inversion analogue l'ouverture d'un espace rendu extensible par la nature expansionniste de la puissance d'action sur soi-même.
>
> (Chadelat 2003: 244)

> [To the closed and defensive nature of societies concerned with the past correspond by a similar inversion the opening of a space made expandable by the expansionist nature of power acting on itself.]

What we have, in effect, is the movement from the heteronymous world of *Richard II*, structured by a theological order and guided by a set of metaphysical beliefs, to the one we find in *Henry V, Julius Caesar* and *Coriolanus* where an autonomous society legislates for itself and politics becomes a real and symbolic site of transformation.

Implicit in this transformation is the notion that power can extend itself indefinitely in space and that space can be extended as far as the reach of power. If Shakespeare will notably expand the resources of the English language and English dramatic expression, this development will take place alongside the territorial expansion of England itself overseas. It is no accident therefore that it should be precisely at the moment when England begins to consolidate (monarchy) internally and expand externally (empire) that it should seek to consolidate the internal legitimacy of English and expand the external use of the language. The coincidence of the two projects can be observed in the linguistic interests of a number of notable military adventurers and propagandists involved in the Tudor campaigns in Ireland. Fynes Moryson, for example, who was a zealous defender of the English cause in Ireland was equally preoccupied with the defence of the English language. Determined to pursue the claims of the vernacular, he maintained:

> they are confuted who traduce the English tounge to be like a beggers patched Cloke, which they should rather compayre to a Posey of sweetest flowers, because by the sayd meanes, it hath been in late ages excellently refyned and made perfitt for ready and brief deliuery both in prose and verse.
>
> (Moryson 1903: 437–8)

Humphrey Gilbert, who used extreme violence in suppressing the rebellion in Munster in the south-west of Ireland in 1579, was similarly preoccupied with the future status of English. His proposal was for the establishment of a university in

London to be called Queen Elizabeth's Academy which would be in a sense the capital's answer to Oxbridge. The Academy would offer extensive oratorical training but would differ from the established universities in one crucial respect: the training would be in the medium of the vernacular, English, rather than in Latin. In addition, Gilbert recommended that each language teacher in the Academy should 'printe some Translation into the English tongue of some good worke' every three years (1869: 3).

The more eloquent the English language, the better it was fitted to be the language of empire, and the more flowers in the bouquet, the more becoming the conquest itself. Gilbert, like a latter-day Quintilian, realizes that no imperial language can do this all by itself, hence the requirement that the trainers of his orators also be translators. Gilbert as soldier and educational theorist was by no means unusual in his interest in translation. As Patricia Palmer points out in *Language and Conquest in Early Modern Ireland*,

> The fact that so many leading translators of the age – Bryskett, Fenton, Googe, Harrington – were also players in the conquest of Ireland confirms the uncanny incongruity between pushing back the frontiers of English and expanding the geopolitical boundaries in which it operated.
>
> (2001: 111)

It is therefore in a larger context of linguistic and territorial expansion attended by the good offices or otherwise of translation that Shakespeare is working as a writer.

We would like to suggest that what we find in his work is a recognition that the construction of the nation and by extension the beginning of empire constitute among other things an exercise in translation and, moreover, that it is translation which becomes an exemplary figure for many of the anxieties attending the nation in its expansionary moment. We will consider Shakespeare's political engagement with the question of translation as it relates to French and Irish Gaelic and concentrate on two of Shakespeare's history plays, *Henry VI, Part 2* and *Henry V*, which provide particularly fruitful insights into the doubts and uncertainties besetting the Tudor mind around the necessary but troubled exchange of translation.

Double dealing

In *Henry VI, Part 2*, the rebel leader Jack Cade enters into dialogue with the King's ally Stafford and sets out the grounds for his suspicion of the trustworthiness of Lord Say. Cade's attitude to Say is primarily dictated by questions of language and more specifically by Say's role as a translator, as a linguistic broker in the Franco-English translation space.

CADE: . . . Fellow kings, I tell you that Lord Say hath gelded the commonwealth and made it a eunuch; and more than that, he can speak French; and therefore he is a traitor.
STAFFORD: O gross and miserable ignorance!

CADE: Nay, answer, if you can: The Frenchmen are our enemies; go to then, I ask you but this, can he that speaks with the tongue of an enemy be a good counsellor.

(IV.ii.178–86)*

Cade's sentiments cannot simply be dismissed as 'gross and miserable ignorance,' as Stafford would have us believe. Cade, in effect, was simply articulating a belief that was widely held in Elizabethan England, namely that language knowledge potentially compromised political fealty. Edmund Spenser in his *A View of the Present State of Ireland* advances a broadly similar argument to that of Cade when he advocates the radical elimination of the Irish language: 'the speech being Irish, the heart must needs be Irish for out of the abundance of the heart, the tongue speaketh' (Spenser 1970: 68).

When Say is captured by the rebels and brought before Cade, he mounts a defence of his linguistic brokerage claiming: 'This tongue hath parley'd unto foreign kings/For your behoof' (IV.vii.82–3). The argument advanced by Say on the necessary, strategic importance of translation in times of conflict is the standard defence of linguistic mediation. Its merits are, however, lost on Cade, and Say is unable to save his life. Cade's indifference to Say's defence is all the more surprising in that Cade is a mirror image of Say not so much in his pretensions to political power as in his past experience of translatorial intervention. We know of this because of the portrait of Cade that York first presents to us when he outlines the former's military prowess in the Irish wars. York focuses initially on the valour and indomitable energy of Cade:

> In Ireland I have seen this stubborn Cade
> Oppose himself against a troop of kerns,
> And fought so long, till that his thighs with darts
> Were almost like a sharp-quill'd porpentine:
> And, in the end being rescued, I have seen
> Him caper upright like a wild Morisco,
> Shaking the bloody darts as he his bells.
>
> (III.i.360–6)

But then York reveals information that is arguably crucial to our understanding of Cade:

> Full often, like a shag-hair'd crafty kern,
> Hath he conversed with the enemy,
> And undiscover'd come to me again,
> And given me notice of their villainies.
>
> (III.i.367–70)

---

* This reference and all subsequent references to Shakespeare's plays are taken from William Shakespeare, *The Complete Works*, ed. W.J. Craig (Oxford: Oxford University Press, 1974) and appear in the text.

The implication in York's account is that Cade was able to act as a translator/ interpreter from Irish Gaelic to English and this accounts in part for the inestimable worth of Cade as a soldier and ally. Indeed, if Cade had not mastered Irish Gaelic he would have been quite unable to communicate with the overwhelmingly Irish-speaking infantry, the 'kerns', and his Irish would have to be very good if he was somehow to go 'undiscover'd'. The rebel Cade like the loyal Say has acted as a linguistic double agent and both have found themselves thrust into the role of translator by the expansionist drive of the English Crown. That both France and Ireland are linked in the political ambitions of the Crown is made apparent in the presentation of York. York himself is explicit in proclaiming his attachment to the 'realms of England, France and Ireland' and we are told by Salisbury that what makes York feared and honoured by the people is both 'thy acts in Ireland,/In bringing them to civil discipline' (I.i.195–6) and 'Thy late exploits done in the heart of France' (I.i.197). The realms of both Ireland and France involve an engagement with language and translation, an engagement that is seen to be fraught with danger not only at the level of actual practice in the field (away) but in terms of perception in the (home) country from which the translators come.

It is interesting to note that the motif of translation is not only expressed in the direct accounts of interpreting practice but is also variously indicated in more oblique ways in the play. A feature of Cade's language in *Henry VI, Part 2* is his relentless punning. Both in his soliloquies and in his exchanges with others Cade is drawn irresistibly towards word play so that it becomes a characteristic marker of his speech. Cade's obsessive fondness of the pun could be seen as indicative of a social unease, a slightly frantic and undisciplined imitation of the corrosive wit of his erstwhile aristocratic masters or as the comic signature tune of the Shakespearean low-life character. However, it also possible to see punning itself as a form of double language so that the double language of interlingual translation (Cade as Gaelic–English translator) is mirrored by the double language of intralingual translation in the form of punning (Delabastita 1993). Not only has Cade spoken a 'double language' in Ireland in his role as interpreter but in England he continues to speak a double language as punster and usurper.

A further echo of Cade's activity as translator is to be found in the metaphor used to describe his political ambitions and his activities in Ireland. When York tells us of Cade's work as an informant in Ireland, we are told that he was in disguise: he went 'undiscover'd' presumably because he wore the distinctive dress of a 'shaghair'd crafty kern'. If he had not, such were the disparities between native Gaelic and Tudor dress he would have been found out instantly (Dunlevy 1989: 43–64). Not only is Cade himself a clothier by profession but when his follower George Beavis looks for an image to describe the political project of Cade, he takes his metaphor from the professional occupation of the rebel leader: 'Jack Cade the clothier means to dress the commonwealth, and turn it, and set a new nap upon it' (IV.ii.6–8).

Theo Hermans has commented on the prevalence of the 'garment metaphor' in Renaissance discourse on translation and it is significant that Cade the clothier ends

￫e translator (1985: 106). The attractiveness of dress as metaphor is
hor itself dress both reveals and conceals. If Cade dresses to disguise
￫entions from the native Irish, his dress in England reveals his social
￫ing in the eyes of both his aristocratic allies and his enemies, useful as a tool
or feared as a rabble rouser, but ultimately outside any hierarchy of inclusion. His
position as interpreter gives him power in the field but it is when he seeks to enlarge
this power to the court that his cover is in a sense blown.

If Matthiessen (1931) sees translation as a quintessentially Elizabethan art and
part of the literary effervescence of sixteenth- and early seventeenth-century
England, it is because translation takes place in the context of and influences other
developments in English society at the time. When Cade lists the charges that he
believes warrant the execution of Lord Say, he includes Say's role in the promotion
of the printing press ('thou hast caused printing to be used' [IV.vi.39–40]) and in
the heightening of language awareness ('thou hast men about thee that usually
talk of a noun and a verb, and such abominable words as no Christian ear can endure
to hear' [IV.vi.43–5]). Cade in his indictment of a fellow translator shows himself to be remarkably aware of the context and consequences of translation even
if the egregious nature of the justification for the killing of Say is doubtless intended
to alienate any possible sympathy for Cade among the audience. The printing press
was of course crucial to the dissemination of translations in Tudor England and
the fortunes of the English Bible in particular are bound up with the revolutionary
possibilities of the new technology (McGrath 2001).

As we saw earlier, a constant preoccupation of the period was with the legitimacy
of the vernacular language as an adequate means of expression. One effect of
translation in many different cultures and historical periods has been an enhanced
linguistic self-awareness. As languages, both modern and classical, come into
sustained and continuous contact with English it is inevitable that there will be more
and more 'talk of a noun and a verb', the English language becoming increasingly
aware of its own specificity and also, through philology, of its relationship to other
languages. Cade in singling out the printing press and grammatical self-knowledge
has perhaps unwittingly identified crucial elements in the elaboration of the
'civilizing' mission of empire where propaganda, proselytism and printing are
conjoined in the workshops of translation.

This primary role for translation is not, of course, without its drawbacks, as
Cade's subsequent career shows. General anxieties around expansion of empire
and consequent vulnerability are manifold in the period and not infrequently cluster
around translation. An example is to be found in a letter to the poet John Donne
written by his close friend, Sir Henry Wotton, one of the most distinguished
English diplomats of the period. At one stage in his career Wotton was secretary
to the earl of Essex who was at that time in negotiations with Hugh O'Neill, the
leader of the Gaelic Irish. Wotton is less than charitable about interpreters in Ireland
whose loyalty he finds more than questionable:

Whatsoever we have done, or mean to do, we know what will become of it,
when it comes among our worst enemies, which are interpreters. I would there

were more O'Neales and Macguiers and O'Donnells and Mac-Mahons and fewer of them.

(Pearsall Smith 1907: 308)

The central problem of translation in general and interpreting in particular is that of control. Anderson says of the interpreter that 'his position in the middle has the advantage of power inherent in all positions which control scarce resources' (1976: 218). We have already seen in the last chapter how interpreters in asylum settings exercise more power than is commonly supposed. The proximity is both desired, of course, and dreaded. The desire comes from a clear wish to control and manipulate a situation. The dread results from the fear of being misled either by the native interpreter or by the non-native interpreter changing sides and going native.

The choice for the architects of empire was between heteronymous and autonomous systems of interpreting. A heteronymous system involves recruiting local interpreters and teaching them the imperial language. The interpreters may be recruited either by force or through inducements. An autonomous system is one where colonizers train their own subjects in the language or languages of the colonized (Cronin 2002: 55–6). The conflicting merits of both systems are clearly outlined in a letter of Pedro Vaz de Carminha, dated 1 May 1500. In this letter we find an account of a Portuguese admiral asking whether two Tupis should be taken by force to act as interpreters-informants. A majority of Portuguese officers are reported as claiming that:

> it was not necessary to take men by force, since those taken anywhere by force usually say of everything that they are asked about that they have it in their country. If we left two of the exiles there, they would give better, very much better information than those men if we took them; for nobody can understand them, nor would it be a speedy matter for them to learn to speak well enough to be able to tell us nearly so much about that country as the exiles will when your Majesty sends them here.

(de Carminha 1947: 49)

The 'exiles' were those Portuguese whose punishment for breaking the law took the form of banishment to live among the indigenous peoples in Portugal's newly discovered colonies.

The Portuguese officers might have added that the return of the native is rarely comforting. Return offers the promise of closure, the synthesis of retrospection, the gathering in after the voyage out. However, the Prodigal Son, as we saw in the case of Owen in Brian Friel's play *Translations*, is a figure of disquiet and Ulysses' arrival in Ithaca is marked by a bloodbath. The Bible and Homer intimate that return usually disturbs the settled community. The dilemma for interpreters in colonial contexts is whether they can return as *native*. In other words, what is apparent in Wotton's letter to Donne is his unhappiness with having recourse to heteronymous interpreters and the questions this raises for control in situations of conflict.

However, the autonomous interpreters too are dogged by suspicions around the tension between linguistic agility and political fidelity. So when Cade, for example, returns to England from Ireland he is both unsettled and unsettling. The one who has conversed with the enemy has now become the enemy. Cade has with respect to his allegiance to the Crown gone native and behaved like the kerns he affected to deceive. Lord Say, who also performs as an autonomous interpreter, falls victim to the image of the translator/interpreter as duplicitous double and is condemned in the eyes of Cade and his followers for his linguistic fraternizing with the French enemy.

Forging the nation

If we move on to consider an earlier play in Shakespeare's history cycle, *Henry V*, it is possible to see the relationship between translation, nation and empire play itself it out in a somewhat different context. In a famous scene from the play soldiers from the various nations that will go on to constitute the United Kingdom engage in a series of sharp exchanges:

FLUELLEN: Captain Macmorris, I think, look you, under your correction, there is not many of your nation –
MACMORRIS: Of my nation! What ish my nation? Ish a villain, and a bastard, and a knave, and a rascal? What ish my nation? Who talks of my nation?
FLUELLEN: Look you, if you take the matter otherwise than is meant, Captain Macmorris, peradventure I shall think you do not use me with that affability as in discretion you ought to use me, look you; being as good a man as yourself, both in the disciplines of wars, and in the derivation of my birth, and in other particularities.
MACMORRIS: I do not know you so good as myself: so Chrish save me, I will cut off your head.
GOWAN: Gentlemen both, you will mistake each other.
JAMY: A! that's a foul fault.

(III.ii.136–52)

In this scene Fluellen, Jamy and Macmorris, the Welsh, Scottish and Irish soldiers, are busy translating themselves into the new language and political order of (Great) Britain, the Irish language ghosting the final 's' in Macmorris's famous question, 'What ish my nation?', so that he, like so many stage Irishmen after him, will become the emblematic figure of translation or mistranslation. However, what we would like to consider here is the relationship between translation and artifice and the significance of that relationship for the construction of national identity.

To take translation itself, is there something about the activity that is vaguely fraudulent, as we have suggested in an earlier work (Cronin 2003: 129–30)? History indeed has many examples of fictitious translation, from Macpherson's eighteenth-century Ossianic forgeries to twentieth-century Hungarian 'translations' of non-existent English-language science fiction novels. If translators are urged to produce versions that 'read like the original' for end users with no knowledge of the original, one could argue that they are being asked to produce a skilful knowledge of the original, or, in a sense, to deliver a highly skilful fake.

Staying with this idea it is arguable that there is a crucial link between *translation and forgery* and *translation and the forging of the nation*. It is frequently observed that what Tudor England, Classical France and Romantic Germany had in common was a desire to provide cultural legitimacy for the emerging nation through a close and unstinting involvement in the activity of translation (Delisle and Woodsworth 1995: 39–76). What translations and translators were doing in the critical period of political consolidation and national expansion was *forging* the language, the vernacular that would be appropriate and adequate to the ambitions of the new body politic. In other words, the forging of a new national identity implies the forgery of translation, the reading of the translation as if it were the original. Put another way, these translated subjects, Fluellen, Jamy and Macmorris, must now be presented as English or more properly British originals. The drama of their encounter is that they must now behave as if they were always already English speakers. Their identity forged in the military alliance of the conquering nation must be seen as their original condition because if they, in the words of the Englishman Gowan, continue to 'mistake each other' and revert to their original condition and language, the national and imperial project is threatened by dissent and disaffection.

What ish my nation? will of course be the language-haunted question that will dominate European politics throughout the Age of Empire. A rising cultural nationalism in the nineteenth century will seek to expose the 'forgery' of empire through a return to the 'originals' of the constituent languages and cultures of empire. In the Irish case, for example, as the nineteenth century draws to a close, the translation traces become not the residue of shame (an imperfect original) but the kernel of the new language (Hiberno-English) of the Irish literary renaissance.

In Shakespeare's presentation of the transactions of translation and their con-sequences in periods of political conflict, we are offered an insight into both the genesis and the decline of empire. The intrinsic duality of the translation exchange means that the eloquence of civility is always vulnerable to the return of the originals, always potentially destabilized by new forms of forgery (irredentism) that draw their power from claiming to be closer and more 'faithful' to the original. If Shakespeare reminds us in different ways of just how fraught the translation process is and how it is not only knaves but their masters who double their tongues, Joyce, that great student of Shakespeare, was closer than he perhaps realized to an important political and translation truth when Stephen Dedalus famously declared, 'I go to encounter for the millionth time the reality of experience and to forge in the smithy of my soul the uncreated conscience of my race' (Joyce 1977: 228). Bragg's contention that the supreme fiction of translation has meant that Shakespeare is truly a writer not for an age but for all time must be qualified by Shakespeare's own awareness that in forging the uncreated conscience of his own race, both age and time would watch over the handiwork of the translator as forger of nation and empire.

Metaphor and relational semantics

Translation not only exercised the minds of Shakespeare and his contemporaries as part of the praxis of national and imperial expansion. It also lay at the heart of the very language they would use to give voice to the new dispensation. Eric Cheyfitz in his *The Poetics of Imperialism: Translation and Colonization from 'The Tempest' to 'Tarzan'* has the following to say about metaphor in the sixteenth century:

> for Europeans, metaphor occupies the place of both the foreign and the domestic, the savage and the civilized, it occupies the place of both nature and culture; it is, at once, the most natural of languages or language in its most natural state and the most cultivated or cultured. Metaphor is nature; metaphor translates nature into culture.
>
> (1991: 121)

The fundamental problem, however, for Tudor cultural commentators is whether culture is somehow made 'unnatural' by this translation of nature into culture. Even more alarming is the possible pairing of the 'un-national' and 'unnatural' – a recurrent trope in the demonology of cultural nationalism – in the Tudor rhetorical engagement with difference through translation. The danger is all the more real in that in this period there is a decisive shift in thinking about language from referential semantics to relational semantics. Pioneers in this paradigm shift in Renaissance linguistics were Lorenzo Valla and Juan Luis Vives.

Valla in his study of the changes in Latin over time demonstrated that language was not an ahistorical object which emerged always already made but rather it was basically the socio-historical creation of a speech community. Vives for his part demonstrated that words which were previously thought to be similar, such as *homo* and *anthropos*, meant in fact somewhat different things. The net effect of these demonstrable differences between the semantic fields of various words was to prove that no two languages operated in the same way (Waswo 1987). Thus, the work of these scholars and others initiated a fundamental semantic shift in the Renaissance from a view of language simply representing reality (referential semantics) to a view of language generating that selfsame reality (relational semantics). The shift carried with it implications for how translation might be conceptualized and also for what its effects might be on cultural engagement.

In the first instance, relational semantics called into question more naïve or literalist notions of translation equivalence. If translation theoreticians from Cicero and Jerome onwards had cast doubt on the possibilities of one-to-one, referential equivalence, the findings of the language scholars appeared to justify their scepticism. In particular, the translation of figurative speech, long held to test the limits of the word-for-word fetishization of fidelity, was an exemplary case of the inadequacy of referential semantics. Figurative language, as that which presented the particular genius of a language community in the eyes of many, was precisely that feature of language which the community had specifically created and which did not fit easily into the speech of other different and distinct language communities.

A further consequence of the semantic shift for translation was what words, whether in the original or translation, could do to reality. If language is seen to create reality, what figurative language expresses in a particularly dramatic or heightened form is the ability of other languages to generate entirely different sets of meanings or ways of viewing the world. In the case of referential semantics, a belief in a common Adamic origin for language, where language was viewed as a somewhat elaborate exercise of pointing to objects in the real world, provided a basis for a trust in the existence of universal meanings. In other words, the objects pointed to by the words place their own limits on what differences might exist. With the advent of relational semantics, this was no longer the case. To some extent, it is possible to argue that what William Shakespeare's *The Tempest*, for example, dramatizes is precisely a world which must come to terms with the generative consequences of this new vision of semantics.

If the conventional relationship between words and reality is changed, then translation acquires wholly new powers. Now words in translation can shape our vision of the real and cause us to experience reality differently. If Caliban learns the language of his master Prospero, then in the changed universe of relational semantics, what he carries through from his mother tongue into his translated speech can alter the world as much as Prospero's imaginative ruminations. So the translator as agent of metamorphosis may not only effect change but become metamorphosized in the process. If metaphor in particular and figurative language generally are about the matching of the like and the unlike, the bringing together of the alien and the domestic, then it seems similarly true that translation is primarily a metaphorical operation in its bringing together of difference and that all metaphor is fundamentally a translational operation (Cronin 1995: 227–43). If translation has a transformative power which is allied to the metaphorical and the figurative what are the consequences for how translators are viewed in a situation of violent cultural encounter?

Metamorphosis

Not unexpectedly, Marina Warner begins *Fantastic Metamorphoses, Other Worlds* with the opening lines from Ovid's *Metamorphoses* and she goes on to articulate what will be a central thesis of her book, namely that in the Ovidian vision:

> Metamorphosis is the principle of organic vitality as well as the pulse in the body of art. This concept lies at the heart of classical and other myths, and governs the practice and scope of magic; it also, not coincidentally, runs counter to notions of unique, individual integrity in the Judaeo-Christian tradition.
>
> (Warner 2002: 2)

Location is not a matter of indifference for the metamorphic, however, and Warner's own readings of the literature of the fantastic led her to conclude that 'tales of metamorphosis often arose in spaces (temporal, geographical, and mental) that were crossroads, cross-cultural zones, points of interchange on the intricate connective tissue of communications between cultures' (ibid., 17).

For the sixteenth-century English, Ireland was one of those cross-cultural zones, a part of the Old World that ushered them into the New World of military and colonial expansionism. It is part of the argument in this chapter that Ireland provides a context for the anxieties attending tales of metamorphosis in Shakespeare and that the figure of translation is a way of exploring the metamorphic journey of the Tudors on their way to elaborating new conceptions of identity. The argument will be illustrated by a reference to a play of Shakespeare's that convinced at least one critic, Sir D. Plunket Barton, that 'Shakespeare must have made an Irish tour shortly before the production of the play', namely *As You Like It* (Plunket Barton 1919: 66).

What is immediately apparent in the arcadia of Arden is that linguistically it is a point of interchange, English and French and quite possibly Irish, existing in the golden world of the Duke's sylvan kingdom. Jaques, Amiens, Le Beau, Orlando provide us with the echoes of another literature and language so that the Merry England of the greenwood forest is not the original space of pure language but one that is already inhabited by language difference. More specifically, if the forest is to become the scene of multiple transformations, an appropriate arena for tales of metamorphosis, then it must be framed as a particular kind of place. The tutelary presence of the banished Duke is crucial in this respect as he will seek to change the misfortune of exile into the good fortune of redemption. When we first meet the Duke, he is eager to persuade his followers of the good luck of their bad luck:

> Sweet are the uses of adversity,
> Which like the toad, ugly and venomous,
> Wears yet a precious jewel in his head;
> And this our life exempt from public haunt,
> Finds tongues in trees, books in the running brooks,
> Sermons in stones, and good in everything.
> I would not change it.
>
> (II.i.12–18)

Amiens's comment is that the Duke has in a sense got it wrong, that he has in fact changed everything to maintain the pleasing fiction of the paradisiacal woods:

> Happy is your Grace,
> That can translate the stubbornness of fortune
> Into so quiet and so sweet a style.

It is because the Duke has set himself the task of translation that his new condition has become bearable. He translates the rustic reality before him into a courtly world of high literacy (books/sermons) so that in speaking the new language of Arcady his followers can find comfort in their radically altered circumstances. In a world which already bears traces of the plurilingual it is hardly surprising that it is translation that Amiens thinks of when trying to describe the transformative rhetoric of his master. If translation is typically thought of as a transaction between two languages, one doubling up as another, then doubles are everywhere in *As You Like It* with two characters called Oliver, two called Jaques and (in the folio edition) two dukes called Frederick.

But there is a darker side to the golden world of the court in exile and it is ironically highlighted by the other instance in the play where we find the verb 'translate'. Touchstone, the clown, is trying to dissuade William from wooing Audrey and bamboozles the hapless suitor with a show of wordy learning. Thus, if William does not desist from courting Audrey: 'Thou perishest; or to thy better understanding, diest; or, to wit, I kill thee, make thee away, translate thy life into death, thy liberty into bondage' (V.i.57–60).

Touchstone, like fools and clowns everywhere, uses the licence of language to articulate truths that might otherwise be unpalatable. As the Duke senior notes, 'He uses his folly like a stalking-horse, and under the presentation of that he shoots his wit' (V.iv.112–14). The Duke's own translation strategy is an apparently benign substitutionalism, the metaphorical recasting of Arden as another Eden. Touchstone's take on translation, on the other hand, is markedly dystopian. It is a form of unmasking, a way of revealing the menace behind ordinary language. Translation involves change but the change is decidedly for the worse, life becomes death, liberty becomes bondage. So what does this translation duality, this other doubling in a play replete with doubles, point to and what is the role of metamorphosis in the acting out of these contraries?

In order to try and answer this question it is important to cite two textual contexts for Shakespeare's play. Lisa Hopkins (2002: 1–21) has described *As You Like It* as part of a variety of cultural responses to Sir Walter Ralegh's account of his 1595 expedition to Guiana in search of the mythical city of El Dorado, *The Discoverie of the Large, Rich and Bewtiful Empire of Guiana*. More importantly for us, Ralegh's exploits in the New World began in the Old – in Ireland where he was intimately involved in the military campaigns of English territorial expansion in the late sixteenth century. As has been noted by a number of critics, from Barton Plunkett to Hopkins, there are multiple references to Ireland in the play, from the name Rosalind (from the Irish Rosaleen) to references to Irish wolves, rats, rhymers, women (who 'ripened' early) and a possible Irish-language source for the word 'ducadame' in Jaques's song which turns up in a well-known Irish tune of the sixteenth century, 'Eileen Aroon'. The world of *As You Like It* could be said to encompass two kinds of Old World, the Anglo-Norman antecedents of the English monarchy and the Irish world across the sea peopled by bards, song, strange women and treachery. If the one is a world transformed, that is England has already undergone French influence, the other is a world waiting to be transformed.

Another textual context for thinking about translation and metamorphosis is of course Ovid's own work, *Metamorphoses*, which enjoyed great currency in sixteenth-century England. In one ten-year period in the 1560s alone, we get three different part or full translations of Ovid's *Metamorphoses*: the anonymous 1560

Fable of Ovid Treting of Narcissus, Thomas Peend's 1565 *Pleasant Fable of Hermaphroditus and Salmacis* and Arthur Goulding's 1567 *Metamorphosis* (Oakley Brown 2001: 48–84). Ovid, of course, is mentioned in *As You Like It* when Touchstone declares to Audrey that, 'I am here with thee and thy goats, as the most capricious poet, honest Ovid, was among the goats' (III.iii.7–9). In a play where a series of secular transformations see boys metamorphose into women, the dispossessed restored to their rightful inheritance and 'convertites', to use Jaques's phrase, transformed by spiritual illumination, it is hardly surprising that the literary celebrant of the metamorphic, the 'capricious poet', should get an honourable mention. Jonathan Bate (1993) has, of course, traced Shakespeare's literary indebtedness to Ovid but we want to focus here on an aspect of Ovid's text that has remained largely uncommented upon in the context of the imperial and translation politics of Shakespeare's world.

In Book V of *Metamorphoses* we encounter Emathion, an old man who loved justice and revered the gods; since age has made warfare impractical, he 'fought with the tongue'.* He is decapitated by Chromis and the narrative in the final moment focuses on Emathion's head which, we learn, 'fell straight on the altar, and there the still half-conscious tongue kept up its execrations'. In Book XI, the death of Orpheus is described, his body dismembered by the scorned Ciconian women. The poet tells of Orpheus' head and lyre floating on the stream while 'mournfully the lifeless tongue murmured'. Book VI contains the terrifying scene of the rape of Philomela by Tereus who attempts to conceal his crime by cutting out her tongue. Metamorphosis then is not simply a benign shift in state, a progressive molting into otherness, triggered by the benevolent timetables of Mother Nature, but can involve a violent alteration of state, a brutal transformation of one's condition.

In the foundational narrative of the nation-state of Rome that is the *Metamorphoses* anger and violence are everywhere. In this respect, the seemingly gentle pastoral of *As You Like It* would appear to be its very antithesis. If we look more closely at the language of the play, however, we begin to pick out more disturbing imagistic parallels with the turbulent Ovidian world. They are to be found in the image Orlando uses in his opening exchange on the injustice of his treatment at the hands of his brother Oliver: 'Wert thou not my brother, I would not take this hand from thy throat till this other had pulled out thy tongue for saying so' (I.i.63–6). When Charles, the wrestler, is thrown, perhaps fatally, by Orlando, and Duke Ferdinand inquires how he is, Le Beau answers, 'He cannot speak, my lord' (I.ii.236), and the body of the luckless grappler is borne unceremoniously off the stage. The Duke senior detailing his idyll 'finds tongues in trees' (II.i.15) and Orlando in announcing his love for Rosalind repeats the image, 'Tongues I'll hang on every tree' (III.ii.136). Rosalind doubling up as Ganymede informs Orlando on the subject of wives and wit, 'You shall never take her without her answer, unless you take her without her

---

* Translations are from F.J. Miller (trans.) *Ovid: the Metamorphoses*, 2 vols, London: Harvard University Press.

tongue' (IV.i.181–2). So underlying the gentle parley of the good denizens of the greenwood forest is an undercurrent of violent change, a potential damming up of speech, which must be seen in the context of a general backdrop of dispossession in the play, whether it be the usurpation of the dukedom, the banishment of Rosalind, the threatened expropriation of Oliver or the plot to deprive Orlando of his rightful inheritance.

Here we can return to Shakespeare's earlier play with a significant Irish dimension, *Henry VI, Part 2*. A striking aspect of the play is the alarming headcount. Suffolk is beheaded so that he may talk no more. Lord Say is decapitated, as is Sir James Cromer and in the end the rebel leader, Jack Cade. Not only do heads literally roll but the sometime tactic of Iraqi insurgents is never far from the lips of the characters in the history play. Two female characters in the play provide us with examples. In Act I, scene ii, while Gloucester reports a dream where he sees the heads of the dukes of Suffolk and Somerset displayed on his broken staff, his vengeful wife, Eleanor, has her own vision of what the future should hold:

> Were I a man, a duke and next of blood,
> I would remove these tedious stumbling-blocks
> And smooth my way upon their headless necks;
> And, being a woman, I will not be slack
> To play my part in Fortune's pageant.
>
> (I.ii.62–6)

In Act IV, scene iv, lines 5–6, Queen Margaret mourns the demise of Suffolk asking: 'Here may his head lie on my throbbing breast;/But where's the body that I should embrace?'

It is noteworthy in the case of the named victims in *Henry VI, Part 2* that three out of the four – Suffolk, Say and Cade – have been involved in various forms of language contact with an adversary and two – Cade and Say – acted as interpreters. The notion of embodied agency evoked earlier in the chapter has a direct bearing on how we view translation, power and transformation in the Shakespearean context.

The fact of Cade or Say having a body situated in place and time means that not only will their body give expression voluntarily or involuntarily to their world-view, but the fact of embodied agency means that they are immediately aware of the consequences of their interpreting activity. The benign version of this is the torment of the lovers' bodies in *As You Like It* where at close quarters they try to translate their affections into a language acceptable to the beloved. In situations of conflict, however, not only as a speaking body are interpreters affecting the bodies of others but as an embodied agent they are uniquely vulnerable to torture and possible death should they fail to perform according to the wishes of their superiors. In the case of interpreting, as we have noted, there is no appreciable time difference between the act of translation and the moment of reception. Message and messenger become as one. The conditions of utterance cannot be separated from the context of utterance. ·

And the conditions and context of utterance bring us back to zones of conflict. Thomas Churchyard in his *A Generall Rehearsall of Warres* (1579) describes the extreme violence of the campaign in Munster (Ireland's most southerly province) led by the Elizabethan scholar, translator and soldier, Sir Humphrey Gilbert. We are told that Gilbert lined 'each side of the waie leadying into his own Tente' with 'the heddes of all those . . . which were killed in the daie'. The defeated coming to surrender passed through the 'lane of heddes' where 'thei sawe the heddes of their dedde fathers, brothers, children, kinffolke, and freendes, lye on the ground before their faces, as thei came to speak with the saied Colonell' (Churchyard 1579: iii.v). But it is not the severing of the head alone that guarantees conformity to the new political and military order. Words must be marshalled to legitimize this violent metamorphosis.

Patricia Palmer speaks about ventriloquism, the simulation of textual compliance by the defeated. As she notes, 'Ventriloquism touches against the terrible paradox that lay at the heart of linguistic colonisation in sixteenth-century Ireland: the grafted tongue followed after the severed head' (Palmer 2001: 58). John Derricke in his *Image of Irelande* (1581), for example, offers the reader an imagined scene in which after Rory Óg O'More, one of the Irish Gaelic leaders, has been captured and slain, his head, displayed on Dublin Castle, cautions his listeners against rebellion. Derricke writes:

> suppose that you see a monstrous Deuill, a truncklesse head, and a hedlesse bodie liuying, the one hid in some miskin & dunghill, but the other exalted, yea mounted vppon a poule (a proper sight, God wot, to beholde) vanting itself on the highest toppe of the Castell of Dublin, vttering in plaine Irishe the thynges that ensewe.
>
> (Derricke 1883: 92)

The lifeless head then begins its sorry tale:

> These things to confirme, I Rorie am he,
> Who sometime mounted alofte in the Skie,
> And fortune castying a fauour to me,
> Prouoked me higher, and higher to flie,
> . . .
> All men that heare this, take warnyng by me.
> (ibid., 95–7)

Rory Óg O'More was a Gaelic speaker but his utterances after death, though allegedly in 'plaine Irish', textually metamorphose into English. In Touchstone's words, Rory Óg's killing not only means his life has been translated into death but the act of posthumous translation itself signifies that for him and his followers, political and cultural liberty has been translated into military and linguistic bondage.

Thus, bearing in mind the Irish political context of both *Henry VI, Part 2* and *As You Like It* and the Ovidian backdrop of violent change, the remarkable clustering of imagery, comment and/or dramatic action around tongues and heads in the two plays is less than surprising. Focusing attention on the head and tongue not only sits easily with a form of art, drama, that is primarily concerned after all with spoken speech but in the image of the severed tongue the playwright finds a potent metaphor for the linguistic fallout of war, whether that be enforced speechlessness, coercive or covert translation or the perils of translatorial embodied agency.

Simon Schama in his account of the incidence of human concerns on the representations of landscape sees the English greenwood as inextricably bound up with a notion of liberty. Citing the Forest of Arden in *As You Like It*, he claims: 'Greenwood was not, then, like Dante's *selva oscura*, the darkling forest where one lost oneself at the entrance to hell. It was something like the exact opposite: the place where one found oneself' (Schama 1995: 141).

The problem was what kind of self you were likely to find after the passage through this metamorphic space: what, if you like, is found or gets lost in Duke senior's translation. The forest after all was by the account of all the Tudor adventurers the most formidable redoubt of the native Irish, the sixteenth-century equivalent of the Vietnamese jungle. If the savagery of the Irish was taken to be axiomatic, this was in part to do with the spaces they inhabited, bogs and woodlands. And what characterized these spaces was that you never quite knew where you stood. Ralph Lane, leader of the first settlement in Roanoke in the New World, who had overseen the extermination of the O'Moores from Laois to Claremorris in the Old, complained bitterly in Ireland of 'the tediousness of the brokenness of this lost kingdom in the daily confusions of it' (*Calendar State Papers* 1869: 482). Sir Walter Ralegh, half-brother to Sir Humphrey Gilbert, mentioned earlier, who was closely involved in punitive expeditions in Munster in the 1580s speaks of being in 'a strang country newly sett downe' where he felt like 'a fish cast on dry land, gasping for breath, with lame legs and lamer loonges' (cited in Hennessy 1883: 143). The poet John Donne warned his friend Sir Henry Wotton who was setting out for Ireland of the dangers of 'Irish negligence' and of what he referred to as 'Lethargies' (cited in Hadfield and Maley 1993: 9).

The Forest of Arden may be another kind of 'lost kingdom' if only because the Duke senior has indeed lost his kingdom but it is also a kingdom where nothing is what it appears to be, from wise clowns to female Ganymedes. The 'daily confusions' are to an extent set right by the not so natural magic of Rosalind with the neat conjugal pairings and the timely restoration of property rights but Arden shows not so much the permanence of liberty as its fragility. In the context of aggressive territorial ambition it is not so much the inhabitants of a mythical Merry England who will inhabit the forests as the hunted-down adversaries of imperial expansiveness in the Old World of Ireland and the New World of the Americas. If translation is to the fore in understanding the particular political tensions of the period and is artfully incorporated into the Shakespearean *oeuvre*, it is because it is the operation that best describes a world like our own, where questions of identity remain obdurately centre stage, heads continue to roll and armies march.

Actionable intelligence

As if to illustrate the continuing relevance of these preoccupations, the invasion of Iraq by the coalition forces in 2003 provided graphic evidence of the immediate and often tragic connection between the situatedness of interpreters and their extreme vulnerability as embodied agents. As Domenico Maceri noted,

> Interpreting is the most dangerous civilian job among employees of private contractors with the US Labor Department. Interpreters' deaths accounted for more than 40 per cent of the more than 300 death claims filed by all contractors operating in Iraq.
>
> (2005: 1)

Interpreters working with US forces began to wear black ski masks, sunglasses and caps to hide their identity and body armour and helmets to protect them from attack, as well as using American nicknames and spending months on end housed in American bases (Spetalnick 2004: 1–2; Maceri 2005: 1–2). The extent of the implication of translation and interpreting in the military operation in Iraq can be gauged from revenue figures for the Titan Corporation of San Diego, California. Its contract with the US military stipulated that it provide up to 4,800 'skilled contract linguists' and in 2004 the contract was worth $675 million to Titan. Over 6 per cent of the company's $1.8 billion total revenue for 2003 came from its translation and interpreting contract with the US army (Washburn 2004: 2).

In an eerie echo of the theatre of Shakespearean war, a Titan interpreter and Iraqi Kurd, Luqman Mohammed Kurdi Hussein, was captured by Iraqi insurgents in October 2004 and a video of his beheading was posted on the internet (Krane 2005: 2). Earlier, in August 2004, guerrillas followed an interpreter to his home near Samarra, north of Baghdad, and killed him with a bullet through the head. Beside his body was a note vowing to kill 'collaborators' (Spetalnick 2004: 1). The rumoured price on the head of interpreters was $5,000 (ibid., 2). A US Army reservist First Sergeant Stephen Valley claimed, 'There was a period when it seemed translators were being targeted on a daily basis. There was virtually no way to protect these people' (Krane 2005: 2). One Iraqi translator/interpreter reported on the continued human cost of interpreting in a situation of conflict:

> The Coalition Forces and Titan which recruit translators do nothing to protect them after they leave work or provide for the living of those translators, who, out of fear, force themselves into voluntary house-confinement, or for the orphaned children and widowed wives of those translators who lost their lives not for any offence but for practicing their profession. . . . We gather frequently underground or talk about our problems while walking in backstreets and narrow city lanes. American patrols pass by and sometimes automatically shoot at the least sense of threat if not instigation. . . . I myself, I am tired of hiding to tell you the truth. The other day a car in a place on my way back from the internet café where I go stealthily entered horror into my

heart and sleepless to me [*sic*]. Next day I was relieved when I knew they were not targeting me.

(Friel 2005: 4)

If 'translators', 'linguists', interpreters are being targeted with particular ferocity, there is nothing to suggest that the situation is unlikely to change in our century due to the changing nature of warfare itself. This was apparent from the evolution of the military conflict within Iraq as described by John Pike, a director of GlobalSecurity.org:

The challenge military intelligence has in Iraq is that this is not a war most of them were organized, trained and equipped to fight. . . . They were basically geared up for the major combat operation phase of the war. They have not been primarily focused on counterinsurgency – they don't like it, it's not much fun, it's not what they had planned on doing in Iraq.

(cited in Taylor Martin 2004: 1)

Traditional Cold War theories of large-scale combat between conventional forces are no longer tenable as an increasingly salient feature of violent conflict is the rapid mobilization and dispersal of combatants who are not part of identifiable national armies belonging to particular nation-states (Kaldor 1999). One effect of this change in the nature of conflict is that the archive of empire, the information network that sustained the Great Powers in the imperial age, is once again coming to the fore as a crucial element in the relationship between translation itself and power. 'Actionable intelligence' (Taylor Martin 2004: 1) becomes the watchword of counter-insurgency operations but of course intelligence is only 'actionable' if it is in fact intelligible.

Underlining the link, Domenico Maceri has argued that the role of translators and interpreters in Iraq was 'vital' because the war was 'not only about force but about information'. He quoted a US Army commander to the effect that 'his men could not do two-thirds of their job without interpreters' (Maceri 2005: 1). Thus, if the shift from modern to postmodern war means that intelligence gathering becomes a priority for military strategists and that in an informational society even warfare itself becomes primarily a question of accessing particular kinds of information, then translators and interpreters are set to become more exposed than ever in the conflicts of the present and the future. If interpreters were specifically targeted as 'critical links' by insurgents in Iraq, and Sudanese interpreters were rounded up for interrogation and worse after the visits of the British and American politicians Jack Straw and Colin Powell to Darfur (Friel 2005: 4), then there is every reason to believe that in our century, translators and interpreters will find themselves at the very heart of the new informational or intelligence wars. They will in a sense become 'vital' players in a new form of risk society (Beck 1992) where 'to feel safe in the world', it will be necessary to 'understand that acquiring knowledge in multiple languages is necessary, not just in English' (Maceri 2005: 2). Not one of the least paradoxes of the situation is that as they are recruited to make the world less risky for the countries or organizations which employ them, they will find their own lives increasingly at risk.

As translators and interpreters become more and more implicated in what might be described as the informational economy of conflict then questions which have haunted translation and interpreting through the centuries will recur with renewed relevance and urgency in our century. As we noted earlier, a central problem of translation in general and interpreting in particular is that of control. Proximity is both sought after and feared. The fear comes from the risk of being misled either by the native interpreter or by the non-native interpreter gone native. The difficulty for the imperial agent is dealing with this monstrous doubleness, the potential duplicity of interpreters. The shortfall of qualified US Army interpreters has meant, for example, that 'intelligence soldiers trying to extract information from inmates at Abu Ghraib have been forced to use Iraqi translators of dubious reliability' (Taylor Martin 2004: 2).

We have already noted examples from history of the difficulties relating to heteronymous interpreting practices. The remedies sought were various and the shift to autonomous modes of interpreting is notable in Champlain's decision to set up the institution of *interprète-résidents* whereby young French adventurers went and lived among the tribes with whom the French traded and learned the language of the indigenous peoples of Canada. Later in the same century, as a result of a decree drawn up by Colbert, the French court in 1669 arranged to train French-born children known as 'enfants de langue' in Turkish, Arabic and Persian (St-Pierre 1995: 16–17). These trainee interpreters were assigned to French ambassadors and consuls abroad where they learned and perfected their knowledge of different foreign languages. So foreign-language instruction in imperial countries was frequently linked to the move towards more autonomous modes of interpreting. The establishment of new courses in language training and cultural awareness by the US Army in Fort Huachucha in Arizona, the base where army interrogators and intelligence officers are trained, and the drive to recruit soldiers in the United States who are Arabic speakers, were twin elements of a shift in the direction of an autonomous mode of interpreting in the contemporary era.

A very real dilemma for interpreters in situations of conflict is whether they can return as *native*. If they do, the risk, of course, is that they *go native*. In 1830 Captain Fitzroy, later captain of the *Beagle*, abducted a number of Fuegians on his first trip to Tierra del Fuego. His crew gave them nicknames that stuck, Jemmy Button (exchanged for a mother-of-pearl button), York Minister and Fuegia Basket. Jemmy Button was a huge success in England and became noted for his fastidiousness about cleanliness and dress. He learned English and was presented along with Fuegia Basket to Queen Adelaide. Button's English sojourn did not last indefinitely and in 1833 he was back in Tierra del Fuego along with York Minister and Fuegia Basket. They had travelled there on the *Beagle* with a young English naturalist, Charles Darwin (Beer 1996: 38–40).

One reason for the repatriation of the Fuegians to Tierra del Fuego was the belief that their knowledge of English language and culture would facilitate trade in the area. Years later, W. Parker Snow, in his *A Two Years' Cruise off Tierra del*

Fuego, the Falkland Islands, Patagonia and the River Plate: a Narrative of Life in the Southern Seas, gives an account of meeting Jemmy Button, 'quite naked, having his hair long and matted at the sides, cropped in front, and his eyes affected by smoke' (Beer 1996: 69). Parker Snow goes on to note that Jemmy's tribe were the least reliable – they had learnt a double language and behaviour. Not only did Jemmy speak the indigenous language but he also spoke English, the language of the imperial trader. As a result, the English found that Jemmy's tribe was considerably more adroit in its dealings with them than other tribes and more likely to manipulate than be manipulated.

The returned native had indeed gone native but because he was not wholly native he was even more dangerous as a native. Here 'abduction' in the more usual sense of the word becomes 'abduction' in the sense of retrospective hypothesizing. This is the type of hypothesizing we find in the Victorian detective story, where clues allow Sherlock Holmes to retrace a certain path back to secure origins. The interpreter is returned to his language and culture of origin, he has retraced the path from his B language to his A language, but the origins have now become uncertain, a potential site of duplicity.

In the contemporary setting there is another sense in which the 'return of the native' becomes both dangerous and problematic in the context of heteronymous modes of interpreting. The interpreter and legal expert Ellen Ruth Moerman has written of the frequently ad hoc local recruitment of interpreters in situations of conflict and of the terrible consequences for those who are left behind once the outside forces leave:

> When the military or the press or human aid organizations move into an area whose language they do not master, they rarely plan the need for interpreters in advance. And even if they do, they will decide to rely on cheaper locals. When their task is finished, they will depart, leaving the locals behind, giving little or no consideration to the risks to which these interpreters are exposed. And yet, we know that interpreters who work with the 'occupiers' of a country or a region are often seen as 'sleeping with the enemy'. We know of the dozens that were murdered in ex-Yugoslavia, dozens are now being murdered in Iraq, even publicly executed on television, are now having to live with the enemy permanently instead of going home. They will remain suspicious strangers in their own country long after the foreigners have gone home.
>
> (Moerman 2005: 13)

The heteronymous mode of interpreting can, as we saw, bring with it anxieties around fidelity and control. Speaking about 'translators', US Major Clint Nussberger, intelligence chief for the 24th Marine Expeditionary Unit in Iraq, claimed that, 'They are an important lifeline. Trust is very important' (Spetalnick 2004: 1). However, the recruitment of local interpreters is not simply to do with their knowledge of 'local' languages, terrain and culture; it also means that a foreign organization, whether public body or private company can often avoid legal duties 'which an interpreter might be able to derive from human rights law, contract law in general or employment law in particular' (Moerman 2005: 14). In addition, the 'foreign party gets out of the cost of providing healthcare, safe working conditions, a disability pension, pensions and looking after the family etc. etc. when the interpreter is killed on duty' (ibid., 14).

The problem now is that the native may indeed return home but he or she may not return from home alive. In the words of one Iraqi interpreter, 'My life is always in danger, but most of all when I go home to visit' (cited in Spetalnick 2004: 1). The localness of the interpreter, which is perceived as a linguistic, cultural and 'intelligence' asset, is also that which makes the interpreter uniquely vulnerable to the political pressures of the locale. The desire on the part of foreign organizations to benefit from local knowledge without a concomitant commitment to local responsibilities is part of a dangerous disconnect that makes global–local interactions a one-way street which is, in more than one sense of the word, a dead-end street. When Zygmunt Bauman describes 'liquid modern culture' as a '*culture of disengagement, discontinuity and forgetting*' (2004: 117; his emphasis), there is an obvious parallel with a culture of translation logistics and management which disengages from the local lives of interpreters and forgets about them as they contend with ostracism, persecution and worse.

The interpreter's visibility

One area where the interpreter has literally become visible rather than invisible is the cinema screen. There is of course a long and largely unwritten history of translation and interpreting featuring in motion pictures but it is noteworthy that within two years alone, two major Hollywood films, *Lost in Translation* (2003) and *The Interpreter* (2005), feature issues of translation and interpreting as central rather than peripheral concerns, concerns flagged in their very titles. If we want to understand how translators and interpreters are seen to function in cultures and societies, it seems legitimate to investigate not only actual working conditions, rates of pay and training or educational opportunities for the profession but also the manner in which they are represented in cultural or imaginary artefacts. Indeed, a greatly neglected resource in the teaching of translation theory and history is cinema, whose familiarity and accessibility make it a compelling form of instruction for undergraduates and postgraduates who often possess a broad cinematographic knowledge base and highly developed visual literacy.

Silvia Broome (Nicole Kidman) works as an interpreter for the United Nations in New York in Sydney Pollack's film, *The Interpreter*. She reports a suspicious conversation she overheard on her headphones after hours, containing an implied threat on the life of the leader of the fictional African Republic of Matobo. As she in her turn becomes an object of suspicion, the US secret service are called in and one of the officers, Tobin Keller (Sean Penn), asks the UN security staff for information on her background. He is informed that she was born in the United States, grew up in Africa, had a British mother and a white African father, studied music in Johannesburg, linguistics at the Sorbonne and several languages in different parts of Europe. The comment of the UN security official (Clyde Kusatsu) is that Silvia Broome 'is the UN'. So the interpreter is immediately identified as a cultural composite, a literally embodied intercultural agent, who becomes a metonym for the United Nations itself.

Keller, however, is not satisfied with this briefing and wants more intelligence on Broome. He wants to know whether she is married, if she has children, if she belongs to any clubs, what her religious background is, whether she votes Democrat or Republican. Finally he asks, 'Who is she?' The film is in part an attempt to answer Keller's question. How difficult the task turns out to be is apparent in a scene towards the end of the film where one of Keller's agents tries to establish where Silvia Broome has gone after disappearing from her apartment. He has checked with hotels and more especially with her friends but nobody seems to know where she has gone because they do not 'really know her'. The agent's lapidary conclusion is that 'no one knows her'. The weakness of the ties to her friends would seem to be borne out by the interpreter's fundamental unknowability, as if her very linguistic and cultural connectivity (the United States/Matobo/ South Africa/several European languages and one indigenous African language) resulted in a curious form of isolation. Her parents and siblings were the victims of state violence in Matobo so that she is literally left on her own, a point that is repeatedly emphasized in the film.

At one level, of course, Silvia Broome is akin to Owen in Brian Friel's *Translations*. She is alone or apart from others because of her ability to master several languages. At another level, she is not so much unknowable as not knowable in terms of conventional expectations about race, ethnicity and gender. She is white and constantly asserts her African rather than US/European identity, even when the 'politics of my skin', as she puts it, become a problem in her relationship with her lover, the Matoban rebel leader, Ajene Xola (Curtis Cook). What makes her hard to know is not that she moves effortlessly between English, French, Spanish and Ku (the fictional African language in the film) but that she carries in her person a polyidentity that confounds the monolingual and monocultural stereotypes of the unitary nation-state. If the security official treats Broome as a metonym of the UN, it is equally plausible to treat her as a metonym of the state of Matobo which is as internally complex and fractured as any UN gathering. In this sense, one can argue that the interpreter is not so much an exceptional ('prodigal') figure as one who is unexceptional in her multilingualism and complex cultural allegiances, a condition which is arguably a much more widespread default value for much of humanity than any purist fantasy of single, monophone, national origin.

If *The Interpreter* as a film is primarily concerned with the visual, language figures prominently in its representation of what it is that interpreters do. In an early exchange between Broome and Keller, the secret service agent wants to establish the interpreter's feelings about the Matoban leader, Edmond Zuwane (Earl Cameron). She says that she wouldn't mind if he was 'gone' and Keller retorts, 'dead?' Broome's immediate response is that 'dead and gone are not the same thing' and that if 'she interpreted dead as gone at the UN she would be out of a job'. Keller then accuses her of 'playing with words' and she argues in her defence that she believes in diplomacy, in what the UN is attempting to achieve through the medium of words. The charge that the UN is a glorified verbal playground also comes from a very different source in the film, the Matoban rebel leader, Kuman Kuman, who on learning that Broome works as an interpreter in the UN claims that the UN is 'layers of languages, signifying nothing'. Kuman Kuman is killed shortly after this conversation by a bomb on the bus carrying him but his accusation does not shake Broome's belief that, as she tells Keller, 'words and compassion are the better way even if slower than the gun'.

It is hard to dissociate this discussion of the rights of language and diplomacy in the UN context from the row over the refusal of the UN to sanction the invasion of Iraq by the coalition forces. However, more generally, the film raises the issue of interpreting and language mediation as a form of triangulation or, to use Gillian Rose's term, a 'broken middle' (Rose 1992: 32) that prevents the violent and dogmatic synthesis of binary opposites. It is because words matter that interpreting matters. When Nils Lud (Jesper Christensen), the head of Zuwane's security detail, questions Broome about her reasons for leaving Africa and coming to the UN, she responds that she has come for some 'quiet diplomacy'. Her answer provokes the comment from Lud, 'With respect, you are only an interpreter', to which she replies that 'countries have gone to war because they have misinterpreted each other'. Broome's response gives us a clue as to why it is the interpreters rather than the political leaders who should be centre stage in a film set in the headquarters of the United Nations. One of the tasks that Silvia's brother Simon (Hugo Speer) was engaged in before his murder was compiling lists of the names of victims of the regime. This is a sombre echo of a childhood game between brother and sister when they used to compile lists of odd and unusual things in notebooks such as the list of '739 interesting words' that we get a glimpse of towards the end of the film ('bodaceous, hypotenuse, shellac'). What the lists do is to break a local cultural taboo against the naming of the dead but also a wider political taboo against the naming of the acts of certain governments against their own people as genocide or crimes against humanity. In other words, naming things correctly, being careful in the use of terminology (not confusing 'gone' and 'dead'), is fraught with ethical consequence. In the 'small world' of the United Nations if the interpreters are the long-distance links that bring countries closer to each other in the realm of mutual comprehension then their linguistic and cultural tact prefigures in a sense what might be careful intercultural negotiation in a multilingual world.

The difficulty for Silvia Broome is not only that no one claims to really know her but more worryingly that nobody claims to believe her. The promotional material for the film claims that 'the truth . . . needs no translation' but what exercises the minds of many of the characters in the film is whether there can be any truth without translation. Tobin Keller's first reaction after interviewing the interpreter about her claim to have overheard an assassination plot is to tell a colleague (Catherine Keener) 'She's a liar.' Silvia Broome is subsequently shown attached to a lie detector though the results of the tests are inconclusive. Thus, at one level, the suspicion in which she is held, the speculation that she is speaking a double language and is therefore not to be trusted, has been a recurrent feature of attitudes towards interpreters, as we have seen in this chapter. At another level, however, it is through her eyewitness account of the deterioration of the human rights situation in Matobo under Edmond Zuwane that Silvia Broome translates the situation in Matobo into a language that Tobin Keller can understand.

She, of course, is not neutral, having been emotionally close to Xola and having taken up arms against Zuwane's government, an absence of neutrality which is emphasized towards the end of the film when she threatens to kill Zuwane with a gun. Her absence of neutrality does not indicate, however, that she is deliberately lying but rather that as an embodied agent she has been subject to the depredations of the regime which has destroyed all of her close family and she thus cannot remain detached or indifferent. Truth about what is happening in Matobo does need the assistance of the 'translator' or interpreter but the truth may not be what governments want to hear.

It is the business of interpreters, needless to say, to hear what is being said and to be heard as they interpret. In her first exchange with Keller, Broome claims that as an interpreter she does not concentrate on faces but rather listens to voices. This statement is self-contradictory as there would be little point in the glass-fronted interpreting booths that we see in the film if the interpreters did not have to see facial expressions and gestural language in order to function effectively. The motif of the voice is ever present in the film as Broome is constantly challenged on her ability to recognize voices and this culminates in her encounter with the Matoban leader Zuwame where she asks him to read out the epigraph to his account of his role in the Matoban struggle for freedom:

> The gunfire around us makes it hard to hear but the human voice is different from other sounds. It can be heard over noises that bury everything else, even when it is not shouting, even if it is just a whisper. Even the lowest whisper can be heard over armies when it is telling the truth.

The theme of the voice is not simply crucial to the development of the plot (what did Broome actually hear in Ku over her headphones?) but it highlights the fundamental importance of orality as a dimension to the activity of the interpreter. Zuwane might indeed have been talking about interpreters who rely not on guns but on the 'human voice' in their interface with others in situations of conflict. It is the presence, the actuality of those voices, which again makes the circumstances or context of utterance hard to ignore. It is when the interpreting stops, when the people are no longer named and the voices are silenced, that truth becomes the most spectacular victim of gunfire and armies.

4   The future of diversity

For the god Enki careless talk costs lives. In Neal Stephenson's novel *Snow Crash* the Chaldean god turns out to be an ur-hacker, alarmed at the spread of the Asherah virus. This virus, doubtless to the joy of creationists, has made evolution in Sumeric society impossible. In a bid to stop the spread of the virus Enki produces a 'nam-shub', a type of spell which prevents everyone from speaking the Sumeric language. The Asherah virus, which uses oral and verbal forms of transmission, is thus prevented from infecting any new subjects. The danger of speaking only one language is that development stops. Out of that hygienic silence for Stephenson's narrator arose the myth of the Tower of Babel, an elegant metaphor for the programming skills of Enki and a parable for the regressive menace of monoculturalism and monolingualism (Stephenson 1993).

The translation 'virus' notoriously uses oral and verbal means of transmission as it disseminates new ideas, insights, sensations, perspectives across societies and cultures. Over the centuries political and ecclesiastical authorities have often been alarmed at the speed with which subjects and believers can become 'infected' with the new ideas of dissent or revolution reaching them through the medium of translation. Various forms of 'nam-shubs' have been tried from covert intimidation to death at the stake to produce the desired silence and check the viral spread of dissidence, a bleaker reading in other words of Enki's mute achievement. What is most objectionable in the existence of translation is the way in which it acts potentially not just as a viral agent destroying cherished pieties but as a bridge which connects different experiences, belief systems and cultural practices and opens the door to a whole new way of experiencing and interpreting the world. In considering this, it may be useful to reflect on the very concepts of 'bridge' and 'door' and see what they might tell us about translation before seeing what an understanding of translation informed by these considerations can contribute to thinking about the future of cultural and linguistic diversity from an interdisciplinary perspective.

Bridge and door

Georg Simmel notes in his essay 'Bridge and Door' that a particular quality of humanity is the ability to connect and separate but one cannot exist without the other. Each always presupposes the opposite:

By choosing two items from the undisturbed store of natural things in order to designate them as 'separate', we have already related them to one another in our consciousness, we have emphasized these two together against whatever lies between them. And conversely, we can only sense these things to be related which we have previously somehow isolated from one another; things must first be separated from one another in order to be together. Practically as well as logically, it would be meaningless to connect that which was not separated, and indeed that which also remains separated in some sense.

(Simmel 1997a: 171)

Therefore any culture of connectivity or connectedness implies a degree of separateness and without separateness there is nothing to connect. If translation is proverbially a bridge-building exercise, and much is said about how it bridges gaps between cultures, it must not be forgotten that translation has as much a vested interest in distinctness as in connectedness. To put this another way, translation scholars must be to the forefront in campaigns to protect and promote the teaching of diverse languages as there is little point in being in the business of connection if nothing is left to connect. It is the existence of separate languages and cultures and skilled practitioners in these languages that makes bridge-building a feasible and worthwhile exercise. The fulsome rhetoric of global communications bringing us all closer together in the global village is in effect a form of bad faith if there is a failure to recognize that connectedness has as a necessary prerequisite the identification and maintenance of separateness.

Conversely, what is separate does not remain unaltered by connection and indeed must be understood as a function or dimension of connection: 'Only for us are the banks of a river not just apart but "separated"; if we did not first connect them in our practical thoughts, in our needs and in our fantasy, then the concept of separation would have no meaning' (Simmel 1997a: 171). Animals can find ingenious ways of getting from one point to another but Simmel would see path-building as a specific human achievement which connects a beginning and an end and allows the connection to endure. It is movement frozen in space. Therefore, we can only speak of separate cultures and languages because they are in a sense always already connected to other languages and cultures, whether German linguistic self-consciousness sharpened by French political ambition in the early nineteenth century or Brazilian-Portuguese distinctness emerging out of geopolitical distance. Just as connectedness without separateness is a non sequitur so similarly a notion of separateness without connectedness would result not in separateness but in indistinctness. It is because we pick out things to connect that they can be perceived as different. Otherwise, they are in a sense non-existent, all background and no figure.

For Simmel, the door also connects and separates but whereas the bridge connects the finite with the finite, the door connects the finite (being) with the infinite (world). Because doors can be opened, they provide paradoxically a greater sense of isolation from space outside than, for example, a wall:

The latter [a wall] is mute, but the door speaks. It is absolutely essential for humanity that it set itself a boundary, but with freedom, that is, in such a way that it can also remove the boundary again, that it can place itself outside it.

(Simmel 1997a: 172)

Though there is no difference in structural meaning in which direction a bridge is crossed, the 'door displays a complete difference of intention between exiting and entering' (ibid., 173). Entering a space that is shut off by a door is evidence of a human ability to establish structure and significance in the flux of things, to create a finite framework of meaning, but the possibility of exiting through the door illustrates the ability 'at any moment of stepping out of this limitation into freedom' (ibid., 174) into the infinite realm of the potential. So to what extent are concepts of the bridge and the door operative with respect to what goes on in translation and what might they tell us about very real identity predicaments in the contemporary world?

In his discussion of the origin and source of Barthélemy d'Herbelot's *Bibliothèque orientale* (1697), Nicholas Dew emphasizes the author's indebtedness to Katib Chelebi's bibliographic encyclopedia, the *Kashf al-zunūn 'an asāmīl-kutub wa-l-funūn* ('The Uncovering of Ideas: On the Titles of Books and the Names of the Sciences'), which contained a list of over 14,000 works in Arabic, Turkish and Persian. Dew challenges the notions of 'centre' and 'periphery' for the seventeenth century, arguing that:

The very notion of 'centre and periphery' seems inadequate, given that the Ottoman metropolis was the centre for book-trading networks stretching across the whole Ottoman Empire, and given that Istanbul intellectuals like Katib Chelebi, and his student Hezarfenn, used travellers from Europe to learn about and translate European scientific texts.

(2004: 241)

Dew's basic contention is that Istanbul is a bridge-city, a translation hub, inhabited by a 'bordering creature' (to use Simmel's term) such as Katib Chelebi. So like Baghdad and Cairo, 'world cities' in an earlier period (Abu-Lughod 1989), Istanbul connects different cultural areas and, in establishing these contacts, also allows for the emergence of identities in the known world which are defined in turn against the West or the East or the North or the South, the poles of definition partly dependent on your geopolitical situation (Bayly 2004). Pascale Casanova points to a similar phenomenon for Latin American writers in another 'bridge-city', Paris, in the twentieth century:

Cette sorte de réappropriation nationale, qu'autorise en quelque sorte la 'neutralité' ou la 'dénationalisation' de Paris, est aussi soulignée par les historiens de l'Amérique latine qui ont montré comment les intellectuels de ces pays se sont découverts 'nationaux' à Paris, et plus largement en Europe.

(Casanova 1999: 52)

[This kind of national reappropriation which was in some way authorized by the 'neutrality' or 'denationalization' of Paris is also emphasized by Latin American historians who showed how the intellectuals of these countries discovered their 'national' identity in Paris and more generally in Europe.]

Bridges separate as much as they connect and separateness, as we saw in the last chapter on immigration, is as much a feature of the 'bridge-city' as connectedness. If translations are the Ashera viruses of dissemination that spread from culture to culture, they are also the 'nam-shubs' that stop infinite spread through the constitution of separate literatures, cultures and vernaculars (Delisle and Woodsworth 1995). Not all translations, of course, spread at the same speed, or into or from the same languages, or in the same conditions. Like the door, directionality makes for crucial differences in meanings. Casanova acknowledges the close fit between cultural prestige and the concentration and directionality of translatorial power:

Dans l'univers littéraire, si l'espace des langues peut, lui aussi, être représenté selon une 'figuration florale', c'est-à-dire un système où les langues de la périphérie sont reliées au centre par les polyglottes et les traducteurs, alors on pourra mesurer la littérarité (la puissance, le prestige, le volume de capital linguistico-littéraire) d'une langue, non pas au nombre d'écrivains ou de lecteurs dans cette langue, mais au nombre de polyglottes littéraires (ou protagonistes de l'espace littéraire, éditeurs, intermédiaires cosmopolites, découvreurs cultivés . . .) qui la pratiquent et au nombre de traducteurs littéraires – tant à l'exportation qu'à l'importation – qui font circuler les textes depuis ou vers cette langue littéraire.

(Casanova 1999: 37)

[In the world of literature, if languages can also be represented using a 'floral figure', that is to say a system where languages on the periphery are linked to the centre by polyglots and translators, then it is possible to measure the literariness (the power, prestige, the volume of linguistico-literary capital) of a language, not by the number of writers and readers in this language, but by the number of literary polyglots (or main players in the literary arena, publishers, cosmopolitan intermediaries, well-educated talent spotters . . .) who know it and by the number of literary translators – for export as well as for import – who cause texts to be translated into or out of this literary language.]

A language may have many millions of speakers and a rich literary tradition but if it is bereft of translators or of opportunities for translation wider perceptions of its 'literariness' will suffer. Francesca Orsini illustrates the consequences of this logic for literature in the vernacular languages of India such as Tamil, Bengali and Urdu. As Orsini argues, although much is made of the 'decentring' of English through the successes of non-American and non-British writers in the Anglophone world in recent decades, the reality is that major publishers seeking out the next 'big' Indian novel will only go for English-language works: 'The phrase "translated from" has started to acquire negative connotations: difficult, obsolete, non-global' (2004: 331). In the absence of the infrastructure of literariness that Casanova alludes to, Orsini notes, 'The global does not incorporate the regional literatures of India. It cold shoulders them' (ibid., 331). Though these languages and literatures are under pressure from English in India, English has little in turn to fear from them.

Orsini's bleak diagnosis is echoed in Pierre Lepape's denunciation of the 'dictature de la "world literature"'. What Lepape has in mind is the dominance of works by J.K. Rowling, Umberto Eco and Paulo Coelho in the world publishing market which is primarily based on their initial success in the English-speaking world. As two out of the three authors he mentions are translated authors, they come to represent metonymically the great mass of authors who never make it into the exclusive club of 2–3 per cent of translated titles in English. The global fortunes of the Happy Few contrast with the fate of many of the world's writers and publishers at the world's leading book fair in Frankfurt where up to 400,000 titles (including 100,000 new titles) are presented each year:

> A Francfort, les pavillons réservés aux pays d'Asie, d'Afrique et d'Amérique latine sont de plus en plus éloignés du centre de la manifestation et chaque année plus désertés, les éditeurs de moins en moins nombreux et de moins en moins sollicités par les acheteurs de droits.
>
> (Lepape 2004 : 24)

> [In Frankfurt, the stands from Asian, African and Latin American countries are further and further away from the centre of the fair and as each year goes by they are more and more poorly attended. There are fewer and fewer publishers with fewer and fewer people looking to buy rights from them.]

The unwillingness to take risks with translated titles from authors largely unknown to the target reading public, a problem we referred to in Chapter 1, is of course crucially determined by the changing economics of publishing.

The Bertelsmann Group, whose subsidiaries account for 40 per cent of all book sales in the United States, demanded that publishers under its wing look for profit margins of at least 15 per cent and show an annual increase in profits of 10 per cent. These figures were considerably in excess of what had previously been the norm for publishing (Clark 2000). In addition, there is little point in publishing a book if it never gets to the reader and herein lies the second problem of selling translated titles into a large Anglophone market. Distribution in the United States is largely in the hands of three distributors, Barnes & Noble, Borders and Book-A-Million. With an annual turnover of approximately $8 billion, they are able to dictate draconian conditions to publishers, exacting extra fees for prominent shelf profile or refusing to take titles that are suspected of not selling quickly enough (ibid.).

Qualifying her model of the world literary scene as one of intense rivalry between national literatures, Casanova sees the contemporary situation not as one that opposes, for example, France, the US and Great Britain but as one of:

> la lutte entre le pôle commercial qui tente de s'imposer comme nouveau détenteur de la légitimité littéraire à travers la diffusion d'une littérature qui mime les acquis de l'autonomie (et qui existe aussi bien aux États-Unis qu'en France) et le pôle autonome, de plus en plus menacé aux États-Unis comme en France et dans toute l'Europe par la puissance du commerce de l'édition internationale.
>
> (Casanova 1999 : 235)

> [the struggle between the commercial end of publishing which attempts to establish itself as the new source of legitimacy through the promotion of a literature which mimics the features of independence (and which can be found in France as much as in the United States) and the independent sector which is coming under more and more pressure from the commercial power of international publishing in the United States, in France and throughout Europe.]

The American avant-garde has just as much to fear in this new dispensation as the European. In a sense, what is implicit in the new publishing order in the twenty-first century is the incorporation of the predicament of translated literature into a more general issue of the survival of a literature that is not purely commercially driven.

In other words, to isolate the issue of translation from the larger question of the relation of culture to profit is to marginalize translation from broader struggles for cultural diversity and to run the risk of 'renationalizing' literary debates through the simple binarisms of the US vs. the Rest or the West vs. the Best. What the bottom line instrumentalism of global media (and publishing) corporations illustrate is less an ethnocentric triumphalism (Bertelsmann is after all German and Murdoch Australian) than a return on investment ruthlessness where *pace* Derrida the only margins that count are those that collocate with profit.

The decline of diversity

A sense of the imminent demise of cultural diversity is not of course new. Eric Auerbach, for example, in an essay published in the late 1960s claimed that:

> Our earth, the domain of *Weltliteratur* is growing smaller and losing its diversity. Yet *Weltliteratur*, as it was conceived by Goethe, does not merely refer to what is generically common and human; rather it considers humanity to be the product of fruitful intercourse between its members.

And he adds that when the process of modern standardization is fully complete, a person:

will have to accustom himself to existence in a standardized world, to a single literary culture, only a few literary languages, and perhaps even a single literary language. And herewith the notion of *Weltliteratur* would be at once realized and destroyed.

(1967: 301)

A similar pessimism as to the survival of cultural specificity also informed much of the writings of the postwar Frankfurt School theorists. In view of the economic constraints we have alluded to, the threat to the linguistic ecology of the planet (Maffi 2001: 1–50) and the well-documented imbalance in the directionality of translations, the pessimism of an Auerbach or a Lepape or a Casanova would appear to be well founded. However, it is worth considering whether such pessimism and apocalypticism amount not so much to a guide to a solution as to a way of further implicating us in the problem the critics analyse and decry.

Charles Forsdick in his analysis of French travel literature in the twentieth century notes that the perceived decline of diversity is one of the most common pre-occupations of the literature. Travellers go to far-off places, tell their readers that the 'exotic' is an illusion, that everywhere has now become much the same and that they themselves are the last witnesses of differences which are about to disappear for ever:

The implicit sense of erosion [of diversity] that characterizes certain nineteenth-century and earlier twentieth-century attitudes to the distinctiveness of individual cultures may, in its more extreme manifestations, have bordered on apocalypticism; but the transfer from generation to generation of such renewed prophecies of entropic decline uncovers the pervasive and conservative tendency according to which transformation is cast as death and loss.

(Forsdick 2005: 3)

Forsdick (ibid., 16) draws a comparison with Raymond Williams's analysis of the trope of the decline of rural England which Williams saw less as a precise event happening at a specific moment in time than as a 'structure of feeling' running through English writing for centuries. In other words, though the notion of the decline of diversity may be differently accented depending on whether the context is the triumph of the Fordist factory or the predatory designs of globalizing Goliaths, there is a sense in which the theme of the imminent demise of diversity is akin to a recurrent structure of feeling as proposed by Williams (Williams 1979: 156–65).

Things are always getting worse and the cultural critic like the despairing travel writer can only report on a world that is about to lose its distinctiveness and leave us adrift in a 'standardized world'. Chris Bongie discussing the terminal pessimism of Claude Lévi-Strauss's *Tristes tropiques* on the future of diversity observes:

Dire visions such as these however, most often resemble each other not only in their pessimism but also in their propensity for deferring the very thing that is being affirmed: although humanity is settling into a 'monoculture', it is at the same time still only *in the process of*, or *on the point* of, producing a 'beat-like' mass society.

(Bongie 1991: 4; his emphasis)

There is no time like the present to tell us about all that is soon to be past. The attraction of the entropic, of course, is that it does away with the historic. Indeed, Thomas Richards sees the scientific origins of the concept of entropy as a convenient means of ensuring the end of history:

> As a myth of knowledge, entropy, like evolution, would seem to place history outside the domain of human activity. Because it transfers agency from human beings to physical principles, it ostensibly represents a pessimistic relinquishing of all possibilities of social control.

(1993: 103)

As we have seen above, critics in our century concerned with the disappearance of cultural diversity do not, however, simply invoke physical principles of entropic decline. They identify economic and political forces that represent a genuine threat to the continued existence of cultural and linguistic plurality. There is nonetheless a disconcerting familiarity in the repeated threnodies of identity loss and one might argue that in the case of translation one is faced with a form of dual entropy.

What is to be understood by dual entropy here is a combination of the general entropy of the decline of diversity with the specific entropy of the act of translation. The general entropy is a particular vision of translation assimilationism where either everyone self-translates into a 'single literary culture' and 'a single literary language' or 'the single literary culture' and the 'single literary language' get massively translated into every other culture and language so that cultures and languages are left in the long shadow of a Dan Brown or a J.K. Rowling. If the blurb tells us the book has been translated into any number of languages, thus ensuring its fame, then any number of languages have in principle to worry about the cultural and linguistic consequences of that fame. This is more generally globalization as homogenization, standardization and banalization.

Specific entropy, on the other hand, is not so much to do with the perceived role of translation in the triumph of monocultures as it is to do with the very act of translation itself and its inherent entropy. Joachim du Bellay in his *Deffence et illustration de la langue françoyse* articulates a criticism of translation that has become a ritual commonplace in popular commentary on the subject. Translation, for Du Bellay, is almost invariably a form of slavish imitation which does little to enrich the language:

> Que pensent doncq' faire ces reblanchisseurs de murailles, qui jour et nuyt se rompent la teste à imiter? que dy je immiter? mais transcrire un Virgile & un Cicéron? batissant leurs poëme des hemystyches de l'un, & jurant en leurs

proses aux motz & sentences de l'autre. . . . Ne pensez donques, immitateurs, troupeau servil, parvenir au point de leur excellence.

(du Bellay 1970 : 76–7)

[What do they think they are doing these whitewashers of walls who night and day try their hardest to imitate? What am I saying imitate? They transcribe a Virgil and a Cicero, building up their poems using the hemistiches of the one and swearing in their prose by the words and sentences of the other. . . . Do not think, imitators, servile herd, ever to come near to their excellence.]

Du Bellay acknowledges that translation does have a role to play in the development of the French language and literature if it involves aggressive transformation (he uses the metaphor of devouring) but the categorization of most of the translators of his time as dim-witted hacks condemned to a culture of servility has an all too familiar echo in the history of translation (Venuti 1995). That those outside the business of translation should generally perceive it as involving an inevitable loss in meaning, force and expressiveness is perhaps not too surprising. The belief that poetry is what gets lost in translation and that all translators are invariably traitors is a conventional understanding readily sustained by neo-Romantic pieties about the primacy of original expression and the cultural nationalist credo of the sacredness of native speech.

What is somewhat more surprising is the extent to which translation studies has internalized elements of specific entropy. In 2004 at the First Dublin City University Postgraduate Conference in Translation Studies my colleague Jenny Williams and I were asked to give our overall response to the papers presented there. The papers were of a uniformly high standard and there was much to commend. However, I did note that what I referred to as the 'entropic paradox' was present in a quite a number of presentations. What was meant here was the way in which presenters repeatedly drew attention to the importance of translation in culture, language and society and then systematically proceeded, using a variety of tools, to show how existing translations were failing to be adequate or accurate or competent. These analyses were often indeed persuasive and highlighted significant failures of understanding and expression, whether these failures were motivated by political prejudice, linguistic incompetence, gender bias or the material constraints of existing technologies. In other words, the presentations – and in this they are not dissimilar from a myriad of papers presented to translation conferences the world over – showed again and again how translation as transformation involved loss, misrepresentation, partiality and distortion. Even when presentations were explicitly offered within the framework of descriptive translation studies, the descriptions become so ritually focused on absences and approximations that the entropic conclusions were inescapable.

In this way, it can be seen how specific entropy feeds into general entropy. If translations are shown over and over again to be somehow inadequate to the task of carrying texts across and into cultures and languages then it is difficult to see how the activity can be relied upon to perform the crucial task of the maintenance of linguistic and cultural diversity. If general entropy can be partly explained through a structure of feeling that always sees diversity as on the verge of extinction, what explains the persistence of the special entropy not so much in popular commentary as in the discipline of translation studies? One answer might lie in the very nature of academic or intellectual inquiry itself which, as the German thinker Peter Sloterdijk has pointed out, is traditionally fixated on ends rather than beginnings (Sloterdijk and Finkielkraut 2003). When Hegel claimed that the owl of Minerva flies at dusk, his contention was that it is only after an event that we can make sense of it, that only when something is over can we begin to detect patterns. Similarly, when Frank Kermode wanted to investigate the recurrent human need for fiction, he entitled his study, *The Sense of an Ending* (1967).

Kermode's contention is that as human beings are born *in medias res* and have no memory of their birth, and as death signals the extinction of consciousness, we need the fictional stories of other lives to vicariously experience their beginnings and endings (characters are born and die) and thus make sense of our own. What this attraction to endings produces, however, is arguably a culture of belatedness which is drawn inevitably to a sense of loss, of the entropic, as one is always discussing what is already gone, past, no longer, or what indeed might have been. In this context, James Clifford in *The Predicament of Culture* is critical of a tendency in ethnography to see cultures studied as forever in decline, claiming that, 'It is easier to register the loss of traditional orders of difference than to perceive the emergence of new ones' (1988: 15). Thus, the process of inquiry itself carries within it a strong, entropic, end-focused drive.

Cultural negentropy

What we would like to propose is precisely a way of thinking about translation and identity which is grounded in cultural negentropy. This *negentropic translational perspective* is primarily concerned with the 'emergence of new' cultural forms through translation practice and the way in which translation contributes to and fosters the persistence and development of diversity. It is this perspective which informs the discussion of translation in the European Union in Chapter 1 and here we would like to make more explicit the connection between the negentropic translational perspective and the concept of micro-cosmopolitanism that has already been advanced in this work.

Benedict Anderson, the well-known theorist of language and cultural nationalism, discussing the work of the Filipino folklorist Isabelo de los Reyes comments on a passage where the folklorist part-translates a song sung by the indigenous people, the Ilocanos, before they cut down a tree:

> Here Isabelo positions himself firmly within the Ilocano world. He knows what the Ilocano words mean, but his readers do not: for them . . . this experience is closed. But Isabelo is a kindly and scientific man, who wishes to tell outsiders something of this world; and yet he does not proceed by smooth paraphrase. The reader is confronted by an eruption of the incomprehensible original

Ilocano, before being tendered a translation. Better yet, something is still withheld, in the words *barí-barí*, for which Spanish has no equivalent.

(Anderson 2004: 208)

The indigenous Filipino folklorist here makes use of a practice that was common currency among European philologists up to the mid-twentieth century. Leo Spitzer, for example, in his 1948 essay 'Linguistics and Literary History', left the quotations in the original foreign languages on the grounds that

> since it is my purpose to take the word (and the wording) of the poets seriously, and since the convincingness and rigor of my stylistic conclusions depends entirely upon the minute linguistic detail of the original texts, it was impossible to offer translations.

(Spitzer 1988: 35)

Emily Apter claims that Spitzer's position is not 'an argument against translation per se, but rather a bid to make language acquisition a categorical imperative of *translatio studii*' (Apter 2004: 105).

Whether it is the tree songs of the Ilocanos or the canonical masterpieces of European literature, the strategy of partial or non-translation is signalling not so much the ultimate failure of translation (the conventional view) as the necessary complexity of language and culture without which translation would not exist and which justifies its existence in the first place. In other words, it is because so much cannot be translated that much more remains to be translated. Pointing to the impossibility of translation should then be accounted not as further evidence of the entropic, of translation as fundamentally a practice of imitative or even transformative loss, but as proof of the negentropic function of translation in culture. By this we mean that both in what translation tells us about cultures and what cultures tell us about translation we can discern a practice that not only counters cultural apocalypticism and the recurrent End-of-Diversity trope but challenges the repeated devaluation of translation as a particular kind of cultural activity.

Jean Bernabé, Patrick Chamoiseau and Raphaël Confiant in their argument for the necessary specificity of Francophone Caribbean literature call into question a universalism which simply means subservience to the language and literary practices of metropolitan France. They call instead for 'diversalité':

> La littérature créole se moquera de l'Universel, c'est-à-dire de cet alignement déguisé aux valeurs occidentales ... cette exploration de nos particularités ... ramène au naturel du monde ... et oppose à l'universalité la chance du monde diffracté mais recomposé, l'harmonisation consciente des diversités préservées: la Diversalité.

(Bernabé *et al.* 1989: 41)

> [Creole literature will have little time for the Universal, that is to say, this hidden alignment to Western values ... this exploration of our specificity

... brings us closer to the world itself ... and opposes universality with the opportunities of a world which is diffracted but reassembled, the conscious harmonization of the diversities which have been maintained: Diversity.]

Implicit in the notion of 'diversality', opposed to 'universality', is the notion that though the Caribbean may be made up of 'small' islands, the imaginative territory and the linguistic potential of the region are of a wholly different order. When they write that 'notre monde, aussi petit soit-il, est vaste dans notre esprit', they are foregrounding the fractal complexity of a site of the microcosmopolitan (Sheller 2003). Engaging in the 'universality' of the translation of French Caribbean literature is by definition difficult because of the 'diversality' of French Caribbean culture (or cultures) but it is the 'diversality' which means that there is something rather than nothing to communicate or express.

It is also the diversality that hopelessly complicates the easy binarisms of certain contemporary theoreticians of world literature. Franco Moretti, for example, presents a tidy metaphorical opposition between waves and trees in his 'Conjectures on World Literature':

The tree describes the passage from unity to diversity: one tree, with many branches: from Indo-European, to dozens of different languages. The wave is the opposite: it observes uniformity engulfing an initial diversity: Hollywood films conquering one market after another (or English swallowing language after language).

(Moretti 2004: 160)

In Moretti's view, there is a clear division of labour between national and world literature. National literature is 'for people who see trees; world literature for people who see waves' (ibid., 161). Moretti could, however, be accused not of failing to see the wave or the wood for the trees (the failing as he would see it of the national theorist) but of failing to see that trees are their waves in their own right. As we argued in Chapter 1, it is the wave-like properties of the particle or the particular that allow for connections to be made between the local and the global.

We can see this at work in Deborah Kapchan's account of a Moroccan storyteller who performs continuous intralingual translation in the marketplace in Marrakech, translating literary texts written in Classical Arabic into oral renditions performed in Moroccan dialectical Arabic. As Kapchan points out, 'Like public writers, Moroccan storytellers have functioned as brokers of literary culture, acting as bridges between the world of written tales and those of aural imagination' (2003: 136). The translation process occurs at three levels, from the written medium to the verbal, from high literary language to the familiar language of 'home' and from the visual, namely the text, to the auditory and performative. If Goethe uses the image of the marketplace to describe translation practice, what Moulay 'Omarr and the other translator-verbal artists demonstrate in the marketplace in Marrakech is that the translation of tales into the intimate language of the local everyday is a way of bringing the 'world of written tales' into the lives and ken of their listeners.

Conversely, the local event of the translation and the retailing of a story in Moroccan dialectical Arabic contains within it the 'world' of written literature in Classical Arabic. To this extent, using the binary polarities of trees and waves to describe what happens in world literature (and there is no 'world' literature without translation) is to miss an important point about how the local and the not local are imbricated in each other.

Holograms

What Moretti is attracted to is a form of thinking about writing and culture that is beholden to an apparently self-evident duality (parts that make up wholes). But the question that might be asked about the tree/wave model is also one that can be addressed to the linear reductionism of the part–whole paradigm: are there dominant metaphors or paradigms that obscure rather than clarify our thinking on translation among other things? John Urry notes, 'In modern industrial societies, dominant metaphors were those of the clock, modern machinery (train, car, assembly line) and the photographic lens.' In contrast, he argues the 'hologram is a complex metaphor for a complex informational age. Information in a hologram is not located in any particular part of it. Rather any part contains, implies and resonates information of the whole' (Urry 2003: 50). In drawing our attention to the complexity of the part, this hologrammatic vision accords with the attention to the fractal intricacy of the micro-cosmopolitan that we discussed in Chapter 1 but it also does justice to the full complexity of particular translations, whether the Authorized Version (McGrath 2001), an Old Irish hero tale (Tymoczko 1999) or the storyteller's tale in Marrakech, which carry within them a 'world' of information about culture, language, politics, society and other texts, both translated and untranslated.

Implicit in a hologrammatic understanding of translation then is a regard for the particular that incorporates a vision of the whole. What the implications of this perspective are for debates around world literature and how they relate to a commitment to the negentropic possibilities of translation are best illuminated by Emily Apter's evaluation of the legacy of the comparative literature scholar, Leo Spitzer. Apter quotes Spitzer to the effect that:

> philology is the *love* for works written in a particular *language*. And if the methods of a critic must be applicable to works in all languages in order that the criticism be convincing, the critic, at least at the moment when he is discussing the poem, must love *that* language and *that* poem more than anything else in the world.
>
> (Spitzer 1988: 448; his emphasis)

Apter then contrasts Franco Moretti's plea for the distant reading of secondary critical literature as a way of identifying patterns in world literature with Spitzer's close attention to the linguistic detail of texts themselves, arguing that if 'distant reading privileges outsized categories of cultural comparison – national epic, the "planetary" laws of genre – philology affords its micrological counterpart as close reading with a world view: word histories as world histories, stylistics and metrics in diaspora' (Apter 2004: 108). Although translation studies has often had to struggle to assert its separate identity with respect to philology, particularly in continental Europe, it nonetheless shares with philology, as understood by Spitzer and Apter, a 'commitment to a close reading with a world view'. In other words, what translation usually involves is the linguistic, textual and cultural competence to render a text from one language into another (or within languages from one kind of language into another). The literary translator must in a sense love that poem in that particular language if he or she is to put it into another particular language. The hologrammatic dimension is precisely the ability to perceive the full complexity of the work in the 'particular' language, bearing constantly in mind the 'world view'.

This is translation's contribution to 'diversality', to the negentropic, as it shows how diversity persists in the elaborateness of the particular, how translation's commitment to close reading and linguistic attentiveness shows that in the case of each text, the 'monde, aussi petit soit-il, est vaste'. It is precisely, on the other hand, the sensitivity on the part of a translator to a 'world view', to literary texts as literature not museum pieces, that avoids the end-game of philological antiquarianism, so ably criticized by Maria Tymoczko (1999). A further implication of the hologrammatic dimension to translation is the extreme prudence with which translations done by translators who have no command of the source language must be viewed. Edwin Gentzler, for example, points to a baleful outcome in the American literary workshop tradition of a cavalier and reductive reading of Ezra Pound's approach to translation where Pound's actual language skills and extensive cultural knowledge tend to get forgotten about and what remains is a general commitment to 'plain speech' and over-reliance on cribs:

> License has been given to allow translators to intuit good poems from another language without knowledge of the original language or the culture, and, as long as they have some poetic sensibility and good taste, now governed by plain speech and lack of adornment, their translations are accepted.
>
> (Gentzler 2001: 31)

If the whole is in the part, there are no wholes without parts. The commitment to diversality, to the negentropic energies of translation, to the fractal and holo-grammatic complexity of the particular carries with it a duty of language care and language respect which demands the requisite competence in the languages being translated.

In this sense, declining interest in modern languages in the Anglophone world, the closing of language departments, the by now well-documented threat to the linguistic diversity of the planet (Hagège 2000) are issues of pressing political, aesthetic and educational concern to translators and translation scholars as love without knowledge is truly blind and a world-view without close readings is the ultimate form of provincialism, a global projection of myopia. For what we know about cultural contact is that the harder it is to see, the more profound the vision.

Drawing on the work of Victor Segalen, Christopher Prendergast argues that we 'are never "closer" to another culture (and hence liberated from the traps of ethnocentrism) than when we fail to understand it, when confronted with the points of blockage to interpretive mastery' (2004: xi). It is because language acquisition and cultural literacy are the labour of a lifetime that the translation of the foreign text is not an easy task. The possibility of a 'failure' of understanding is always there and it is precisely because of the 'points of blockage to interpretive mastery' that literary translation (but not only literary), for example, can often be a slow, painstaking exercise. An implicit assumption in 'interpretive mastery' for the translator is that all the necessary or available knowledge is at his or her disposal before the translation is embarked upon. That this is more of a utopian hope than a practical reality is suggested by the Swiss writer Nicolas Bouvier when he claims that the ideal translator should know

> tous les âges de la vie, tous les climats des pôles aux tropiques, tous les goûts sur la langue, du curry à l'irish stew, sans oublier les parallèles et les méridiens. Impossible.
>
> (Bouvier 1998: 14)

> [every stage in life, every type of climate from the poles to the tropics, every taste from curry to Irish stew, not forgetting every longitude and latitude. Impossible.]

The impossibility is not the sole prerogative of literary translation, as is borne out by the remarks of an interpreting scholar on the interaction between training and research when he claims that

> trainers need to have a background in a variety of research areas if they are to be effective in dealing with individual student problems. The areas include: sociolinguistics, psycholinguistics, neurolinguistics, text linguistics, translation studies, cognitive linguistics and sciences, neurophysiology, semantics, pragmatics and communication theory.
>
> (Riccardi 1997: 94)

Alessandra Riccardi's comments point to the complexity of the task she is describing but also to the almost inevitable incompleteness of any attempt to describe it. Thus, it is precisely because translation and interpreting are difficult that they represent not hopeless efforts at an impossible task but a more valuable and worthwhile form of seeing in the sense articulated by Segalen and Prendergast. Not only is sense-making or understanding in interlingual and intercultural contact hard work practically and analytically but it is also possible that if it was not, violence, not empathy, would ensue. Nicole Lapierre, for example, in describing the rise of gated communities in modern urban settings expresses a fear that we have already alluded to in Chapter 2:

Partout, on se barricade, à Tokyo comme à Paris. La brutalité des relations grandit quand l'espace des médiations se réduit, la solidité des barrières s'accroît quand s'effacent les zones intermédiaires, et, faute de seuil, l'hospitalité régresse.

(Lapierre 2004 : 42)

[The barriers are going up everywhere, from Toyko to Paris. As the space for mediation shrinks, the brutality of relationships increases. Barriers become more impregnable when the between places disappear and where there is no threshold, hospitality is less common.]

To remove the space of mediation, the intermediary zone of time and difficulty which is the attempt to get to know another culture and another language, is to move from the triangular space of negotiation to the binary space of opposition.

Translation and interpreting, rather than being treated as an unfortunate impediment to the progress of understanding and true love between peoples, are arguably what ensures that people remain interested in each other. Both activities involve the obligation to know, to understand better, to open up the space of mediation in the absence of which individuals and communities remain marooned in the discrete islands of their own prejudice. Collapsing the space brings not proximity but alienation. Hence, the necessary difficulty of language acquisition and the learning of intercultural knowledge for a translator who is embarking on the translation of a text from one language into another cannot be lightly forgone through the palliative agency of a crib. The closing of the gap, that excision of the intermediary space, leads almost inevitably either to the Hegemony of the One (the translator into a dominant language who senses that others may be grateful to have texts appear in that language) or the Tyranny of the Two (there is My Language and Your Language and anything else between disappears). What the fractal, hologrammatic, negentropic dimensions to translation practice imply is a form of ethics which is predicated on complexity, distance and desire. The desire to know means the necessary triangulation of relationships (source text – translator – target text) which is more complex and less readily assimilated than the polar simplicities of binary opposites and involves an inevitable distancing effect but one which brings closeness, not familiarity. The more we know about the other language and text, the closer we get to a sense of the text and the language, the more we realize there is still to know in the infinitely receding horizon of Bouvier's impossible ideal translator.

Emergence

The desire to know is, of course, what draws us to investigate the world around us and the people who inhabit it. It is this desire too which points to a crucial link between translation and the phenomenon of emerging behaviour in everything from ant colonies to human cities. Steven Johnson in his discussion of the genesis of organized complexity, of the manner in which complex, adaptive, self-organizing activity emerges from the repeated actions of simple, rudimentary agents, enunciates a number of principles for the development of such complexity which includes the following, 'Pay attention to your neighbours' or, as he reformulates it, 'Local information can lead to global wisdom' (Johnson 2002: 79). As Johnson puts it in his discussion of research on the behaviour of ant colonies:

> *Local* turns out to be the key term in understanding the power of swarm logic. We see emergent behavior in systems like colonies when the individual agents in the system pay attention to their immediate neighbors rather than wait for orders from above. They think locally *and* act locally, but their collective action produces global behavior.
>
> (ibid., 74; his emphasis)

Ants reacting to the reactions of their neighbour ants has parallels in how humans respond to the conduct of their fellow human beings on the pavements of the world's villages, towns and cities. Johnson, drawing on the work of the urbanist Jane Jacobs in her classic study, *The Death and Life of Great American Cities* (1961), presents the pavement or sidewalk as the primary conduit of information flow between city residents:

> Neighbors learn from each other because they pass each other – and each other's stores and dwellings – on the sidewalk. Sidewalks allow relatively high-bandwith communication between total strangers, and they mix large numbers of individuals in random configurations. Without the sidewalks, cities would be like ants without a sense of smell, or a colony with too few worker ants. Sidewalks provide both the right *kind* and the *right* number of local interactions.
>
> (Johnson 2002: 94; his emphasis)

However, the encounter with others will do little for you if this is all that happens. That is to say, 'Encountering diversity does nothing for the global system of the city unless that encounter has a chance of altering your behavior. There has to be feedback between agents, cells that change in response to the changes in other cells' (ibid., 96). Therefore, the emergence of complex, adaptive behaviour in human communities involves proximity, interaction and feedback. As we saw in Chapter 2, it is not possible to envisage Jacobs's high-bandwith communication without taking into account the dual dimensions of translation and language difference. To this extent, what is missing from both Jacobs's and Johnson's account of the sidewalk utopia of emergent complexity is a role for translation and linguistic alterity. Paying attention to your neighbours is not a strategy likely to succeed if you have no idea what your neighbours are saying. Nor are they likely to pay much attention to you if they have no idea what you are on about. If, as we saw in earlier chapters, the local can no longer be construed as tightly defined communities all speaking the same language and sharing the same culture, then the impact of vernacular cosmopolitanism and internal transculturalism means that the most local of interactions now will almost invariably involve some degree of translation.

Accepting that 'without the open, feedback-heavy connections of street culture, cities quickly become dangerous and anarchic places' (ibid., 146) is to accept that an enabling condition of feedback mechanisms is a central role for translation in the design and development of human communities. In the absence of translation, information does not flow between language speakers and communities and it is arguable that the conditions for the emergence of successful, urban settlements are severely compromised. In other words, as a characteristic of stable, complex systems is the presence of negative feedback which acts as a corrective to elements that might destabilize the system or disrupt its homeostatic equilibrium (the slow handclap that reminds speakers that they are beginning to bore their audience senseless or have offended them so much that it is time to clam up and sit down), then if there is no way of identifying or understanding the linguistic feedback from individuals or communities, this bodes ill for the future stability of a system, whether at the level of a local neighbourhood, a city or the planet.

It is, of course, the potential difficulties of neighbourly interactions that have prompted US writers like Samuel Huntington to be severely critical of any policy that would appear to offer succour to multilingualism in US civil society. Huntington sees the hegemony of English in the United States as precisely that factor which allowed all neighbours to interact and cohere as members of the US polity, irrespective of their linguistic or ethnic background (Huntington 2005). The particular target of Huntington's ire is the alleged counter-hegemony of the Spanish language in the US, leading in his view to a dangerous fragmentation of civil society and the public sphere. Huntington's thesis is in essence a classic modernization argument that has been used to justify the dominance of particular vernaculars in nation-states the world over since the time of the French Revolution and indeed earlier (Anderson 1991). If the nation is to fight with one army, build one society, construct one school system and run one economy, then it had better have one language. If the empire as an extension of the expanding nation is to be effective, then it too must school its subjects (or at least those useful to the imperialists) in the rudiments of the One, True Language. To move from the feudal rabble of squabbling fiefdoms to the onward march of modernity meant speaking with a single voice. So in this view the only good translator is a dead translator as translation, to paraphrase Stephen Dedalus, is an activity which properly belongs to that multilingual nightmare of history from which the monolingual modernist is trying to awake.

One difficulty with this conventional modernization thesis is that it is attempting to shore up the ruins of a nation-state which is no longer there in its former guise (if indeed, it ever existed in the more purist versions of statist nostalgia) to justify a policy of One People, One Language (Bobbitt 2002: xxii). This is not to say that the nation-state no longer exists, quite the contrary, but that developments in human rights legislation, environmentalism, weapons of mass destruction, the world economic order and the area of information technology and telecommunications (Cronin 2003) have greatly altered its remit and operations. Philip Bobbitt, for example, argues that the end of the 'great epochal war' from 1914 to 1990 has meant a fundamental change in the nature of the state itself:

The various competing systems of the contemporary nation-state (fascism, communism, parliamentarianism) that fought that war all took their legitimacy from the promise to better the material welfare of their citizens. The market-state offers a different covenant: it will maximize the opportunity of its people. Not only the world in which we live but also the world that is now emerging is more comprehensible and more insistent once this historical development is appreciated and explored for the implications it holds for the fate of civilization itself.

(Bobbitt 2002: xxvi)

Implicit in the notion of the market-state identified by the former senior adviser to the White House is that the state will seek to maximize the resources at its disposal in order to enhance the opportunities of its citizens. One of these resources in the age of informationalism is of course information itself (Castells 1996). Information is the point where the genesis of the market-state, the emergent complexity of the city and the ever present need for translation converge. Lewis Mumford noted in *The City in History* that the city, among other things, 'may be described as a structure specially equipped to store and transmit the goods of civilization' (1991: 30). One of those goods is information and what cities do supremely well is to act as places where ideas can be stored, retrieved and reworked. That grain cultivation, the plough, the potter's wheel, the sailboat, copper metallurgy, mathematical abstraction, the calendar, precise astronomical observation should be associated with large-scale human settlements on the Sumerian coast and in the Indus Valley which date back to 3500 BCE (ibid., 33) is hardly surprising if we observe that information circulates more rapidly among clusters of individuals (with inevitable feedback loops) than among individuals in isolation.

If certain professions tend to congregate in certain parts of the city, it is in part because clustering allows for the faster and more efficient circulation of information among producers and service providers, and it makes it easier for their customers to locate them. As Johnson argues, 'Information management – subduing the complexity of a large-scale human settlement – is the *latent* purpose of a city, because when cities come into being, their inhabitants are driven by other motives, such as safety or trade' (2002: 109). The structure of cities therefore is a way of managing information, so that we know where we need to go when we want certain kinds of information; that is, we know where it is stored and where to retrieve it. We would not generally go to the financial services quarter to look at paintings any more than we would go looking for advice on investment port-folios in the city's cultural quarter. What the notion of the city as an elaborate interface or as an information management tool implies is that the information can be not only stored but accessed and that the more information a city potentially has to draw on, the greater its capacity for creativity and innovation in an informational age.

One important way of accessing the information held by the communities living in a city is translation, for without translation whole areas of potentially useful information are simply not available for access or retrieval. Translation, in effect, allows for the cultural and linguistic specificity and integrity of the information base of individuals or communities to be respected but at the same time allows for the wider circulation of concepts, attitudes, ideas, aesthetic or cognitive styles. The translational approach which is close to Paul Ricoeur's (2004) notion of equivalence without similarity is thus opposed to Huntington's anti-Babelian vision of the monoglot melting pot where information only circulates on the precondition of language surrender. Such a move paradoxically eliminates the very difference (linguistic, cultural) it claims to celebrate in the championing of a polity with a plurality of ethnic origins. On the other hand, translation participates in the strategic micro-cosmopolitan move of not making difference synonymous with disconnection. Rather than leave speakers and readers shut off from the information pool of the city, translation, whether in the form of written translation or community interpreting, is a way into the resources that are on offer in large human settlements.

It would be a mistake, however, to see translation as solely partaking of emergent complexity and information management at the level of the city, whatever its size. There is another level at which translation can potentially operate and this is in the realm of what one theorist, Robert Wright, has called the construction of the 'global brain' (2000: 48). Simply put, this is the notion that by uniting all the world's disparate pools of information new, innovative and more complex ideas can emerge. If the old adage is that many hands make light work, Wright's argument is that one good mind guiding those hands can make the work much lighter still. In other words, it only takes one person to invent something for the rest of the group to adopt it, so the more potential innovators and the more people with access to information on these innovations the faster the rate of technical or creative advance. So the 'group brain' of the community that learns from its smartest member has a potential global analogue in a mega-pool of knowledge that could be shared with others. The advent of the World Wide Web suggests that Wright's scenario may not be pure fantasy. More importantly, the notion of a 'global brain' suggests that its component parts must be able to communicate with each other if the 'brain' is to function effectively. So rather than see translation in the context of localization as simply facilitating access for users in different languages to information, it is equally plausible to see a multilingual web with translation interfaces as a precondition for the emergence of a form of global intelligence which would be greater than the sum of its parts.

In a sense, this brings us back to the argument in Chapter 1 about the desirability of a 'bottom-up' localization as the provision of local, digitally relevant content in various languages is a two-way process. Not only do language groups get content that is specific to their interests and needs but generating that material means that through translation these specific materials can then be brought into cyberspace. In this way, the 'global brain' fed by the 'group brains' of different languages and cultures would not simply be receiving the same message in every language, a process more likely to produce universal dullness than emergent complexity. Again, as Johnson points out, what is crucial for evolving intelligence is reciprocity: 'Relationships in these [complex, adaptive] systems are mutual: you influence your neighbors, and your neighbors influence you. All emergent systems are built out

of this kind of feedback, the two-way connections that foster higher-level learning'
(2002: 120).

Small worlds and weak ties

A feature of the contemporary impact of informationalism is that the notion of
who is our neighbour gets redefined by the communications technology at our disposal. We may have more regular contact through the internet with a friend at
the other end of the city or on the other side of the globe than with our physical
neighbour in the apartment or house next door. This means in turn that for our
neigbour to get in touch with someone at the other end of the city or on the other
side of the planet they are only one degree of separation away from that person,
that is, they only have to go through you to make the contact. The world becomes
smaller for your neighbour. Two mathematicians, Duncan Watts and Steven
Strogatz (1998: 440–2), in their study of how small worlds come into being drew
on their work in network theory. Starting from a circle of nodes each of which is
connected to its immediate and next-nearest neighbours, they added a few extra
links connecting randomly selected nodes. These long-range links offer the crucial
short cuts between distant nodes and so dramatically shorten the average separation
between all nodes. As Albert-László Barabási observes:

> The surprising finding of Watts and Strogatz is that *even a few* extra links are
> sufficient to drastically decrease the separation between the nodes. These few
> links will not significantly change the clustering coefficient. Yet thanks to the
> long bridges they form, often connecting nodes on the opposite side of the
> circle, the separation between all nodes spectacularly collapses.
>
> (2003: 53; his emphasis)

In human terms, the relatively short number of degrees of separation which
will allow me to contact anyone in the world (between three and six degrees of
intervening persons) is based on

> the fact that a few people have friends and relatives that do not live next door
> any longer. These distant links offer us short paths to people in very remote
> areas of the world. Huge networks do not need to be full of random links to
> display small world features. A few such links will do the job.
>
> (ibid., 53)

The default model adopted by Watts and Strogatz is one that closely resembles
the circumstances of many human beings in that it presupposes a close, inner circle
or 'cluster' of relatives or friends. As the geographers Geraldine Pratt and Susan
Hanson have argued, 'Although the world is increasingly well connected, we must
hold this in balance with the observation that most people live intensely local lives;
their homes, work places, recreation, shopping, friends, and often family are located
within a relatively small orbit' (1994: 10–11). Clustering is of course in part linked

to shared language, culture, history and so on, a phenomenon which can be observed in international gatherings and academic conferences where after the main business has been done (often in English), delegates tend to congregate at break time or in the evening with others from their language group.

In the context of translation, what is implied by the 'small worlds' theory of Watts and Strogatz is that translations from other languages and cultures can operate as these 'distant links' or 'long bridges' that make the world feel like a smaller place. These links can of course be anything from the translations from Russian by Constance Garnett for early twentieth-century England to the work of translators for the television newsroom in Taiwan (Tsai 2005: 145–53). Translators, in a sense, ensure a reduction in those degrees of separation that make other parts of the world seem remote or irrelevant. Conversely, of course, the absence of translation or translators in a culture means that the distant links and the long bridges are not there to ensure the connectivity that permits the 'small orbit' to be brought closer to small orbits elsewhere. In this scenario, the small world of the tightly clustered leaves no room for the Small World of the distantly related.

A further dimension of network theory which has implications for the ways that we think about translation is the importance of what the sociologist Mark Granovetter calls 'weak ties' (1973: 1360–80). Granovetter established on the basis of his research that when it comes to finding a job, launching a new fashion, or letting people know about a new restaurant, weak social ties are much more important than close friendships. So, in the words of Barabási:

> Weak ties often play a crucial role in our ability to communicate with the outside world. Often our close friends can offer us little help in finding a job. They move in the same circles we do and are inevitably exposed to the same information. To get new information, we have to activate our weak ties. . . . The weak ties, or acquaintances, are our bridge to the outside world, since by frequenting different places, they obtain their information from different sources than our immediate friends.
>
> (2003: 43)

If our close friends have access to much the same sources of information as we have, then it stands to reason that new sources are more likely to come from those who move in somewhat different circles from our own. Bearing in mind then the importance of 'weak ties' for innovation and connectivity, we can consider the conventional marginalization of translation in public and academic discourse (Venuti 1995) in a somewhat different light. If translators are deemed to be 'invisible' or their activities are considered peripheral or relatively unimportant, one could argue that they are in effect not considered to be among those 'strong ties' that bind a culture or a community together. They are outside that inner circle or cluster of the defining activities of a culture (writing and speaking in the native language, maintaining indigenous traditions and so on [Anderson 1991]), excluded from the close friendship of cultural intimacy. It is, of course, precisely the fact that translation would be perceived to be a 'weak tie' that accounts for its importance.

It is the weak ties that are the 'bridge to the outside world'. As we saw in our earlier discussion of Simmel and the notion of the bridge (pp. 121–2), what bridges do is to redefine the way we perceive the sides they connect, so cultures that are connected by the 'weak tie' of translation are mutually redefined by the practice. If the Scottish Gaelic origins of the Ossianic 'translations' had a decisive impact on the evolution of European Romanticism in the late eighteenth and early nineteenth centuries through the 'weak tie' of Macpherson, then Gaelic culture would in turn be profoundly affected by the literary movement of Romanticism well into the twentieth century (Stafford 1988). If the 'weakness' of translation may thus in a sense be accounted as its greatest strength the difficulty is that remuneration, working conditions and status are predicated on perception, not effect. The care and attention lavished on close friends are not always extended to casual acquaintances, no matter how great their importance in sourcing new areas of opportunity or expression.

Translation as weak tie should not, however, be confused with translation as brief tie. A danger in the informational, market economy is that instantaneity of communication can lead to a perception of all ties as rapid and ephemeral (Sennett 1998). The short, sharp shock of exchange does not adequately represent, however, the more long-lasting nature of networks. As Walter W. Powell argues, 'in markets the standard strategy is to drive the hardest possible bargain on the immediate exchange. In networks, the preferred option is often creating indebtedness and reliance over the long haul' (1996: 211). The role of literature as a guarantor of linguistic and cultural diversity in an enlarged Europe, as discussed in Chapter 1, draws in essence on the idea of a European literary network which through translation creates 'indebtedness and reliance over the long haul'. Powell claims that network-based practices even in the most pragmatic business relationships ensure the greatest success as regards long-term profitability, as indicated by his case study of networking in the biotechnology industry. It is hardly surprising then that the time and investment needed for translation are in fact contributory factors to the long-term effectiveness and stability of networks of cultural exchange as they generate long-term indebtedness and reliance.

More generally, what has been evident throughout this chapter and indeed hopefully throughout this work is the vital necessity of factoring in translation to any proper understanding of debates around identity in contemporary society. Georg Simmel, whose reflections on doors and bridges opened this chapter, was also preoccupied about what brings people round a table. In his essay 'Sociology of the Meal', he describes how the basic physiological need of bodily nourishment gives rise to an elaborate set of cultural practices around food and eating. Simmel's conclusion is 'that in a whole series of areas of life, the lowest phenomena and indeed even negative values, are not only the gateways for the development of higher things, but also that is the reason why superior things arise' (Simmel 1997b: 134). Thus, human beings' relative physical weakness compared to larger mammals became in fact a strength as they were forced to socialize for protection, and socialization in turn 'brought all the abilities of the intellect and the will to fruition' (ibid., 134). The exercise of these abilities led to humans possessing an influence over their environment far in excess of their initial physical capacity. As we have seen in this volume, in every area of human activity from politics to migration to literature to warfare and emergent systems, translation is one of the 'lowest phenomena' which becomes a gateway for the 'development of higher things'. When we include it among the 'lowest phenomena', we mean that translation is perceived as marginal or peripheral, if indeed it is perceived at all. In other words, if Simmel believed that part of the duty of a cultural theorist was to explain how even the most ordinary of everyday events was rich in human significance, it is equally important for the translation theorist to show that translation, a fundamental feature of the daily lives of countless millions on the planet, has much to tell us about how humans have lived and how they will live in a world where to know who you are means first and foremost knowing who others are. It is time to journey again with Herodotus.

Bibliography

Abley, M. (2003) *Spoken Here: Travels Among Threatened Languages*, London: Heinemann.

Abu-Lughod, J.L. (1989) *Before European Hegemony: the World System A.D. 1250–1350*, New York: Oxford University Press.

Anderson, B. (1991) *Imagined Communities: Reflections on the Origin and Spread of Nationalism*, London: Verso.

—— (2004) 'The Rooster's Egg: Pioneering World Folklore in the Philippines', 197–213, in Prendergast, C. (ed.) *Debating World Literature*, London: Verso.

Anderson, R.B.W. (1976) 'Perspectives on the Role of Interpreter', 208–28, in Brislin, R.W. (ed.) *Translation: Applications and Research*, New York: Gardner Press.

Apter, E. (2004) 'Global *Translatio*: the "Invention" of Comparative Literature, Istanbul, 1933', 76–109, in Prendergast, C. (ed.) *Debating World Literature*, London: Verso.

Arnold, M. [1859] (1961) 'England and the Italian Question', 69–75, in Super, R.H. (ed.), *The Complete Prose Works*, Vol. 1, Ann Arbor: University of Michigan Press.

Auerbach, E. (1967) *Gesammelte Aufsätze zur Romanischen Philologie*, Bern: Francke.

Augustine (1984) *City of God*, trans. John O'Meara, London: Penguin.

Auster, P. (2002) *The Book of Illusions*, London: Faber and Faber.

Bagnoli, A. (2004) 'Constructing the Hybrid Identities of Europeans', 57–67, in Titley, G. (ed.) *Resituating Culture*, Strasbourg: Council of Europe.

Barabási, Albert-Lászlof (2003) *Linked: How Everything Is Connected to Everything Else and What It Means for Business, Science, and Everyday Life*, New York: Plume.

Barber, B. (1996) *Jihad vs. McWorld*, New York: Ballantine Press.

Bate, J. (1993) *Shakespeare and Ovid*, Oxford: Clarendon Press.

Bateson, G. (1973) 'Double Bind', 242–9, in Gregory, *Steps to an Ecology of Mind*, London: Paladin.

Bauman, Z. (1998) *Globalization: the Human Consequences*, Cambridge: Polity Press.

—— (2004) *Wasted Lives: Modernity and Its Outcasts*, Oxford: Blackwell.

Bayly, C.A. (2004) *The Birth of the Modern World 1780–1914*, Oxford: Blackwell.

Beck, U. (1992) *Risk Society: Towards a New Modernity*, trans. M. Ritter, London: Sage.

—— (2002) 'The Cosmopolitan Perspective: Sociology in the Second Age of Modernity', 61–85, in Vertovec, S. and Cohen, R. (eds) *Conceiving Cosmopolitanism: Theory, Context, Practice*, Oxford: Oxford University Press.

Beer, G. (1996) *Open Fields: Science in Cultural Encounter*, Oxford: Clarendon Press.

Beiner, G. (2001) 'To Speak of '98: the Social Memory and Vernacular History of Bliain na bhFrancach', unpublished Ph.D. dissertation, University College Dublin.

Bellamy, R. and Castiglione, D. (1998) 'Between Cosmopolis and Community: Three Models of Rights and Democracy within the European Union', 58–71, in Archibuigi, D., Held, D. and Köhler, M. (eds) *Re-imagining Political Community: Studies in Cosmopolitan Democracy*, Cambridge: Polity.

Benhabib, S. (2002) *The Claims of Culture: Equality and Diversity in the Global Era*, Princeton, NJ: Princeton University Press.

Berman, A. (1984) *L'Épreuve de l'étranger: culture et traduction dans l'Allemagne romantique*, Paris: Gallimard.

Bernabé, J., Chamoiseau, P. and Confiant, R. (1989) *Éloge de la créolité*, Paris: Gallimard.

Bertaud, J.P. (1990) 'Forgotten Soldiers: the Expedition of the General Humbert to Ireland in 1798', 220–37, in Gough, H. and Dickson, D. (eds) *Ireland and the French Revolution*, Dublin: Irish Academic Press.

Bhabha, H. (1994) *The Location of Culture*, New York: Routledge.

Bischoff, A. and Loutan L. (2004) 'Interpreting in Swiss Hospitals', *Interpreting*, 6, 2, 181–204.

Bloom, A. (1987) *The Closing of the American Mind*, New York: Touchstone.

Bobbitt, P. (2002) *The Shield of Achilles: War, Peace and the Course of History*, London: Penguin.

Bongie, C. (1991) *Exotic Memories: Literature, Colonialism and the Fin de Siècle*, Stanford, Calif.: Stanford University Press.

Bouvier, N. (1998) 'Traduire!', 13–14, in Graf, M. (ed.) *L'Écrivain et son traducteur en Suisse et en Europe*, Geneva: Éditions Zoé.

Boyle, N. (1992) *Goethe. The Poet and the Age: the Poetry of Desire, 1749–90*, Oxford: Oxford University Press.

—— (2003) *Goethe. The Poet and the Age: Revolution and Renunciation, 1790–1803*, Oxford: Oxford University Press.

Bragg, M. (2003) *The Adventure of English: 500 AD to 2000: the Biography of a Language*, London: Hodder and Stoughton.

Brah, A. (2004) 'Diasporic Spatiality, Difference and the Question of Identity', 31–9, in Titley, G. (ed.) *Resituating Culture*, Strasbourg: Council of Europe.

Branchadell, A. and West, M.L. (2005) *Less Translated Languages*, Amsterdam: John Benjamins.

Breckenridge, C., Pollock, S. and Bhabha, H.K. (eds) (2002) *Cosmopolitanism*, Durham, NC: Duke University Press.

Brennan, T. (1997) *At Home in the World: Cosmopolitanism Now*, Cambridge, Mass.: Harvard University Press.

Bryson, A. (1998) *From Courtesy to Civility: Changing Codes of Conduct in Early Modern England*, Oxford: Clarendon Press.

Caglar, A. (2002) 'Media Corporatism and Cosmpolitanism', 180–90, in Vertovec, S. and Cohen, R. (eds) *Conceiving Cosmopolitanism: Theory, Context, Practice*, Oxford: Oxford University Press.

Calendar State Papers, Ireland 1598–9 (1869) London: Her Majesty's Stationery Office.

Calhoun, C. (2002) 'The Class Consciousness of Frequent Travellers: Towards a Critique of Actually Existing Cosmopolitanism', 86–109, in Vertovec, S. and Cohen, R. (eds) *Conceiving Cosmopolitanism: Theory, Context, Practice*, Oxford: Oxford University Press.

Canny, N. (2001) *How Ireland Became British*, Oxford: Oxford University Press.

Carew Hunt, R.N. (1957) *A Guide to Communist Jargon*, London: Geoffrey Bles.

Carrasquillo, O., Orav, E.J., Brennan, T.A. and Burstin, H.R. (1999) 'Impact of Language Barriers on Patient Satisfaction in an Emergency Department', *Journal of General Internal Medicine*, 14, 2, 82–7.

Casanova, P. (1999) *La République mondiale des lettres*, Paris: Seuil.

Castells, M. (1996) *The Rise of the Network Society*, Oxford: Blackwell.

—— (1997) *The Power of Identity*, Oxford: Blackwell.

Chadelat, J.-M. (2003) 'Le désenchantement du monde: de *Richard II* à *Coriolan*', in Pironon, J. and Wagner, J. (eds) *Formes littéraires du théologico-politique de la Renaissance au XVIIIè siècle: Angleterre et Europe*, Clermont-Ferrand: Presses Universitaires Blaise Pascal.

Cheah, P. and Robbins, B. (eds) (1998) *Cosmopolitics: Thinking and Feeling Beyond the Nation*, Minneapolis, Minn.: University of Minnesota Press.

Cheyfitz, E. (1991) *The Poetics of Imperialism: Translation and Colonization from the Tempest to Tarzan*, New York and Oxford: Oxford University Press.

Chomsky, N. (1965) *Cartesian Linguistics*, New York: Harper and Row.

Churchyard, T. (1579) *A Generall Rehearsall of Warres*, London: Edward White.

Cicero (1997) 'De optimo genere oratorum', 7–8, in Robinson, D. (ed.) *Western Translation Theory from Herodotus to Nietzsche*, Manchester: St Jerome.

Clark, G. (2000) *Inside Book Publishing*, London: Routledge.

Clifford, J. (1988) *The Predicament of Culture: Twentieth-Century Ethnography, Literature and Art*, Cambridge, Mass.: Harvard University Press.

Clinch, P., Convery, F. and Walsh, B. (2002) *After the Celtic Tiger: the Challenges Ahead*, Dublin: O'Brien Press.

Cohen, J. (ed.) (1996) *For Love of Country: Debating the Limits of Patriotism*, Cambridge: Beacon Press.

Cohen, M. (1992) 'Rooted Cosmopolitanism: Thoughts on the Left, Nationalism and Multiculturalism', *Dissent*, autumn, 478–83.

Cohen, R. (1997) *Global Diasporas*, London: UCL Press.

Committee on Culture, Youth, Education, Media and Sport (2003) *Report on Cultural Industries*, Strasbourg: European Parliament, 14 July.

Coulmas, P. (1990) *Weltbürger: Geschichte einer Menscheitssehnsucht*, Hamburg: Rowohlt.

Coulter, C. (2003a) 'Student "Not Guilty" of Sexual Assault', *The Irish Times*, 4 March.

—— (2003b) 'Garda Will Report Soon on Selection and Use of Translators', *The Irish Times*, 10 March.

Coveney, P. and Highfield, R. (1995) *Frontiers of Complexity: the Search for Order in a Chaotic World*, London, Faber and Faber.

Crépon, M. (2004) 'Penser l'Europe avec Patočkà. Réflexions sur l'altérité', *Esprit*, 310, 28–44.

Cronin, M. (1995) 'Keeping One's Distance: Translation and the Play of Possibility', *TTR*, 8, 2, 227–43.

—— (1996) *Translating Ireland: Translation, Languages, Cultures*, Cork: Cork University Press.

—— (2000) *Across the Lines: Travel, Language, Translation*, Cork: Cork University Press.

—— (2002) 'The Empire Talks Back: Orality, Heteronomy and the Cultural Turn in Interpreting Studies', 45–62, in Gentzler, E. and Tymoczko, M. (eds) *Translation and Power*, Boston and Amherst: University of Massachusetts Press.

—— (2003) *Translation and Globalization*, London and New York: Routledge.

Cronin, M. and Ó Cuilleanáin, C. (eds) (2003) *The Languages of Ireland*, Dublin: The Four Courts Press.

Crul, M. (2000) 'Breaking the Circle of Disadvantage: Social Mobility of Second-Generation Moroccans and Turks in the Netherlands', 121–39, in Vermeulen, H. and Perlmann, J. (eds) *Immigrants, Schooling and Social Mobility: Does Culture Make a Difference*, London: Macmillan.

Cullen, P. (2003) 'Major Social Changes Evident in Past Decade', *The Irish Times*, 20 June.

Daltún, S. (1983) 'Scéal Rannóg an Aistriúcháin', *Teangeolas*, 17, 12–14.

Dantanus, U. (1988) *Brian Friel: a Study*, London: Faber and Faber.

Darwin, C. (1986) *Journal of Researches into the Geology and Natural History of the Various Countries visited by the H.M.S. 'Beagle'*, Part I, in Barrett, P. and Freeman, R.B. (eds) *The Works of Charles Darwin*, Vol. 2, London: Pickering and Chatto.

David, R.A. and Rhee, M. (1998) 'The Impact of Language as a Barrier to Effective Health Care in an Underserved Urban Hispanic Community', *Mount Sinai Journal of Medecine*, 65, 5–6, 393–7.

Davies, N. and Moorhouse, R. (2002) *Microcosm: Portrait of a Central European City*, London: Cape.

de Carminha, P.V. (1947) 'The Discovery of Brazil', 41–59, in Ley, C.D. (ed.) *Portuguese Voyages*, London: J.M. Dent.

Delabastita, D. (1993) *There's a Double Tongue. An Investigation into the Translation of Shakespeare's Wordplay, with Special Reference to 'Hamlet'*, Amsterdam and Atlanta: Ga.: Rodopi.

de Laet, M. and Mol, A. (2000) 'The Zimbabwe Bush Pump: the Mechanics of a Fluid Technology', *Social Studies of Science*, 30, 225–63.

Delanty, G. (2000) *Citizenship in a Global Age*, Buckingham: Open University Press.

—— (2001) 'Cosmopolitanism and Violence: the Limits of Global Civil Society', *European Journal of Social Theory*, 4, 1, 41–52.

Delisle, J. (1999) 'Introduction', 1–6, in Roland, Ruth A., *Interpreters as Diplomats: a Diplomatic History of the Role of Interpreters in World Politics*, Ottawa: Ottawa University Press.

Delisle, J. and Woodsworth J. (eds) (1995) *Translators through History*, Amsterdam: John Benjamins.

Derricke, J. [1581] (1883) *The Image of Irelande*, (ed.) J. Small; notes, Sir Walter Scott, Edinburgh: Black.

Derrida, J. (1985) 'Des Tours de Babel', trans. Joseph Graham, 165–248, in Graham, Joseph (ed.) *Difference in Translation*, Ithaca and New York: Cornell University Press.

Descartes, R. (1637) *Discours de la méthode*, Paris: Colin, 1959.

Dew, N. (2004) 'The Order of Oriental Knowledge: the Making of D'Herbelot's *Bibliothèque Orientale*', 233–52, in Prendergast, C. (ed.) *Debating World Literature*, London: Verso.

du Bellay, Joachin (1970) *Deffence et illustration de la langue françoyse*, Paris: Didier.

Dunlevy, M. (1989) *Dress in Ireland*, London: Batsford.

Eagleton, T. (2004a) *After Theory*, London: Penguin.

—— (2004b) *The English Novel: An Introduction*, Oxford: Blackwell.

Edwards, J. (1995) *Multilingualism*, London: Penguin.

Egerton, P. (ed.) (1847) *Life of Lord Grey of Wilton*, London: Camden Society, repr. 1968.

Eoyang, Eugene Chen (2003) *'Borrowed Plumage': Polemical Essays on Translation*, Amsterdam and New York: Rodopi.

European Booksellers Federation (2004) 'The Book Trade in Europe'. Available online: http://www.ebf-eu.org (accessed 2 March 2004).

Featherstone, M. and Lash, S. (eds) (1999) *Space of Culture*, London: Sage.

Fernández Armesto, F. (1996) *Millennium: a History of Our Last Thousand Years*, London: Black Swan.

Fine, R. and Cohen, R. (2002) 'Four Cosmopolitan Moments', 137–62, in Vertovec, S. and Cohen, R. (eds) *Conceiving Cosmopolitanism: Theory, Context, Practice*, Oxford: Oxford University Press.

Finkielkraut, A. (1987) *La Défaite de la pensée*, Paris: Gallimard; *The Undoing of Thought*, trans. Dennis O'Keeffe, London: Claridge, 1988.

Foley, J. (1984) 'Oral Literature Today', 2570–96, in Caws, M.A. and Prendergast, C. (eds) *Harper Collins World Reader*, New York: Harper Collins.

Forsdick, C. (2005) *Travel in Twentieth-Century French and Francophone Cultures: the Persistence of Diversity*, Oxford: Oxford University Press.

Freyer, G. (ed.) (1982) *Bishop Stock's 'Narrative' of the Year of the French*, Ballina: Irish Humanities Centre.

Friedman, J. (1994) *Cultural Identity and Global Process*, London: Sage.

Friel, B. (1981) *Translations*, London: Faber and Faber.

—— (2005) 'Human Problems facing Translators and Interpreters Worldwide Today', *Translation Ireland*, 16, 1, 4–6.

Ganahl, R. (2001) 'Free Markets: Language, Commodification and Art', 23–38, in Apter, E. (ed.) *Translation in a Global Market*, special issue of *Public Culture*, 13, 1.

Gentzler, E. (2001) *Contemporary Translation Theories*, Clevedon: Multilingual Matters.

Giblin, C. (1995) 'Hugh McCaghwell, O.F.M., Archbishop of Armagh (+1626): Aspects of his Life', 63–94, in Millet, B. and Lynch, A. (eds) *Dún Mhuire Killiney 1945–1995: Léann agus Seanchas*, Dublin: Lilliput.

Giddens, A. (1990) *The Consequences of Modernity*, Stanford, Calif.: Stanford University Press.

Gilbert, H. (1869) *Queene Elizabethes Academy*, (ed.) F.J. Furnivall, *Early English Text Society* e.s., 8, 1–12.

Gill, M. (2003) 'Speech'. Available online: http://www.fep-fee.be/speechmg.htm (accessed 12 November).

Ging, D. and Malcolm, J. (2004) 'Interculturalism and Multiculturalism in Ireland: Textual Strategies at Work in the Media Landscape', 125–35, in Titley, G. (ed.) *Resituating Culture*, Strasbourg: Council of Europe.

Gleick, J. (1987) *Chaos: Making a New Science*, London: Cardinal.

Glick-Schiller, N., Basch, L. and Blanc-Szanton (eds) (1992) *Towards a Transnational Perspective on Migration: Race, Class, Ethnicity and Nationalism Reconsidered*, New York: New York Academy of Sciences.

Goethe, J.W. von (1960) 'German Romance [von Carlyle]', 220–3, in *Schriften zu Literatur und Theater*, 15, J.G. Cotta'sche Buchhandlung Nachfolger: Stuttgart.

Goldhill, S. (2004) 'Literary History without Literature: Reading Practices in the Ancient World', 175–96, in Prendergast, C. (ed.) *Debating World Literature*, London: Verso.

Granovetter, M.S. (1973) 'The Strength of Weak Ties', *The American Journal of Sociology*, 78, 1360–80.

Grant, C. (1994) *Delors: Inside the House that Jacques Built*, London: Brealey Publishing.

Griffin, G. (1944) *The Collegians*, Dublin: Talbot Press.

Gundara, J.S. (2000) *Interculturalism, Education and Inclusion*, London: Paul Chapman Publishing.

Hadfield, A. and Maley, W. (1993) 'Irish Representations and English Alternatives', in Bradshaw, B., Hadfield, A. and Maley, W. (eds) *Representing Ireland: Literature and the Origins of Conflict 1534–1660*, Cambridge: Cambridge University Press.

Hagège, C. (1986) *L'Homme de paroles*, Paris: Fayard.

—— (2000) *Halte à la mort des langues*, Paris: Odile Jacob.

Hall, Stuart (1991) 'The Local and the Global: Globalization and Ethnicity', in King, A.D. (ed.) *Culture, Globalization and the World System*, London: Macmillan.

—— (2002) 'Political Belonging in a World of Multiple Identities', 25–31, in Vertovec, S. and Cohen, R. (eds) *Conceiving Cosmopolitanism: Theory, Context, Practice*, Oxford: Oxford University Press.

Hall, S. and du Gay, P. (1996) *Questions of Cultural Identity*, London: Sage.

Hamilton, A. (1904) *The Chronicles of the English Augustinian Canonesses Regular of the Lateran at St. Monica's in Louvain*, Vol. 1, Edinburgh: Sands and Co.

Hampers, L.C., Cha, S., Gutglass, D.J., Binns, H.J. and Krug, S.E. (1999) 'Language Barriers and Resource Utilization in a Pediatric Emergency Department', *Pediatrics*, 103, 6, 1253–6.

Hannerz, U. (1990) 'Cosmopolitans and Locals in World Culture', 237–51, in Featherstone, M. (ed.) *Nationalism, Globalization and Modernity*, London: Sage.

Hayes, R. (1945) 'Priests in the Independence Movement of '98', *The Irish Ecclesiastical Record*, 25, 45–59.

—— (1979) *The Last Invasion of Ireland: When Connacht Rose*, Dublin: Gill and Macmillan.

Healy, M. (1939) *The Old Munster Circuit*, Cork and Dublin: Mercier Press.

Held, D. (2002) 'Culture and Political Community: National, Global and Cosmopolitan', 48–58, in Vertovec, S. and Cohen, R. (eds) *Conceiving Cosmopolitanism: Theory, Context, Practice*, Oxford: Oxford University Press.

Hennessy, J.P. (1883) *Sir Walter Ralegh in Ireland*, London: Kegan Paul, Trench.

Hermans, H.J.M. (2001) 'The Dialogical Self: Towards a Theory of Personal and Cultural Positioning', *Cultural Psychology*, 7, 3, 243–81.

Hermans, T. (1985) 'Images of Translation: Metaphor and Imagery in the Renaissance Discourse on Translation', 95–108, in Hermans, T. (ed.) *The Manipulation of Literature: Studies in Literary Translation*, London: Croom Helm.

Herodotus (1996) *The Histories*, trans. Aubrey de Selincourt, rev. edn, London: Penguin.

Herrera, D.A. (2004) 'School Success of Moroccan Youth in Barcelona: Theoretical Insights for Practical Questions', 69–80, in Titley, G. (ed.) *Resituating Culture*, Strasbourg: Council of Europe.

Hiebert, D. (2002) 'Cosmopolitanism at the Local Level: the Development of Transnational Neighbourhoods', 209–23, in Vertovec, S. and Cohen, R. (eds) *Conceiving Cosmpolitanism: Theory, Context, Practice*, Oxford: Oxford University Press.

Hobsbawm, E. (1983) 'Inventing Traditions', 1–14, in Hobsbawm, E. and Ranger, T. (eds) *The Invention of Tradition*, Cambridge: Cambridge University Press.

—— (1990) *Myths and Nationalism since 1780; Programme, Myth, Reality*, Cambridge: Cambridge University Press.

Hoffman, E. (1991) *Lost in Translation*, London: Minerva.

Holborow, M. (1999) *The Politics of English*, London: Sage.

Hollinger, D.A. (1995) *Postethnic America: Beyond Multiculturalism*, New York: Basic Books.

Hopkins, L. (2002) 'Orlando and the Golden World: the Old World and the New in *As You Like It*', *Early Modern Literary Studies*, 8, 2, 1–21.

Hoppenrath, D. (2002) 'Localisation in the Global Village', *Localisation Focus*, 1, 2, 14–15.

Houston, M. (2003) 'Medicine Without Frontiers,' *The Irish Times*, 7 July.

Hughes, J.L.J. (ed.) (1960) *Patentee Officers in Ireland, 1173–1826*, Dublin: Irish Manuscripts Commission.

Huizinga, J. (1936) 'Erasmus über Vaterland und Nationen', in *Gedenkschrift zum 400. Todestag des Erasmus von Rotterdam*, Basle: Verlag Braus-Riggenbach.

Hung, E. and Pollard, D. (1998) 'Chinese Tradition', 365–74, in Baker, M. (ed.) *Routledge Encyclopedia of Translation Studies*, London: Routledge.

Huntington, S. (1993) 'The Clash of Civilizations', *Foreign Affairs*, 72, 3, 22–50.

—— (2005) *Who Are We? America's Great Debate*, New York: Free Press.

Hutchinson, J. (1987) *The Dynamics of Cultural Nationalism and the Creation of the Irish Nation State*, London: Allen and Unwin.

Jackson, D. (1973) 'The Irish Language and Tudor Government', *Éire-Ireland*, 8, 1, 21–8.

Jacobs, J. (1961) *The Death and Life of Great American Cities*, New York: Vintage.

Jay, G.S. (1997) *American Literature and the Culture Wars*, Ithaca, NY, and London: Cornell University Press.

Jennings, B. (ed.) (1964) *Wild Geese in Spanish Flanders 1582–1700*, Dublin: Irish Manuscripts Commission.

Jensen, I. (2004) 'The Practice of Intercultural Communication: Reflections for Professionals in Cultural Encounters', 81–92, in Titley, G. (ed.) *Resituating Culture*, Strasbourg: Council of Europe.

Johnson, S. (2002) *Emergence: the Connected Lives of Ants, Brains, Cities and Software*, London: Penguin.

Joyce, J. (1939) *Finnegans Wake*, London: Faber and Faber.

—— (1977) *A Portrait of the Artist as a Young Man*, London: Panther.

Kaldor, M. (1999) *New and Old Wars*, Cambridge: Polity Press.

Kapchan, D. (2003) 'Translating Folk Theories of Translation', 135–51, in Rubel, P. and Rosman, A. (eds) *Translating Cultures: Perspectives on Translation and Anthropology*, Oxford and New York: Berg.

Karter, A., Ferrara, A., Darbinian, J., Ackerson, L. and Selby, J. (2000) 'Self-Monitoring of Blood Glucose', *Diabetes Care*, 23, 4, 477–83.

Kenan, L. (2002) 'Translation as a Catalyst for Social Change in China', 160–83, in Tymoczko, M. and Gentzler, E. (eds) *Translation and Power*, Boston and Amherst: University of Massachusetts Press.

Keogh, D. (1993) *The French Disease: the Catholic Church and Irish Radicalism 1790–1800*, Blackrock: Four Courts Press.

Kermode, F. (1967) *The Sense of an Ending; Studies in the Theory of Fiction*, New York: Oxford University Press.

King, R. (1995) 'Migrations, Globalisation and Place', 5–44, in Massey, D. and Jess, P. (eds) *A Place in the World? Places, Culture and Globalisation*, Vol. 4, Oxford: Open University Press.

Klein, N. (2002) *Fences and Windows: Dispatches from the Front Line of the Globalization Debate*, London: Flamingo.

Krane, J. (2005) 'The Most Dangerous Civilian Job in Iraq: Dozens of Translators for US Military Have Been Killed', 1–3. Available online: http: //msnbc.msn.com.id/7911356 (accessed 23 August 2005).

Kundnani, A. (2004) 'The Rise and Fall of British Multiculturalism', 105–12, in Titley, G. (ed.) *Resituating Culture*, Strasbourg: Council of Europe.

Kymlicka, W. (1995) *Multicultural Citizenship: a Liberal Theory of Minority Rights*, Oxford: Clarendon Press.

—— (2005) 'The Uncertain Future of Multiculturalism', *Canadian Diversity*, 6, 1, 82–5.

Lacarrière, J. (1981) *En cheminant avec Hérodote*, Paris: Seghers.

Lally, C. (2005) 'B of I Hires Language Experts for Immigrant Customers', *The Irish Times*, 5 July, 11.

Lapierre, N. (2004) *Pensons ailleurs*, Paris: Stock.

Lash, S. and Urry, J. (1994) *Economies of Signs and Space*, London: Sage.

Latour, B. (1987) *Science in Action: How to Follow Scientists and Engineers Through Society*, Milton Keynes: Open University Press,

Law, J. and Mol, A. (2003) 'Situating Technoscience: an Inquiry into Spatialities', Centre for Science Studies, Lancaster University, UK. Available online: http://www.comp. lancs.ac.uk/sociology/papers/Law-Mol-Situating Technoscience.pdf (accessed 30 March 2005).

Lebedeva, Anna (2001) 'A Modest Business Ambition', *metro eireann*, 2, 8, 12.

Lee, J.J. (1989) *Ireland 1912–1985: Politics and Society*, Cambridge: Cambridge University Press.

Lefebvre, H. (1991) *The Production of Space*, Oxford: Blackwell.

Lentin, A. (2004) 'The Problem of Culture and Human Rights in the Response to Racism', 95–103, in Titley, G. (ed.) *Resituating Culture*, Strasbourg: Council of Europe.

Lepape, P. (2004) 'La dictature de la "world literature"', *Le Monde Diplomatique*, March, 24–5.

Lepreux, J. (1875) 'Documents relatifs à l'établissement à Douai des Récollets anglais', *Analectes pour servir à l'histoire ecclésiastique de Belgique*, 12, 266–79.

Leroy Ladurie, E. (1976) *Montaillou, village occitan de 1294 à 1324*, Paris: Gallimard.

Levi, P. (1958) *Se questo è un uomo*, Milan: Einaudi.

Lindo, F. (2000) 'Does Culture Explain? Understanding Differences in School Attainment between Iberian and Turkish Youth in the Netherlands', 109–20, in Vermeulen, H. and Perlmann, J. (eds) *Immigrants, Schooling and Social Mobility: Does Culture Make a Difference*, London: Macmillan.

Looby, B. (2002) 'Translator Vendor Web Services – the Future of Localisation', *Localisation Focus*, 1, 1, 10–12.

McArdle, J. (1995) *Irish Legal Anecdotes*, Dublin: Gill and Macmillan.

McCarthy, M. (2000). 'The Baha'i Commissioner', *metro eireann*, 1, 8, 14.

Maceri, D. (2005) 'The Most Dangerous Civilian Job in Iraq', *The Japan Times*, 19 July, 1.

McGrath, A. (2001) *In the Beginning: the Story of the King James' Bible and How It Changed a Nation, a Language and a Culture*, London: Hodder and Stoughton.

McIntosh, A. (2002) *Soil and Soul: People versus Corporate Power*, London: Aurum.

MacIntyre, A. (1999) *Dependent Rational Animals*, London: Duckworth.

Mackey, J.P. (ed.) (1994) *The Cultures of Europe: The Irish Contribution*, Belfast: The Institute of Irish Studies.

McPeake, M. (2001) 'Embodying Ireland: Representing Woman as Nation and Community in Irish Writing', unpublished Ph.D. dissertation, University of Miami.

Maffi, L. (2001) 'Introduction: on the Interdependence of Biological and Cultural Diversity', 1–50, in Maffi, L. (ed.) *On Biocultural Diversity*, London and Washington: Smithsonian Institution Press.

Malena, A. (2003) 'Presentation', *TTR*, 16, 2, 9–13, (special issue on translation and (im)migration).

Malik, K. (1996) *The Meaning of Race: Race, History and Culture in Western Society*, London: Palgrave.

Mallove, E.F. (1991) *Fire from Ice: Searching for Truth behind the Cold Fusion Furor*, London: John Wiley and Sons.

Mandelbrot, B. (1977) *The Fractal Geometry of Nature*, New York: Freeman.

Marincola, J. (1996) 'Introduction', ix–xxviii in Herodotus, *The Histories*, trans. Aubrey de Selincourt, rev. edn, London: Penguin.

Mason, I.G. (1999) 'Cosmopolitanism: Then and Now'. Available online: http://www.stlawrenceinstitute.org/vol 14mas.html (accessed 12 April 2005).

Matthiessen, F.O. (1931) *Translation: an Elizabethan Art*, Cambridge, Mass.: Harvard University Press.

Méchoulan, É. (2003) 'Intermédialités: le temps des illusions perdues', *Intermédialités*, 1, 1, 9–27.

Meizoz, J. (1997) *Ramuz, un passager clandestin des lettres françaises*, Geneva: Zoé.

Memmi, A. (1979) *La Dépendance*, Paris: Gallimard.

Micklethwait, J. and Wooldridge, A. (2000) *A Future Perfect: the Challenge and Hidden Promise of Globalization*, London: Heinemann.

Mirandé, A. and Enríquez, E. (1979) *La Chicana. The Mexican-American Woman*, Chicago: University of Chicago Press.

Moerman, E.R. (2005) 'Interpreters under Fire', *Translation Ireland*, 16, 1, 12–15.

Moretti, F. (2004) 'Conjectures on World Literature', 148–62, in Prendergast, C. (ed.) *Debating World Literature*, London: Verso.

Moryson, F. (1903) *Shakespeare's Europe, Unpublished Chapters of Fynes Moryson's Itinerary, with an Introduction and Account of Fynes Moryson's Career*, (ed.) C. Hughes, London: Sherratt and Hughes.

Mulgan, G. (1998) *Connexity: Responsibility, Freedom, Business and Power in the New Century*, London: Vintage.

Müller, M. (1871) *Lectures on the Science of Language*, 2 vols, London: Longmans, Green and Co.

Mumford, L. [1961] (1991) *The City in History*, London: Penguin.

Murphy, P. (1995) *Toss the Feathers: Irish Set Dancing*, Cork: Mercier Press.

Musgrave, R. (1995) *Memoirs of the Different Rebellions*, 4th edn, Enniscorthy: Round Tower.

Nerrière, J.-P. (2004) *Parlez Globish*, Paris: Eyrolles.

Ní Dhonnchadha, M. (2000) 'Irish Language Interpreting in the Courts Since the 1850s', unpublished MA dissertation submitted to Dublin City University.

Niranjana, T. (1992) *Siting Translation: History, Poststructuralism and the Colonial Context*, Berkeley, Calif.: University of California Press.

Nussbaum, M. (1997) *Cultivating Humanity: a Classical Defence of Reform in Liberal Education*, Cambridge, Mass.: Harvard University Press.

Oakley Brown, L. (2001) 'Ovid's *Metamorphoses* in England', 48–84, in Ellis, Roger and Oakley-Brown, Liz (eds) *Translation and the Nation: Towards a Cultural Politics of Englishness*, Clevedon: Multilingual Matters.

O'Brien, J.A. (ed.) (1954) *The Vanishing Irish: the Enigma of the Modern World*, London: W.H. Allen.

Ó Cinnéide, C. (2004) 'Citizenship and Multiculturalism: Equality, Rights and Diversity in Contemporary Europe', 43–55, in Titley, G. (ed.) *Resituating Culture*, Strasbourg: Council of Europe.

Ó Cléirigh, T. (1985) *Aodh Mac Aingil agus an Scoil Nua-Ghaeilge i Lobháin*, Dublin: An Gúm.

O'Clery, C. (2004) 'US Invested Twice as Much in Ireland as in China', *The Irish Times*, 18 May.

O'Donnell, R. (1998) *1798 Diary*, Dublin: Irish Times Books.

Office of Refugee Application Commissioner (2004). Available online: http://www. orac.ie/Pages/Statistics.htm (accessed 20 May 2004).

Ong, W.J. (1982) *Orality and Literacy: the Technologizing of the Word*, London: Routledge.

Onyejelem, C. (2001a) 'Learning to Understand Two English Languages', *metro eireann*, 1, 12, 17.

—— (2001b) 'Employers Should Learn from My Experience', *metro eireann*, 2, 4, 2.

Orpen, G.H. (ed.) (1892) *The Song of Dermot and the Earl: an Old French Poem from the Carew manuscript no. 596 in the Archiespiscopal Library at Lambeth Palace*, Oxford: Clarendon.

Orsini, F. (2004) 'India in the Mirror of World Fiction', 319–33, in Prendergast, C. (ed.) *Debating World Literature*, London: Verso.

O'Toole, F. (1985) 'Going West: the Country versus the City in Irish Writing', *The Crane Bag*, 9, 2, 111–16.

Palmer, P. (2001) *Language and Conquest in Early Modern Ireland*, Cambridge: Cambridge University Press.

Peacock, A. (ed.) (1993) *The Achievement of Brian Friel*, Gerrards Cross: Colin Smythe.

Pearl, M. (2003) *The Dante Club*, London: Vintage.

Pearsall Smith, L. (1907) *The Life and Letters of Sir Henry Wotton*, Vol. 1, Oxford: Clarendon Press.

Peters, M. (2001) 'Profile: Bosnia Community Development Centre', *metro eireann*, 1, 11, 4.

Picard, J.-M. (2003) 'The French Language in Medieval Ireland', 57–77, in Cronin, M. and Ó Cuilleanáin, C. (eds) *The Languages of Ireland*, Dublin: The Four Courts Press.

Pieterse, J.N. (1995) 'Globalization as Hybridization', 45–67, in Featherstone, M. (ed.) *Global Modernities*, London: Sage.

Pitkin, K. and Baker, D.W. (2000) 'Limited English Proficiency and Latinos' Use of Physician Services', *Medical Care Research and Review*, 57, 1, 76–91.

Plunket Barton, D. (1919) *Links Between Ireland and Shakespeare*, Dublin: Maunsel.

Pöllabauer, S. (2004) 'Interpreting in Asylum Hearings: Issues of Role, Responsibility and Power', *Interpreting*, 6, 2, 143–80.

Povinelli, E. (2001) 'Editor's Note', ix–xi, in Apter, E. (ed.) *Translation in a Global Market*, special issue of *Public Culture*, 13, 1.

Powell, W.W. (1996) 'Inter-organizational Collaboration in the Biotechnology Industry', *Journal of Institutional and Theoretical Economics*, 512, 197–215.

Pratt, G. and Hanson, S. (1994) 'Geography and the Construction of Difference', *Gender, Place, Culture*, 1, 1, 5–29.

Prendergast, C. (2004) 'Introduction', vii–xiii, in Prendergast, C. (ed.) *Debating World Literature*, London: Verso.

Preston P. and Kerr, A. (2001) 'Digital Media, Nation-states and Local Cultures: the Case of Multimedia "content" production', *Media, Culture & Society*, 23, 1, 109–31.

Quintilian (1997) 'Institutio oratoria', 19–20, in Robinson, D. (ed.) *Western Translation Theory from Herodotus to Nietzsche*, Manchester: St. Jerome.

Reiss, H. (ed.) (1970) *Kant's Political Writings*, Cambridge: Cambridge University Press.

Riccardi, A. (1997) 'Conference Interpreting: the Background to Research and Training', in Gambier, Y., Gile, D. and Taylor, C. (eds) *Conference Interpreting: Current Trends in Research*, Amsterdam and Philadelphia: John Benjamins.

Richards, T. (1993) *The Imperial Archive: Knowledge and the Fantasy of Empire*, London: Verso.

Ricoeur, P. (2004) *Sur la traduction*, Paris: Bayard.

Ritzer, G. (1993) *The McDonaldization of Society*, Thousand Oaks, Calif.: Pine Forge Press.

Roberts, J.M. (2001) *The Triumph of the West*, London: Weidenfeld and Nicolson.

Robertson, R. (1992) *Globalization: Social Theory and Global Culture*, London: Sage.

Robinson, D. (1997) *Western Translation Theory from Herodotus to Nietzsche*, Manchester: St Jerome.

Robinson, T. (1995) *Stones of Aran: Labyrinth*, Dublin: Lilliput Press.

Rose, G. (1992) *The Broken Middle: Out of Our Ancient Society*, Oxford: Blackwell.

Ruhs, M. (2003) *Emerging Trends and Patterns in the Immigration and Employment of Non-EU Nationals: What the Data Reveal*. Available online: http://www.policyinstitute.tcd.ie (accessed 17 May 2004).

Sabine, G.H. (1961) *A History of Political Theory*, New York: Holt, Rinehart and Winston.

Sarver, J. and Baker, D.W. (2000) 'Effect of Language Barriers on Follow-Up Appointments after an Emergency Department Visit', *Journal of General Internal Medicine*, 15, 4, 256–64.

Sassen, S. (1991) *The Global City: New York, London, Tokyo*, Princeton, NJ: Princeton University Press.

—— (1998) 'The State and the Global City', 195–218, in Sassen, S., *Globalization and Its Discontents*, New York: The New Press.

Scarpetta, G. (1981) *Éloge du cosmopolitisme*, Paris: Grasset.

Schäler, R. (2002a) 'Cultural Adaptation – More Than What Meets the Eye?', *Localisation Focus*, 1, 1, 9.

—— (2002b) 'The Cultural Dimension in Software Localisation', *Localisation Ireland*, 1, 2, 21–3.

Schama, S. (1995) *Landscape and Memory*, London: HarperCollins.

Scholte, J.A. (2000) *Globalization: a Critical Introduction*, Basingstoke: Macmillan.

Seleskovitch, D. (1998) 'Allocution de clôture', 287–91, in Israel, F. (ed) *Quelle formation pour le traducteur de l'an 2000?*, Paris: Didier.

Sennett, R. (1998) *The Corrosion of Character: the Personal Consequences of Work in the New Capitalism*, New York and London: W.W. Norton.

—— (2002) 'Cosmopolitanism and the Social Experience of Cities', 42–7, in Vertovec, S. and Cohen, R. (eds) *Conceiving Cosmopolitanism: Theory, Context, Practice*, Oxford: Oxford University Press.

Sheller, M. (2003) *Consuming the Caribbean: from Arawaks to Zombies*, London and New York: Routledge.

Shields, K. (2000) *Language, Poetry and Identity in Twentieth-Century Ireland*, Bern: Peter Lang.

Shiels, W.J. and Wood, D. (eds) (1989) *The Churches, Ireland and the Irish*, Oxford: Oxford University Press.

Shirinzade, M. (2001) 'Scents of the Sea and of Lilac and Mimosa Flowers', *metro eireann*, 1, 10, 20.

Shiva, V. (1993) *Monocultures of the Mind; Perspectives on Biodiversity and Biotechnology*, London: Zed Books.

Silberman, S. (2000) 'Talking to Strangers', *Wired*, May, 215–28.

Simmel, G. [1909] (1997a) 'Bridge and Door', 170–74, in Frisby, D. and Featherstone, M. (eds) *Simmel on Culture*, London: Sage.

—— (1997B) 'Sociology of the Meal', 130–6, in Frisby, D. and Featherstone, M. (eds) *Simmel on Culture*, London: Sage.

Simon, S. (1999) *L'Hybridité culturelle*, Montreal: L'île de la tortue.

Sloterdijk, P. and Finkielkraut, A. (2003) *Les Battements du monde: dialogue*, Paris: Pauvert.

Spenser, E. (1970) *A View of the Present State of Ireland*, (ed.) W.L. Renwick, Oxford: Clarendon.

Spetalnick, M. (2004) 'Lost in Translation: Iraqi Interpreters Live in Fear', *Reuters International*, 26 December, 2004. Available online: http: www.occupationwatch. org/article.php?id=8513 (accessed 7 February 2005).

Spitzer, L. (1988) *Representative Essays/Leo Spitzer*, Stanford, Calif.: Stanford University Press.

St-Pierre, P. (1995) 'Être jeune de langue à l'âge classique', *Circuit*, 16–17.

Stafford, F.J. (1988) *The Sublime Savage: a Study of James Macpherson and the Poems of Ossian*, Edinburgh: Edinburgh University Press.

Stephenson, N. (1993) *Snow Crash*, New York: Bantam Books.

Sturge, K. (1997) 'Translation Strategies in Ethnography', *The Translator*, 3, 1, 21–38.

Suarez-Orosco, M. (1991) 'Migration, Minority Status, and Education: European dilemmas and responses in the 1990s', *Anthropology and Education Quarterly*, 22, 2, 99–120.

Taylor, C. (1995) *Philosophical Arguments*, Cambridge, Mass.: Harvard University Press.

Taylor Martin, S. (2004), 'Shortage of Interpreters Foreshadowed Prison Excesses', *St Petersburg Times*, 20 May, 1.

Tennent, M. (ed.) (2005) *Training for the New Millennium*, Amsterdam: John Benjamins.

Theroux, P. (1984) *The Kingdom by the Sea*, London: Penguin.

Titley, G. (2004) 'Resituating Culture: an Introduction', 9–18, in Titley, G. (ed.) *Resituating Culture*, Strasbourg: Council of Europe.

Tollefson, J.W. (1989) *Alien Winds: the Reeducation of America's Indochinese Refugees*, New York: Praeger.

Tomlinson, C. (2003) *Metamorphoses: Poetry and Translation*, Manchester: Carcanet.

Tomlinson, J. (2004) 'Global Culture, Deterritorialisation and the Cosmopolitanism of Youth Culture', 21–9, in Titley, G. (ed.) *Resituating Culture*, Strasbourg: Council of Europe.

Toury, G. (1980) *In Search of a Theory of Translation*, Tel Aviv: Porter Institute.

Treaty on European Union. Available online: http://europa.eu.int/en/record/mt/top.html (accessed 2 April 2004).

Tsai, C. (2005) 'Inside the Television Newsroom: an Insider's View of International News Translation in Taiwan', *Language and International Communication*, 5, 2, 145–53.

Tylor, E. (1871) *Primitive Culture: Researches into the Development of Mythology, Philosophy, Religion, Language, Art and Custom*, vol. 1, London: Murray.

Tymoczko, M. (1999) *Translation in a Postcolonial Context*, Manchester: St Jerome.

Tymoczko, M. and Ireland, C. (2003) 'Language and Tradition in Ireland: Prolegomena', 1–27, in Tymoczko, M. and Ireland, C. (eds) *Language and Tradition in Ireland: Continuities and Displacements*, Amherst and Boston: University of Massachusetts Press.

UNESCO (2004) 'Universal Declaration on Cultural Diversity'. Available online: http://unesdoc.unesco.org.images/0012/001271/127160m.pdf (accessed 30 March 2004).

United Nations Population Division (2002) *International Migration 2002*, New York: United Nations.

—— (2003) *World Population 2002*, New York: United Nations.

—— (2005) *International Migration and Development*, New York: United Nations.

Urry, J. (2003) *Global Complexity*, London: Sage.

Uzomah, H. (2001). 'New Video Explains Health Services', *metro eireann*, 1, 12, special anniversary supplement, vi.

van der Meer, J. (2002) 'Impact of Translation Web Services', *Localisation Focus*, 1, 2, 9–11.

van Niekerk, M. (2000) 'Creoles and Hindustanis. Patterns of Social Mobility in Two Surinamese Immigrant Groups in the Netherlands', 92–108, in Vermeulen, H. and Perlmann, J. (eds) *Immigrants, Schooling and Social Mobility: Does Culture Make a Difference*, London: Macmillan.

Venuti, L. (1995) *The Translator's Invisibility: a History of Translation*, London: Routledge.

—— (1998) *The Scandals of Translation*, London: Routledge.

Vergerio, P.P. (2002) 'The Character and Studies Befitting a Free-Born Youth', 2–91, in Craig W. Wallendorf, ed. and trans., *Humanist Educational Treatises*, Cambridge, Mass.: Harvard University Press.

Vertovec, S. and Cohen, R. (eds) (2002) *Conceiving Cosmopolitanism: Theory, Context, Practice*, Oxford: Oxford University Press.

Wadensjö, C. (1998) *Interpreting as Interaction*, London: Longman.

Wallerstein, I. (1996) *Open the Social Sciences: Report of the Gulbenkian Commission on the Restructuring of the Social Sciences*, Stanford, Calif.: Stanford University Press.

Ward, Tanya (2002) *Asylum Seekers in Adult Education: a Study of Language and Literacy Needs*, Dublin: City of Dublin VEC and County of Dublin VEC.

Warner, M. (2002) *Fantastic Metamorphoses, Other Worlds*, Oxford: Oxford University Press.

Washburn, D. (2004) 'Many Iraq Interpreters Unskilled, Soldiers Say', 1–3. Available online: http: www.signonsandiego.com.news/world/iraq/20040521-9999-1 (accessed 23 August 2005).

Waswo, R. (1987) *Language and Meaning in the Renaissance*, Princeton, NJ: Princeton University Press.

Watts, D.J. and Strogatz, S.H. (1998) 'Collective Dynamics of "small-world" Networks', *Nature*, 398, 440–2.

Welch, R. (1993) *Changing States: Transformations in Modern Irish Writing*, London and New York: Routledge.

White, Kenneth (1978) *La Figure du dehors*, Paris: Grasset.

Whitelock, D., McKitterick, R. and Dumville, D. (eds) (1982) *Ireland in Early Medieval Europe*, Cambridge: Cambridge University Press.

Williams, R. (1979) *Politics and Letters*, London: New Left Books.

—— (1981) *Culture*, London: Fontana.

Woloshin, S., Schwartz, L.M., Katz, S.J. and Welch, H.G. (1997) 'Is Language a Barrier to the Use of Preventive Services?', *Journal of General Internal Medicine*, 12, 8, 472–7.

Wright, R. (2000) *NonZero: the Logic of Human Destiny*, New York: Pantheon Books.

Yengoan, A. (2003) 'Lyotard and Wittgenstein and the Question of Translation', 25–43, in Rubel, P. and Rosman, A. (eds) *Translating Cultures: Perspectives on Translation and Anthropology*, Oxford and New York: Berg.

Yoshikawa, M. (1987) 'The Double-Swing Model of Intercultural Communication Between the East and the West', 35–48, in Kincaid, L. (ed.) *Communication Theory: Eastern and Western Perspectives*, London: Academic Press.

Young, I.M. (1990) *Justice and the Politics of Difference*, Princeton, NJ: Princeton University Press.

Zachary, G.P. (2000) *The Global Me: New Cosmopolitans and the Competitive Edge*, London: Nicholas Brealey.

Zohar, D. and Marshall, I. (1994) *The Quantum Society*, New York: William Morrow.

Zolo, D. (1997) *Cosmopolis: Prospects for World Government*, trans. David McKie, Cambridge: Polity Press.

Zuber, R. (1968) *Les 'Belles Infidèles' et la formation du goût classique: Pierrot d'Ablancourt et Guez de Balzac*, Paris: Colin.

Index

heteronymous interpreting practice 113,
115
heteronymous translation 40–1
Hiebert, David 60, 62
Hobsbawm, Eric 18, 32
Hoffman, Eva 70
Hollinger, David 10
holograms 132–5
Hopkins, Lisa 107
Hoppenrath, Detlev 29
human beings: attachments 71; bodily
expression 78; socialization 142–3
human rights 70–1; individual vs. nation 9;
legislation 137
Huntington, Samuel 137
hyper bourgeoisie 11

identity 1, 4, 18; autonomous self 50;
continuity over time 3; debate 1;
defence of difference 15; dialogical self
50, 69; and difference 63; economic
entitlement 3; ethnocentric 9; flexibility
9; forms of 3; generic 63; and ideology
1; interpreting 75–119; polyidentity 9;
primary 10; and radical divisiveness
72; specific 63; violent conflict 5
identity papers 1–5
identity politics 20
ideographs 25
immigrant communities 61; and linguistic
integration 61
immigrants 4; attitude to translation 56;
contributions to society 71; income 64;
language classes 52; phases of
settlement 60–1; private sector 63–4;
public services 63; scepticism of 60;
social mobility 64; target language
54; translation and interpreting
services 48
immigration 43–74
immutable mobile 27, 29, 33
imperialism 10
Indochinese refugees 52–3
information: access to 138; distribution
138
information technology 8, 137; and
temporal investment 39–40
informationalism 8, 132, 138
intelligence: actionable 112–16; inquiry
and endings 129; reciprocity and
evolution 139
intercultural contact zone 6
intercultural knowledge, mediation space
between 135

intercultural training 10
interculturalism 4, 48–9; functionalist
approach 48; post-structural approach
48
International Monetary Fund (IMF) 9, 15
interpreter 4; attitudes towards 118;
conflict and local recruitment 115–16;
in conflict situations 86; conflicting
interests of 4; and criminal courts 57;
deaths in Iraq 112–13; dilemma of 77;
dual function of orality 81; dual
translation 93; duality and allegiance
88; and ethnic minority patients 57;
historical roles 4; identity and practice
4, 5; importance of orality 119;
intelligence gathering 85; intelligence
wars 112–14; interventionist 90; laws
governing 86; legal power 91; and the
legal system 89–94; localness of 116;
long term survival of 86; loyalties
85–6; as a mouthpiece 77–8; neutrality
119; oral vs. textual 81; potential
duplicity of 113; prestige of 79–81; as
prodigal figures 76–7; religious
loyalties 84; representative figures 88;
returning as native 101, 113–15; as a
spy 81; testimonies 79–82; trainee 113;
trust of 118; understanding of politics
and culture 84; unknowability of 117;
visibility of 5, 116–19; vs. translator
78; vulnerability as embodied agents
112; vulnerability of 109, 116; in war
zones 4
Interpreter, The (film) 116–19
Interpreter of the Irish Tongue 86
interpreting: arena of interaction 87;
autonomous 85, 101–2; heteronymous
85, 101–2; historical practice 76;
interaction and resistance 87; and oral
culture 92; oral practice of 75; problem
of control 113; written records 76
intrinsic translation 64–70; and curricula
68–9
Iraq 4; invasion of 112; local recruitment
of interpreters 115–16
Ireland: Bosnian refugees 57; colonization
process 84–5; economic migration 51;
immigrants and linguistics 51; language
status 87; legal transcripts 90;
migration patterns 50–2; multilingual
past 58–9; political context and
Shakespeare 111; political interpreting
87; post-Union and linguistic
assimilation 91; reconquest of 84–5;